The Family's Role
in Soviet Education

LUDWIG LIEGLE is currently a professor at the Institute of Education of the University of Tübingen. Previously he was on the staff of the Institute of Education of Ruhr University at Bochum, which sponsored the research that has led to his published works. A frequent contributor to the literature on the sociology of education, Dr. Liegle is the author of *Familie und Kollektiv im Kibbutz* and editor of *Kollektiverziehung im Kibbutz,* studies for which he prepared himself by acquiring a working knowledge of Hebrew and spending a year at several kibbutzim in Israel. *The Family's Role in Soviet Education,* originally published as *Familienerziehung und sozialer Wandel in der Sowjet-union,* was co-sponsored by the East-Europe Institute at the Free University of Berlin. To collect the data, which are largely based on original sources inaccessible outside the USSR, the author learned Russian and spent months of research in the Soviet Union.

LUDWIG LIEGLE

The Family's Role
in Soviet Education

Translated by Susan Hecker

Foreword by Urie Bronfenbrenner

SP SPRINGER PUBLISHING COMPANY / NEW YORK

Originally published as *Familienerziehung und sozialer Wandel in der Sowjetunion* (Heidelberg: Quelle & Meyer, 1970), volume 5 in the series Erziehungswissenschaftliche Veröffentlichungen (Scientific Publications in Education), edited by Oskar Anweiler and Siegried Baske, and issued by the Osteuropa-Institut at the Free University of Berlin

© 1970, Osteuropa-Institut Berlin

Translation © 1975 by Springer Publishing Company, Inc.

Springer Publishing Company, Inc.
200 Park Avenue South
New York, New York 10003

75 76 77 78 79 / 10 9 8 7 6 5 4 3 2 1

Library of Congress Cataloging in Publication Data

Liegle, Ludwig.
    The family's role in Soviet education.

    Translation of Familienerziehung und sozialer Wandel in der Sowjetunion.
    Bibliography: p.
    Includes index.
    1. Family—Russia. 2. Children—Management.
I. Title.
HQ637.L513   301.42'0947   75-4862
ISBN 0-8261-1760-0

Printed in the United States of America

Contents

1 EDUCATIONAL FUNCTIONS OF THE FAMILY: IDEOLOGICAL FOUNDATIONS AND LEGISLATION   1

2 SOCIOECONOMIC CONDITIONS OF THE FAMILY AND THE ROLE OF WOMEN   30

3 THE FAMILY AND PRESCHOOL EDUCATION   55

Foreword

The publication in the United States of Professor Liegle's insightful and comprehensive study of the Soviet family and Soviet education provides a much-needed corrective to the spotty and often distorted view that prevails in our own country, not only on the part of the general public but even among social scientists, including specialists in the field.

One of many surprises I experienced as an American scholar working in the U.S.S.R. was the discovery that even the educated American's knowledge of Soviet reality was as replete with gross omissions and distortions as the contemporary Russian's view of the United States. To be sure, on my first visit to the U.S.S.R. (now some 15 years ago) I expected to see not the stereotyped picture presented in our popular press and political speeches, but the objective reality as I had come to know it from our responsible magazines and newspapers, such as the *New York Times,* and, more importantly, from the writings of the Sovietologists, scholars who had specialized in the study of the Soviet Union. It was with some resistance and disillusionment, therefore, that I gradually came to the realization that my "objective picture" did not correspond to the reality. The latter turned out to be considerably more complex, contradictory, protean, pragmatic, and unpredictable. Yet, paradoxically, this new, unexpected, more complicated picture was easier to understand, for, like schizophrenia in Harry Stack Sullivan's brilliant essay on the subject, when seen from inside, it turned out to be "more simply human than otherwise."

Nowhere was the disillusioning clash between expectation and reality more pronounced than in the area of my own specialty—the development of the child in family, school, and society. What I had read about, and what I expected, was a politicization of the process of childrearing, reaching into the earliest years of life through the involvement of the family in the goals and methods of communist upbringing. The cherished Western values of family privacy, tradition, loyalty, and distinctiveness of value orientation would appear, if at all, I surmised, only among the older generation, or minority groups and dissidents. The Soviet family, I was led to expect, would not, because it could not, maintain a wall between itself and the rest of the community, for communist ideology and the corresponding Soviet reality as I had read about it stood in direct contradiction to the revered Anglo-Saxon adage, honored no less in America than in the land of its origin, "A man's home is his castle."

Accordingly, it came as a surprise to me that there was more emphasis on privacy, less involvement in external social and political concerns, and, in general, more separation from the outside world in the Soviet family than in its American counterpart. All the developments I had been led to expect from my reading—the infusion of communist ideology into family life and childrearing, the intrusion of the outside community into family affairs, the greater equalization of sex roles, the weakening of family ties—were hardly the salient features of the contemporary Russian home. What stood out instead was a fascinating dynamic between two powerful, mutually adapting systems. The first was the family, whose values and patterns of behavior, including childrearing, appeared to be far more deeply rooted in Russian culture than in Marxist-Leninist theory and practice. The second was the larger society, which, while offering some important supports to the family in the form of health care and basic economic security, at the same time imposed inexorable pressures and demands, again less ideological in character than economic and practical: the necessity for women to work, both from the viewpoint of national needs and family finances; the shortage of housing; fluctuation in the availability of food products and consumer goods; the complexity of family work schedules; and the sheer amount of time required to stand in line and shop in the highly bureaucratized Soviet retail-sales system. This continuing accommodation between culturally rooted patterns of family life and childrearing on the one hand and the sometimes shifting requirements of economic and national life on the other shaped the course of what actually happened to children not only in the home but also in the school, the courtyard, and the other settings in which Russian youngsters live and grow.

Why has this phenomenon, so obvious to anyone who lives and works in Soviet society, so eluded American specialists and scholars writing on the Soviet family and Soviet education? This question has puzzled some Soviet social scientists, but should not present difficulties to anyone who knows our own society well. Throughout recent history, we in America have tended to view the Soviet scene, in all its aspects, primarily in ideological terms. Even to a greater extent than the Russians themselves, we have insisted on interpreting every feature of Soviet life principally, if not exclusively, from a Marxist-Leninist perspective.

Fortunately, our European colleagues have not been so one-sided in their approach. They have been able to look at Soviet society not as a special case requiring a singular mode of analysis, but as yet another complex, contemporary culture requiring for its understanding a comprehensive analysis, and then synthesis, of many diverse sources of influence, including but not limited to political ideology and its implementation. Professor Liegle's study represents a brilliant example of this integrative approach. To give us an understanding of the Soviet family, its role in childrearing, and its relation to other institutions, he draws on many disciplines—history, law, economics, political science, sociology, psychology, pedagogy, and public health. Moreover, in all these areas the treatment is not that of the dilettante seizing upon flashy bits and pieces; rather, in every area the material presented reflects the thoroughness and careful judgment of the scholar, without pretentiousness or unnecessary detail. Particularly impressive is Professor Liegle's command and discriminating treatment of the now substantial scholarly work of Soviet social scientists in the fields of the family, child development, preschool education, and educational psychology. Just as it did in Europe, the publication of this volume in the United States will serve to introduce this Soviet work for the first time to most American readers who have been unaware of its existence.

But Liegle's perceptive eye does not restrict itself to scholarly books and journals. Some of his most revealing material is drawn from his extensive reading of the popular press and from his personal interviews and observations during visits to the U.S.S.R.

Even more impressive than Liegle's scholarship and broad range of source material is his ability, in the parlance of the day, "to get it all together," to develop from the mass of material a picture that is as comprehensible as it is comprehensive and that reaches and communicates the Soviet reality. His achievement calls to mind an oft-quoted and much beloved line from Pushkin: "There one finds the Russian spirit, the smell of Russia." Pushkin always loses by translation, but, fortunately for the readers of this book, Liegle does not.

Urie Bronfenbrenner

SOME USEFUL TERMS

Komsomol   Communist Youth Organization for ages 15-27

Pioneers   the children's mass organization for ages 9-15; closely linked with the Komsomol

USSR   Union of Soviet Socialist Republics

RSFSR   Russian Soviet Federated Socialist Republic, largest of the fifteen union republics of the USSR

CPSU   Communist Party of the Soviet Union

APN   Academy of Pedagogical Sciences (Akademia Pedagogiceskiy Nauki)

kolkhoz   collective farm

comrades' courts   people's courts, comprising lay people, which function in factories, villages, and residential areas and handle misdemeanors and disputes

Introduction

Scientific interest in the educational systems of Eastern Europe, particularly that of the Soviet Union, has increased in recent years. The numerous reliable studies and data available on the development and current state of the Soviet school system indicate that the centrally organized educational system exercises important functions in implementing planned social change. It is well known that the goals of Soviet social change include not only the creation of an effective industrial society but also the realization of a qualitatively "new" society, the "communist" society, based upon socialization of the means of production and the rearing of a "new" man, the "communist" man. This new person shall subordinate his personal interests to those of the communist society and identify with its value system as expressed in Marxist-Leninist ideology and authoritatively represented by the Communist Party. For this reason, educational institutions serve to transmit not only knowledge and skills to the younger generation but also uniform ideological-political values as well.

The communist society's comprehensive claim upon the individual and the "collectivist" character of Soviet society and Soviet pedagogy frequently lose sight of the fact that the individual is formed not only through purposeful education in societal institutions but also through direct social experiences outside these institutions, particularly through family experiences and upbringing. These educational processes in the out-of-school area are only partially susceptible to planned intervention by the state. As long as we consider only the centralist and collectivist aspects of social processes, including education, we indirectly proceed from adherence to the notion of planning for people and for society, and this is exactly what the concrete experiences in the Soviet Union do not fully justify.

The steady decrease in the birthrates in the Soviet Union, which in the long run will impair the physical reproduction of society; the growing social differentiation, which contradicts the sought-after ideal of a "classless" society; the increase in the divorce rates, in juvenile delinquency, and in job turnover—these are only some of the processes which Soviet planning has to evaluate negatively. Of course, these processes are themselves connected with certain socioeconomic factors of the "system"; but they also have to be understood as subjective and "spontaneous" reactions by the people toward the demands of the system. Moreover, under the conditions of centralized economic and educational planning and a collectivist ideology, many contradictions develop between the requirements and norms of society on the one hand and the attitude and value orientation of people and certain social processes on the other. The validity of this statement seems to be substantiated by the fact that the younger generation is not being raised exclusively in a collectivist manner, that is, in the state educational institutions and in the spirit of communist ideology. Instead, the Soviet family has remained that social group which continually influences the child from birth to maturity. It is the individual family, and not an organized children's collective, which generally determines that crucial developmental phase of early childhood when the personality is most malleable.

Of course, the family cannot be studied in isolation from those social, economic, and political realities of a society any more than the school and other institutions can. These realities modify the family's structure and functions, and, in turn, every society depends upon the family's fulfillment of its biological and spiritual functions of reproduction. The view that family and society are mutually dependent is particularly emphasized in Marxist social theory. A recent work on Soviet family sociology points out:

> Every socioeconomic system has its particular forms of marriage and family. The development of the economic structure of society brings about a change in family and marriage ties.
>
> As a small cell, as a segment of society, the family exerts a certain influence upon that society. The initial formation of the individual's personality as a member of society takes place in the family collective (Solov'ëv 1962, pp. 3-4).

If, however, one acknowledges the view that the family is a "product of society and, to a certain degree, its reflection" ("Sem'ja i ee rol' " 1966, p. 103), one may consider the analysis of the family's structure and functions, particularly its educational functions, as an important instrument for the analysis of society on the whole. One will thus be able to draw conclusions about the socioeconomic progress of society from the socioeconomic conditions of family life; and from the actual upbringing in the family one will be able to draw conclusions about the degree of integration attained by Soviet society and the degree of acceptance which the value system of communist education has achieved in popular consciousness.

The few studies on the Soviet family available until now betray a dearth of information on the actual conditions of family life and the concrete forms and goals of family education. Even the recent book by the American sociologist H. K. Geiger (1968) is mainly based on the obsolete data of a survey of Soviet emigrés by Malte Bischoff (1956) and on a similar emigré sample completed at Harvard University. The fact that this study considered the statements of people who were only slightly representative and who, in addition, were generally hostile to the Soviet state necessarily reduces its objectivity. Moreover, as the basis of their reports, Geiger (1968), Mace (1963), and other authors selected interpretations of political and pedagogical documents, commentaries on Soviet legislation on marriage and family, and personal travel impressions from visits to the USSR. There is a need, then, for a study of the Soviet family and family education that is based upon research data gathered during the past few years by various branches of Soviet social science and evaluates these data systematically.

The present study attempts to meet this need. It is based on the conviction that only through a confrontation of official documents—laws, educational policy programs, pedagogical theories, etc.—with empirical data can the contradictions in Soviet societal development and the ambivalent attitude of the communist state toward the family be made clear. Since, in a closed society like the Soviet, the "outsider" is not granted the possibility of making independent scientific inquiries, the results of their own research, even if frequently ideologically colored, must become the basis of an objective examination.

This study is limited in that it must largely restrict itself to a description of the family and social structure in the European part of the USSR. The strong traditionalism in the Central Asian republics and the persistence of national values and customs in the everyday life of the people in these areas urgently call for in-depth study. Equally important would be an analysis of the processes of social change in the development centers of Siberia. The available Soviet ethnological data, however, offer an insufficient foundation for such studies.

Educational Functions of the Family: Ideological Foundations and Legislation

In fulfilling its functions the family is dependent upon that system of values and rules which is expressed in the ideology and in the legislation of a society. This is particularly true in Soviet society, where a marked and uniform value system influences state policy, legislation, and every aspect of social life, and where the family has been exposed to planned social change that has created new conditions for its functioning.

Soviet family policy has been discussed in many publications. But most presentations by Western authors are severely limited in their information value by ideological prejudice. This prejudice is expressed in the underlying assumption that communist philosophy and social practice are aimed at "the attempt to abolish the family" (Timasheff 1960). The impression is given that the Soviet state, relying upon the teachings of Marxism, is guided by a policy and legislation that are hostile to the family. Remnants of such a one-sided interpretation of Soviet family policy and legislation are still found in the most recent American standard work about the Soviet family, that of H. K. Geiger (1968).

On the other hand, some of the early publications have successfully tried to give an objective presentation and evaluation (Koenig 1946; Schlesinger 1949). They have made it clear that every society, including that of the USSR, seeks to influence the family in terms of its interests and in conformity with its value system. The Soviet attempt to limit the family's economic and educational functions and to have them assumed by society as much as possible should not be equated with an attempt to abolish the family as such. Schlesinger expressed this view in stating that "Soviet policy—as distinct from some ideologies popular at certain times—has never discarded the institution of the Family; but the fact that Marxist criticism was directed against the traditional man-dominated family

1

has saved the Soviet from any disputes about the mother's right to get whatever public benefits are provided for families with children, and has helped it to look for possible solutions of the population problem and for suitable surroundings for the new generation without being limited by the Family ideology" (Schlesinger 1949, p. 7).

This statement holds true not only for policy and legislation practice of the Soviet state but also for its ideological foundation, the teachings of Marxism.

THE MARXIST FOUNDATION OF SOVIET FAMILY POLICY

Marx and Engels sharply polemicized against the marriage and family forms they encountered in Western European society. Their analysis of contemporary forms of marriage and family provided only one part of their critical analysis of early capitalist and bourgeois society, while their prognosis of new marriage and family forms represented one part of their projected communist social order. In both realms, analysis and prognosis, Marx and Engels undoubtedly were caught in a certain contradiction, which in turn permitted future interpreters a free hand to emphasize either aspect of their statements.[1]

Their analysis of the early capitalist bourgeois society led Marx and Engels to believe that marriage and the family were in a process of dissolution and that this process was based upon the property and production relations in society. They saw the dissolution of the family in the ruling classes of the bourgeoisie as an internal moral decay; however, because of the economic dependency relations within the family, this dissolution could not lead to the family's external disintegration. They considered the bourgeois family a degenerate institution undermined by the enslavement of the woman, by infidelity, and by prostitution; and this could be reformed only through the abolition of capital. According to Engels, the "modern family" was "based upon the open or disguised domestic slavery of the woman. . . . In the great majority of cases today the husband must be the earner, the breadwinner of the family, at least in the propertied classes, and that gives him a dominant position which needs no special legal privilege" (Engels 1946, p. 51).

Marx and Engels believed that the patriarchal bourgeois family, and the choice of partner and marriage morality in bourgeois strata, were morally corrupted by the ties to "capital." Its lack of capital-created dependency relationships, however, enabled them to characterize the "proletarian family" as that unit where "sexual love becomes the actual rule in the relation toward the woman. . . . Here all property, for whose preservation and hereditary transmission monogamy and male domination were created, is absent, and with it also every impulse to make male domination valid" (Engels 1946, p. 48).

While the proletarian family is thus idealized and made the model of a future family form based upon individual sexual love, equality and freedom of divorce, the *Communist Manifesto* speaks of the "proletarian's forced lack of family" under capitalism (Marx and Engels 1966, p. 133). In contrast to the dissolution process of the bourgeois family, a process primarily conceived of as moral decay, in his report on the "Condition of the Working Class in England," Engels described the dissolution process of the proletarian family in the following manner:

> The woman's employment in a factory completely dissolves the family which forms the foundation of the current state of society, and this dissolution has the most demoralizing results for the married couple as well as the children. A mother who does not have time to take care of her child, to give him the basic affection during his first years, a mother who hardly gets a chance to see her child, cannot be a mother to this child. . . , and children who grow up under such conditions are later completely unable to adjust to family life; they can never feel at home in their own families because they have learned only an isolated life and therefore have to contribute to the already widespread general undermining of the family among workers (Marx and Engels 1966, p. 87).

There is an apparent contradiction between the idealization of the proletarian family as the model of the future family and the statement about actual "dissolution" of this family under conditions brought about by women's employment in industry, although such employment should be the rule in communist society. Rather than solving this contradiction, Marx and Engels assimilated and theoretically eliminated it in their vision of the future communist society, where changed production relations will lead to a restructuring of the ties between husband and wife and between parents and children. Marx described this historical development of the family dialectically in *Das Kapital:*

> As dreadful and disgusting as the dissolution of the old family within the capitalist system seems, big industry is nevertheless creating the new economic foundations for a higher form of the family and of the relations between both sexes. This new form assigns a crucial role to women, young people and children of both sexes in socially organized production processes outside the household (Marx and Engels 1966, p. 184).

Engels argued in a similar vein in his work *The Origin of the Family, Private Property and of the State.* He also named two important measures that should compensate for the threatening dissolution of the family due to the woman's employment in a factory: the creation of public household services and the societal upbringing of children:

> With the transition of the means of production into common property, the single family ceases to be an economic unit of society. Private housekeeping is transformed into a social industry. The care and education of children becomes a public affair; society cares for all children equally, be they legitimate or illegitimate (Engels 1946, p. 53).

Another aspect of the change in marriage and family forms is seen in Engels' answer, in *Foundations of Communism,* to the question, "What influence will the communist social order exert over the family?"

> It [the social order] will make the relation between the two sexes a purely private affair which concerns only the persons involved and in which society is not to interfere. It can [do] this, since it does away with private property and educates the children communally, thus destroying the two foundations of marriage as we have known it: the wife's dependency upon her husband and the children's upon their parents due to private property (Marx and Engels 1966, p. 131).

Although Marx and Engels advocated a change of sexual ties and family order, the individualization and "privatization" of marriage,[2] women's emancipation through financial independence, and a restriction of the family's functions in favor of social production, service, consumption, and education, they did not favor abolition of the family as an institution. However, they failed to specify which roles were to be assigned to the wife's familial functions and which to the educational functions of the family; they did not mention whether freedom of divorce and the spreading of factory work among women were reconcilable with parental responsibility for one's own children. Nor did they discuss whether the transfer of household chores as well as of the care and education of children to societal institutions might not deprive marriage and the family of essential psychological and social foundations and perhaps lead to a reduction in the desire of women to have children. Another problem lies in the fact that Marx and Engels made the change of human ties in marriage and in the family exclusively dependent upon production relations, that is, upon the economic basis of society or of family life, but they rejected a mutual economic dependency and responsibility in the ties between husband and wife, between parents and children.

The contradictory and problematic nature of Marxist teachings about marriage and family can perhaps best be demonstrated by the way the Soviet Union has taken over and modified these teachings in social ideology and applied them in political practice. It must be remembered that rural Russian society was decades behind England or Germany in entering the phase of early capitalism and industrialization, and the social teachings of Marx and Engels are related to an analysis of this condition. The October Revolution of 1917 took place at a time when industrial transformation had just begun in Russia. The Bolsheviks were willing to plan and implement the social change of Soviet society according to the basic principles of Marxism. It was as much a matter of transforming the property and production relations as it was of transforming the prerevolutionary Russian family order.

THE EARLY SOVIET PERIOD:
CAMPAIGN AGAINST THE "OLD" FAMILY

It has already been indicated that, in accordance with Marxist philosophy, official Soviet policy never attempted to abolish the family. For Lenin, the central problem did not lie in the alternative between either presence or absence of the family, but rather in its structure and social orientation, and mainly in the transformation of women's position in the family and society. The main task, as Lenin saw it, was "to include the woman in social productive work, to tear her away from domestic slavery, to free her from the depressing and forced subordination under the eternal and exclusive world of kitchen and child care" (*Sočinenija* 1941-1958, Vol. XXX, p. 383). In contrast to Klara Zetkin, Lenin describes the Party's solution of the woman question in the following manner:

> We are bringing the women into the social economy, into legislation and government. All educational institutions are open to them, so that they can increase their professional and social capacities. We are establishing communal kitchens and public eating-houses, laundries and repairing shops, infant asylums, kindergartens, children's homes, educational institutes of all kinds. In short, we are seriously carrying out the demand in our programme for the transference of the economic and educational functions of the separate household to society (Schlesinger 1949, p. 79).

For Lenin and the Bolsheviks, then, the central point was fighting the "old" family in the course of industrializing and the nationalization of the means of production. Industrialization could succeed only if the woman had a place in the national economy, but it goes without saying that inclusion of the highly illiterate female population into production could be accomplished only by a planned social change that affected the traditional family structure on the one hand and expanded public services and educational institutions on the other. However, aside from legal equality and admission into educational institutions, the woman's outside work activity actually represents an important aspect of her emancipation, not only in the Soviet Union but also in all industrial societies.

Of course, because of the short-term character and radical nature of the planned social change, the inclusion of the Soviet woman in the national economy has led to a one-sided delineation of her functions. Even though her continuing tie to the family should not be dissolved, in the very determination of her role she was required to acknowledge a certain priority of societal over individual interests. One of the central themes of the early revolutionary years was expressed by Bucharin and Preobraženskij in *The ABC's of Communism*, a commentary to the first Bolshevik party program, which stated that the individual person belongs "not to himself, but to society" (Bucharin and Preobraženskij 1923, p. 226). With respect to the determination of the woman's roles, this meant that her economic and educational functions in the family would be deemphasized and subordinated to her economic and political functions in society. Household and educational work, until then her main occupation, were to be increasingly taken over by public institutions.

Even before the 1917 Revolution the female population had participated to a considerable degree in the economic life of the nation. Dodge (1966, p. 32) points out that, if all age groups are taken into consideration, the first decades after the revolution saw an actual decrease in the proportion of women in the total number of the working force. As a matter of fact, up to 13.3% of the 10- to 15-year-olds took part in economic life as late as 1926, but this number decreased to no more than 3.6% in 1959 (due, among other things, to the lengthening of compulsory schooling). Until 1926, women's employment activity was almost exclusively confined to the agricultural sector, where, because of the need of their labor from the time they were very young, they were prevented from attending school. In 1926, 90.8% of working women were engaged in agriculture, representing 49.7% of all agricultural workers (independent farmers made up three-quarters of the working population at this time); only 9.2% were employed in the industrial and service sectors. In the same year, only 42.7% of the female population between the ages of 9 and 49 could read and write—as opposed to 71.5% of the male population.[3]

The first decisive changes in the social structure on the whole, and in the employment and educational structure of the female population in particular, occurred during and after the years of forced industrialization and collectivization under Stalin (1929-1930). By 1939, 26.9% of all working women were employed outside agriculture; in the agricultural sector, however, they were no longer engaged in family farming, but in the almost completely collectivized state industries, where they made up 54.3% of the collective farmers. In the same year only 18.4% of the female population between the ages of 9 and 49 were recorded as illiterates.[4]

The decade after 1926 saw the stepped-up integration of the USSR's female population into the industrial and collective planned economy as well as into educational institutions. Particularly with respect to an increase in educational level, these measures represented the first steps toward the emancipation of women, but they also led to sudden and frequently involuntary separation from the family unit, to a heavy work overload, and to an often arbitrary exploitation of the female work forces by the state. As will be shown, a certain conflict between their work and household roles has remained an unsolved problem, for the "liberation" from household and educational duties which Marx and Engels called for in connection with integrating women into the production process and into educational institutions was not realized and women themselves did not cease to identify with these traditional duties.

Society's priority over the individual extends not only to his employment in the national economy but also to his tie to the ideological value system of the society. The early Soviet period was characterized by a strong politization of every facet of social life in connection with the Bolsheviks' campaign to consolidate their power. The ideological campaign, often detrimental to family unity, was encouraged by the Party's ideological propaganda and by educational institutions. Children could be incited against their parents, who represented the "old" family (for example, in the case of the property-owning kulaks). The Second Komsomol (Communist Youth Organization) Congress (1919) called upon its members to help the young Cossacks "who are rising against their fathers" (Geiger 1968, p. 53). At the Third Komsomol Congress (1920), Lunačarskij, the then Commissar for Public Education, stated that the Bolsheviks wanted to free youth from the conservative influence of their parents in order to stamp them with the revolutionary spirit.[5]

A "left" minority of the Bolshevik party expanded the campaign for successful implementation of the Bolshevist revolutionary goals—a campaign against the "old" family and for the propagation of a gradual state takeover of the family's economic and educational functions—into a campaign against the institutions of marriage and family as a whole. Party functionaries such as Bucharin and Slepkov, as well as scientists like Volfson, Sabsovich, and Strumilin, announced the "dying out of the family under communism" and the loss of its economic and educational functions. At the same time, a number of them, including authors such as Kollontaj, publicized a revolution in sexual relations that led in the end to "free love." Discussion about the family was frequently pushed into the background by the struggle over the sex question. Neither the teachings of the classical leaders of Marxism nor the Soviet Party leadership supported these extreme views. Lenin clearly turned against the "bourgeois" morality of "free love"[6] and Krupskaja rejected Sabsovich's[7] suggestion of completely removing children from their families and educating them in communes.

Despite the internal Party disagreements on the fundamental role of marriage and family under communism, the first legislative acts of the Soviet government included the decree of December 19, 1917, which introduced divorce, and the legal code of October 17, 1918, which required the registration of births, deaths, and marriages. This illustrates the great importance that the Soviet leadership attributed to questions of family policy and primarily to women's emancipation. In 1926, the first RSFSR Code on Marriage and Family was enacted; it confirmed the abolition of church marriages and the introduction of civil marriages (which since the Revolution had been handled by registration bureaus), and it strengthened the demands for the wife's legal equality with her husband in questions of property, work, salary, educational opportunities, and freedom of divorce. Lenin's statements and these laws form the decisive foundations of any presentation and assessment of Soviet family policy.

The legal code of 1918, which stipulates the mutual rights and duties of marriage partners as well as of parents and children, underscores the economic and educational functions of the family. Just as the married couple owe each other support in the event that one of them becomes unable to work, parents are "required to take care of the development of their minor children, of their education and their training for a useful activity.... Parents are entitled to decide the type of education and instruction of the children.... Parents are obliged to provide board and living expenses for their minor children...." On the other hand, children are required to support parents who are unable to work as soon as they themselves are working and earning money. If they misuse their rights or fail to fulfill their duties toward their children, parents can be legally deprived of their parental rights. These rights and duties also apply in principle to divorced couples, to the support of a child after divorce, and to illegitimate children.[8]

The above-mentioned legal provisions illustrate the Soviet state's intent to protect the family and, in particular, the interests of children. Early Soviet marriage and family legislation, however, poses a crucial problem because, at that time, the Soviet state widely repudiated any control or protection over marriage. The decree of November 19, 1926,[9] supplemented the marriage and family legislation of 1918 and facilitated divorce to such an extent that the desire of one partner sufficed to declare the marriage dissolved without a hearing in the marriage license bureau. At the same time a law was passed which said that the same rights and duties derive from a nonregistered common-law marriage as from a registered marriage. In light of the growing frequency of common-law marriages, this law was supposed to guarantee a minimum legal protection for the wife and for children resulting from such unions.

Neither the renunciation of control over the stability of marriage relations nor the entire policy and legislation concerning the family can be simply taken as evidence of Soviet intentions to abolish the institutions of marriage and family. The teachings of Marxism (particularly those of Engels) looked upon the "freedom of divorce" as an individual's right and considered it crucial for women's emancipation; its propagation expressed the utopian view that personal ties needed no state regulation in a socialist society. In addition, the early Soviet period harbored a strong distrust of the marriage form inherited from feudal Russia. This distrust was directed equally against the religious foundation of the patriarchal structure and the insolubility of marriage, and against those traditions among Central Asian ethnic groups which permitted not only forced marriages arranged by parents but also the buying and kidnapping of a wife. Charčev (1964, p. 181) reports that such practices were still widespread in the early Soviet period. The idea behind the liberalization of the right of divorce was to make it possible for women to leave involuntary and unsatisfactory ties and to contribute to the democratization of marriage and family relationships.

In actuality, however, the formal facilitation of divorce did not lead to the emancipation of women, but rather to an increase in irresponsible attitudes on the part of husbands toward marriage and family. According to Charčev (1964, p. 169), there were one and more divorces for every five marriages during the

1930s. As mentioned earlier, common-law marriage was also recognized as a legal institution in 1926 in order to give women a minimum of legal protection; but unstable marriage relations remained synonymous with unstable family relations, and it was chiefly women and children who suffered as a result. The rapid spread of child neglect and juvenile delinquency in the 1920s and 1930s became a social and educational problem of top priority. These phenomena stemmed from the disintegration of many families in connection with the rising divorce rate, as well as from the effects of the Civil War and the forced collectivization of 1929-1930. As of July 20, 1927, the end of a three-year plan against child neglect, 105,000 children were in need of public care within the boundaries of the RSFSR alone.[10]

The decree of November 19, 1920,[11] which legalized abortion, must be mentioned as the final aspect of early Soviet marriage and family legislation. Prefaced by a fundamental condemnation of abortion, this decree was supposed to allow women a less damaging way to free themselves from unwanted offspring than by resorting to illegal operations performed by "babas." The legalization of abortion undoubtedly fulfilled a certain positive function in view of the already mentioned increase in irresponsible attitude toward marriage and family and in view of the lack of contraceptives. Like the facilitation of divorce, however, the legalization of abortion led to a decrease in the birthrate which the Soviet state found intolerable in the long run. Between 1926 and 1937 the number of births per 1,000 inhabitants fell from 44.0 to 38.7, and the natural population increase fell from 23.7 to 19.8.[12] A League of Nations study in 1946 stated that "there is evidence of wide fluctuation in the birthrates between 1928 and 1938. The Soviet code had legalized abortion. . . . The response to these provisions was at first only moderate, but by the middle of the thirties the number of births in the Soviet Union was sharply reduced from over six and one-half million births in 1926 and in 1927 to less than five million births in 1935. The reduction in fertility was also associated with an increase in the frequency of divorce" (Lorimer 1946, p. 126).

POLICY AND LEGISLATION SINCE 1936:
"THE STRENGTHENING OF THE FAMILY"

The early negative experiences with liberal legislation that made marriage a "private affair" (in Engels' sense of the term); the increasing disintegration of marriages and families resulting from misuse of the freedom of divorce, as well as the growing neglect of children and adolescents connected with it; and the stagnation of birthrates—all this induced the Party and the government to choose a new direction in family policy and in marriage and family legislation. Since Soviet society had by no means reached that stage of development in which the family's economic and educational functions could be passed on to social institutions, and since the national economy in the long run needed large manpower reserves, that is, a high birthrate, the "strengthening of the family" appeared to be the only path toward the consolidation of society. Legislation enacted in 1936 and 1944 made it more difficult to get a divorce; common-law marriage was abolished; parental responsibility for the education of children was strengthened; and motherhood and large families were encouraged by the prohibition of abortion (which was reinstated in 1955) and by financial support and social honors for mothers with many children.

A *Pravda* editorial on the 1936 decree, "On the prohibition of abortions, the increase of financial aid for pregnant women, the introduction of state aid for large families, the expansion of maternity hospitals, nurseries, and kindergartens, the increased penalties for nonpayment of alimony, and certain modifications in the divorce laws,"[13] described the new family policy:

> The published draft of the law prohibiting abortion and providing material assistance to mothers has provoked a lively reaction throughout the country. It is being heatedly discussed by tens of millions of people and there is no doubt that it will serve as a further strengthening of the Soviet family. Parents' responsibility for the education of their children will be increased and a blow will be dealt at the lighthearted, negligent attitude towards marriage.
>
> When we speak of strengthening the Soviet family, we are speaking precisely of the struggle against the survivals of a bourgeois attitude toward marriage, women and children. So-called 'free love' and all disorderly sex life are bourgeois through and through, and have nothing to do with either socialist principles or the ethics and standards of conduct of the Soviet citizen. . . . Fatherhood and motherhood have long been virtues in this country. . . . The rise in the standard of living has brought the joy of parenthood within the reach of all adults. The Soviet land cannot complain of too low a birthrate.
>
> Marriage and divorce are, of course, private affairs—but the state cannot allow anyone to mock at women or to abandon his children to the mercy of their fate. The irresponsible profligate who gets married five times a year cannot enjoy the respect of Soviet youth. Nor can a girl who flutters from one marriage into the next with the swiftness of a butterfly enjoy respect. Men and women of this sort merely deserve social contempt. Marriage is a serious, responsible business and one that must not be approached lightheartedly. We alone have all the conditions under which a working woman can fulfill her duties as a citizen and as a mother responsible for the birth and early upbringing of her children.
>
> A woman without children merits our pity, for she does not know the full joy of life. Our Soviet women, full-blooded citizens of the freest country in the world, have been given the bliss of motherhood. We must safeguard our family and raise and rear healthy Soviet heroes (Schlesinger 1949, pp. 251ff.).

Apparently, the main characteristic of the new direction in family policy is the clear and final renunciation of certain early trends toward the devaluation of marriage and the family as social institutions.

Also revealing is the Komsomol's position relating to the new family policy. During the early Soviet period this organization concentrated on educating young people to oppose the "old" family; since 1934-1935 it has emphasized education toward marriage and family responsibilities. Volfson reports a debate that developed in the mid-thirties after publication of a letter to the editor of *Komsomol'skaja pravda:*

> The letter put an outspoken question: ". . . Does a Komsomol need a family? Perhaps he does not need it at all . . . perhaps it is an extra weight which drags the Komsomol back or away from his primary aims and tasks?" The letter evoked an extraordinary response. The *Komsomol'skaja pravda* received about a thousand letters in connection with it, and discussions devoted to it were organized in many establishments and in a number of educational centers.
>
> What did these discussions show? That in the USSR a new generation is already taking shape which is setting up a new form of socialist family, based on equality, mutual affection, common work. It showed that our Youth demands a harmonious co-ordination of productive and social life with the life of the family, that it is determined in its opposition to an attitude of criminal irresponsibility towards the family and to all actions which disrupt the family.
>
> The Komsomol voiced the views of the best and most advanced section of Soviet Youth when in their new programme they said that "the All-Union Lenin Komsomol helps the Soviet State in strengthening the family and in taking care of children and mothers. It fights against the survivals of capitalism in regard to woman" (Schlesinger 1949, p. 314).

The Party's campaign for strengthening the family, or the campaign against an irresponsible attitude toward questions of marriage, family, and family education, has been a matter of public concern since 1936. Numerous placards appeared in the streets and public squares praising the unity of the Soviet family in pictures and slogans.[14] Newspaper articles and brochures propagated the maintenance of strict sexual morality and the fulfillment of parental educational duties as the demands of "communist ethics."

The parents of children who roamed about, who did not participate in societal activities, or whose school work was bad were called to account in their factories. Neglect of parental duty or desertion of a spouse could become the subject of proceedings in "comrades' courts." The decree of May 31, 1935, warned that parents who neglected the education of their children or whose children caroused in the streets in the evening were subject to a fine of up to 200 rubles without legal hearings. The police or the Ministry of Education were to report parental neglect of educational duty to the parents' place of work, and this could lead to effective pressure by "public opinion."[15]

As in all authoritarian regimes, family support and protection were combined with state control, not only of its stability but also of its ideological-political conformity. The Soviet state could undertake the strengthening of the family only if it could at the same time control the family's spirit and educational activity in line with its official ideology. Western democracies take issue with the extent to which Soviet laws and organized "public opinion" with respect to this goal have been implemented and emphasized since 1936, because such measures lead to strong encroachments upon private life. Following the condemnation of Stalinism, much criticism has also been expressed in the Soviet Union concerning excessive public interference in private family affairs, and its replacement by objective "pedagogical enlightenment" is suggested.[16]

The new direction in the family policy introduced in 1936 was continued in the decree of the Supreme Soviet of July 8, 1944, "On the increase of state aid for pregnant women, mothers with many children and unmarried mothers; on increased protection for mothers and children; on the introduction of the title 'Mother Heroine' and the creation of the 'Glory of Motherhood' order and 'Motherhood Medals.' "[17] Marriage and family legislation gave special support to this direction through its population policy goal, a goal that assumed crucial importance because of the great loss of life during World War II.

The 1944 law granted mothers with three and more children a monthly state allowance; mothers with five and more children were awarded orders and tax benefits; and families with less than three children were burdened with a type of "childless tax." To increase the birthrate, the state even encouraged illegitimate births, and went so far as to relieve the fathers of illegitimate children of financial responsibility and to deprive the mothers of their right (which they had until 1936) to sue for paternity and alimony. As our discussion of the Basic Law of 1968 will show, many women sharply condemned this regulation, which remained valid until 1968; they considered it unjust, since it freed men from moral and financial responsibility at the expense of women. In addition, the woman's position was made more difficult by the continuance of the 1936 ban on abortion.

Although the mutual duties and rights of parents and children in the 1944 law corresponded in essence to the principles developed since 1918,[18] the legal determinations concerning marriage and divorce saw significant corrections. The 1944 law requiring marriage registration and the abolition of common-law marriage as a legal institution made it possible for the state to exert control over marital ties, which it had almost completely ignored since 1926. In the words of the prominent Soviet family lawyer G. M. Sverdlov, the Soviet state is interested in the registration of marriages "because this makes possible an influencing of the marital ties in a direction that is both necessary and useful for the state as well as for every individual. . . . The fact that the state acknowledges only registered marriages favors the realization of one of the most important demands of Soviet family law and of socialist ethics, i.e., monogamy" (Sverdlov 1946, p. 36). The obligation to register a marriage is closely connected with making divorce more difficult. In 1936 a married couple was obliged to appear before the marriage registration bureau; the fees for a divorce were increased; and passports had to show a record of divorce. According to the 1944 law, which included a further increase in the divorce fee, divorce was granted only after a legal proceeding in which the couple had to present valid grounds for divorce and the judge had to designate a reconciliation period. The provision that the beginning of legal divorce hearings had to be announced in the local paper could mobilize public opinion against the couple and was annulled on December 10, 1965, by a decree which simplified divorce proceedings.

Except for the already mentioned 1955 relegalization of abortion and the 1965 simplification of divorce proceedings, Soviet marriage and family laws remained unchanged between 1944 and 1968. Even the law project of 1968, which will be discussed in the next section and represents the first new codification of the marriage and family code since 1944, follows the traditions of the 1936 and 1944 laws. As a result, one can say that, since 1944, the Party leadership and public organizations have rarely dealt with family policy in their official statements, and the basic policy of strengthening the family has undergone no legal, economic, or educational change. Official party statements during and after the Khrushchev era concentrate on enumerating a series of state measures favoring the family: increased job protection for pregnant women, larger child allowances, the easing of housework through the gradual development of public services, the improvement of educational work through the expansion of the network of societal educational institutions, a higher standard of living and stepped-up housing construction, more leisure time through a shortened workweek (40 hours), introduction of the five-day workweek (1967), etc.

In speaking of the educational role of the family, official party statements repeat the fact that the family gains importance under communism; however, they demand the assimilation of family education into societal education, as well as societal control over it. At the Twentieth Party Congress, Khrushchev said that family and school are "now, as before, the most important factors in the socialist education of children"; the family must be supported by nurseries, kindergartens, and boarding schools (XX Party Congress, 1956, pp. 49ff.). The Premier emphasized the societal element in education even more strongly at the Twenty-first Party Congress: "We must enhance the role of the state and of society in the education of children and increase state and social support for the family. The planned construction of numerous boarding schools, nurseries, and kindergartens is aimed toward this goal." Khrushchev criticized the necessity for many women to devote themselves exclusively to the household and to the raising of children, for in this manner "active participation in societal life is made more difficult" (XXI Party Congress, 1959, pp. 68ff.). At the Twenty-second Party Congress, Khrushchev clearly opposed the view that the Soviet system is hostile toward the family: "Those who feel that the importance of the family is declining in the transition to communism and in time will completely disappear are totally wrong. In reality the family is growing stronger under communism, and family ties will finally be freed from material concerns and attain a high level of purity and single-mindedness" (Materialy 1961, p. 196). Finally, Khrushchev's comments at the All-Russian Teachers Congress in 1960 clearly express the Soviet state's ambivalent attitude toward the family:

> The example of parents and older family members is very important in the formation of views and ideals, intentions, and habits. . . . It is necessary that Party organizations consider the questions of the education of children in the family as more than a "personal" affair of the parents, and not assume a "neutral" attitude. Family education must be seen as one of the very important aspects of Party work (Khrushchev 1961, p. 31).

The relevance of the Party's statements on educational policy, pedagogy, and its position toward the family as the source of education will become even clearer in the following pages. However, our description of Soviet marriage and family legislation would be incomplete without a discussion of the Basic Law of 1968.

RECENT TRENDS IN LEGISLATION

The legislative commissions of the Supreme Soviet of the USSR have in the course of several years worked out a "Project Concerning the Basic Principles of the Legislation of the USSR and the Union Republics on Marriage and Family." After *Isvestija* and other newspapers published it on April 10, 1968, six weeks of public debate ensued. Thousands of Soviet citizens from every social stratum participated, mainly in the pages of *Isvestija* and *Literaturnaja gazeta.* The editors, in publishing a small number of the letters, acknowledged that the debate was the most extensive in recent years. The chairman of the governmental commission concerned, Solomencëv, reported in *Pravda* on June 27, 1968, that several criticisms expressed by the public had been taken into consideration in the modification of the law project. Finally, on June 28, *Pravda* published a law of the Supreme Soviet, "On the Ratification of the Basic Principles of the Legislation of the USSR and the Union Republics on Marriage and Family." This law established that union republic legislation was to conform to the new "basic principles" that would go into effect on October 1, 1968.

The introduction to the Basic Law explains the principles of family policy:

> One of the most important tasks of the Soviet state is concern for the Soviet family, which harmoniously combines the societal and personal interests of citizens.
> The Soviet Union has created the most favorable conditions for the strengthening and well-being of the family. The citizens' material prosperity is growing continuously; the housing, household, and cultural conditions of family life are being improved.
> The socialist society is devoting great attention to the protection and support of motherhood and to the guaranteeing of a happy childhood.

The communist upbringing of the younger generation and the development of their physical and mental abilities is the family's most important duty. State and society assist the family in every way in the education of children; the network of kindergartens, nurseries, boarding schools, and other children's institutions is being steadily expanded.

The Soviet woman is guaranteed the necessary societal and economic conditions for combining happy motherhood with ever more active and creative participation in productive and political life. Soviet marriage and family legislation is called upon to actively cooperate in the final liberation of family ties from material concerns, in the overcoming of the remnants of the woman's unequal position in domestic life, and in the creation of a communist family, where one's deepest personal feelings find their satisfaction.

Article I lists the most important tasks of marriage and family legislation:

the further strengthening of the Soviet family, which is based upon the principles of communist ethics;

the establishment of family relations based upon a voluntary marital bond between husband and wife, and upon feelings of mutual love, friendship, and respect that are free from material considerations for all members of the family;

the raising of children by the family in organic combination with societal education in the spirit of devotion toward the mother country, in the spirit of a communist attitude toward work and of the children's preparation for active participation in the construction of Communist society;

the comprehensive protection of the interests of mothers and children and the guarantee of a happy childhood for every child;

the final abolition of harmful remnants and customs of the past in family ties;

education toward responsibility with respect to the family (*Isvestija*, April 10, 1968).

The basic principles stipulated in the new law project confirm that the Soviet regime is still committed to its 1936 policy of strengthening the family.

The sequence of its provisions demonstrate the great importance of the new regulations on marriage ties: marriage forms, the rights and duties of the couple, and divorce. They state for the first time in any law that marriage is to be performed "in a solemn manner" (Article 10). In the past decade there has been a shift in the locale of marriage ceremonies from license bureaus to "wedding palaces." The exchanging and wearing of wedding rings, and the reintroduction of the custom of the wedding veil and of inviting friends and relatives, have enjoyed greater popularity. The new law officially approved and emphasized the symbolic importance of the wedding ceremony, which was gradually gaining strength. It was also the first time that any law prescribed a waiting period between the wedding announcement and the marriage registration

(Article 10). Although many lawyers and others favored the introduction of a three- to six-month engagement, the waiting period was fixed at only one month. Even so, it can still serve as an educational measure that encourages reflection and prevents irresponsible marriages.

The basic principles contain two new provisions concerning the mutual rights and duties of the couple. The wife is entitled to full support during pregnancy and for one year after the birth of a child (Article 13), in addition to the customary provision in the event of inability to work. Furthermore, the husband can make no divorce claim during this time without his wife's agreement (Article 14). These important stipulations increase the husband's material and moral responsibility for a pregnant wife and a young mother, and fundamentally recognize the necessity of maternal care and rearing for the small child. The mutual support obligation of spouses was further increased by the abolition of time limits for this obligation, even if the disability occurred up to a year after divorce (Article 13).

The most essential changes in the new marriage and family legislation refer to the expansion of the rights and duties of parents and children, particularly those involving the father and an illegitimate child. Since the decree of July 8, 1944, abolished the wife's right to sue for alimony, responsibility for the support and upbringing of an illegitimate child was largely placed upon the mother and the state; the new provisions reverse this and assign chief responsibility to the father. The father's lack of responsibility for an illegitimate child was the most frequently criticized aspect in the earlier marriage and family law, and it became a focal point in the public debate on the basic principles. Such laxity encouraged a husband's irresponsible attitude toward marriage and family duties, and one-sidedly burdened his wife with the results of "getting into trouble."[19] In contrast, the new provisions provide that the paternity of an illegitimate child can be legally determined (Article 16); when there is no common declaration from the unmarried parents as to the child's origin, the maintenance of a common household before the birth of the infant or the common care and raising of the child serves as proof of paternity. Furthermore, strong public pressure should expand the provisions for the legal determination of paternity. The social status of the illegitimate child is further improved by the fact that he no longer has to forego a surname; if paternity is not established, the mother can determine the surname herself (Article 17).

The educational duties of parents, and the state's control over the fulfillment of these duties, are particularly emphasized. Parents "should raise their children in the spirit of the moral code of the builders of communism" (Article 18). They can be deprived of their parental rights upon the request of state and societal institutions, upon the request of one of the parents or the guardian if they "do not fulfill their educational duties," if they "exercise a harmful influence over the child through amoral, antisocial behavior," or if they are alcoholics or drug addicts (Article 19). The deprivation of parental rights, meanwhile, does not release parents from their obligation to support the child

(Article 19). On the other hand, children are obligated to support disabled parents, but the new provisions free them from this duty "if it is decided by court that the parents have deviated from the fulfillment of their parental duties" (Article 20).

The whole problem of the policy and legislation for strengthening the family in an authoritarian and ideology-based state is also evident in the provisions on the withdrawal of parental rights: the family is promoted as the source of education, but only so long as it maintains conformity with the societal value system in its educational work. It is difficult to ascertain whether, under current political conditions, such drastic measures as the withdrawal of parental rights on political-ideological grounds are really being implemented.[20]

In the course of fifty years, Soviet family policy and marriage and family legislation have increasingly moved further away from the Marxist axiom that marriage and family ties are a private affair.

The strengthening of the family has become synonymous with the strengthening of society, but it has its limits where the interests of the state are concerned. The state leaves much of the education of children up to the family, but does not allow the family any autonomy in this area. It considers family education a part of societal education, which is subject to state intervention.

Those aspects of family policy and legislation which have to do with women clearly illustrate the fact that the strengthening of the family primarily serves the strengthening of society. Although the Soviet woman has to fulfill her traditional roles as housewife and educator-mother in almost a full measure, it is not the fulfillment of these roles but, rather, her contribution to the national economy through outside employment that counts as her first social duty. On the other hand, measures aimed at raising the birthrate—extending maternal protection and state aid for families with many children—cannot disguise the fact that the social and economic pressure toward outside employment, without the possibility of part-time work, makes the woman's fulfillment of her traditional roles extremely difficult. Women's emancipation is still almost fully dependent on the economic interests of the state. As far as the Marxist goal of women's integration into production and educational institutions is concerned, woman's emancipation has been realized to a degree that is unmatched elsewhere in the world. On the other hand, neither the Marxist goal of freeing women from household and educational duties (which has remained one of the goals of family policy) nor the specific desire of women to successfully combine these duties with outside employment has come to pass. The fact that one requirement of women's emancipation has succeeded, but the other has not yet been reached, reflects perhaps not only the economic problems of Soviet society but also the different priorities which have been and are being assigned to the societal and individual aspects of emancipation.

FAMILY AND EDUCATIONAL POLICY

This chapter will discuss some general features of Soviet educational policy and pedagogy which concern the family. Specific problems of family educational policy—such as preschool education, full-day and boarding schools, etc.—will be dealt with in subsequent chapters.

The founders of Marxism asserted that "education of all children beginning at that moment when they can first do without early maternal care" was to be realized "in national institutions and at the cost of the state" (Marx and Engels 1966, p. 129). Lenin felt that the "goal of our program" was the "transference of domestic and educational functions from the individual household to society" (*Vospominanija* 1957, pp. 490ff.). As a result, the main interest of the Soviet state since the revolution has been societal education in organized state institutions. The policy of maximum restrictions on the family's educational functions and their assumption by state institutions was widely accepted as a goal during the early Soviet period. These early programs, together with the propagation of state-sponsored preschool education for all children, testify to the agreement that existed then between the radical minority who predicted the total "dying off of the family under communism" and the Party leadership, which never fully accepted such a radical vision. An excerpt from the *ABC's of Communism* by Bucharin and Preobraženskij is probably characteristic of the general basic concept of educational policy in the 1920s:

> The fundamental and most basic right of children's education also belongs to society. . . . Society may entrust parents with the raising of their children, but the sooner it becomes involved itself, the less reason it has to leave this education to the parents, because the ability to raise children is certainly less frequent than the ability to produce children. . . . The future belong to societal education. Societal education permits the socialist society to most successfully educate the future generation with the least expenditure of energy and means (Bucharin and Preobraženskij 1923, pp. 226-227).

However, while the utopian goal of a societal education for children from birth to maturity was uniformly advocated, there was disagreement over the degree to which children should be taken out of the family and away from parental care and upbringing. Lunačarskij, the Commissar for Public Education, and a number of other school policy-makers supported the radical separation of children and parents. Krupskaja and other leading pedagogues pleaded for a combination of societal and family education.

Shortly before his death (1933), Lunačarskij wrote:

> Our problem now is to do away with the household and to free women from the care of children. It would be idiotic to separate children from

their parents by force. But when, in our communal houses, we have
well-organized quarters for children, connected with the adults' quarters,
there is no doubt the parents will, of their own free will, send their
children to these quarters, where they will be supervised by trained
pedagogical and medical personnel. There is no doubt that the terms "my
parents," "our children," will gradually fall out of usage, being replaced by
such conceptions as "old people," "adults," "children" and "infants"
(Geiger 1968, pp. 47-48).

Radical proponents of a comprehensive societal preschool education, such as
M. Krupenina, felt that the children's home should "supersede individualistic
family education through societal education, remove the child from the hands of
the disintegrated family, and place him a system of organized children's work
communes" (Anweiler 1964, pp. 150-151).

Taking another view, in 1929 Krupskaja sharply criticized *The Cities of the
Future and the Organization of the Socialist Household* by L. M. Sabsovič, who
favored a total societal education for children outside the family. It was to be
based upon a platonic model in state-organized "youth cities" isolated from the
family and the world of grown-ups. Krupskaja argued:

> Projects of this sort can only compromise the cause of societal education,
> and they only show how poorly many people still envision socialism. . . .
> We must endeavor to create such forms of societal education which do not
> tear children away from the influence of the worker and kolkhoz peasant
> milieu, which do not separate them from their parents, but which at the
> same time do eliminate the bad points of contemporary education
> (Krupskaja 1962, pp. 132-133).

The well-known pedagogue S. T. Šackij also supported the combining of
familial and societal education; his primary concern in this connection was the
problem of pedagogical cooperation between teachers and parents.

The moderate idea represented by Krupskaja and Šackij—the combining of
societal and family education—had presumably been supported by the majority
of the Party during the early Soviet period. The idea subsequently gained a
following in the Soviet Union and succeeded. An analysis of the development of
Soviet family pedagogy will show that Khrushchev was not alone in advocating
it, and several reasons more pragmatic than ideological can be cited for this
changing conception. The disintegration of many families in the postrevolutionary years (owing to the hardships of the Civil War and to the liberal divorce
legislation) and the resulting social problems forced people to realize that a
general breakup of the family would lead to the disintegration of society and
that the family was irreplaceable in its economic and educational functions.
Furthermore, the necessary economic and pedagogical prerequisites for the
realization of a comprehensive system of societal education for children from
birth to maturity never existed in the Soviet Union. Finally, popular attitudes

toward the family and family education had to be considered; as the discussion on preschool training and boarding schools will show, the great majority of Soviet parents yield the care and upbringing of their children only under duress. However, Lunačarskij's above-cited opinion demonstrates that even the radical advocates of societal education never envisioned a compulsory total removal of all children from their families.

ORIGIN AND DEVELOPMENT OF FAMILY PEDAGOGY

The first two decades following the October Revolution saw only gradual formation of a uniform pedagogical theory in the Soviet Union. According to O. Anweiler (1964), this was due, on the one hand, to the various competing influences of prerevolutionary Russian pedagogy and, on the other, to Western pedagogy and psychology, which contributed to the origin of "pedology." Efforts toward an independent Soviet pedagogy reflecting the goal of educational policy concentrated upon questions of the institutional education of children. As long as the family's position as an educational factor was still under debate, the pedagogues' concern for the family remained in the background. Except for Krupskaja's and Šackij's unsystematic contributions to questions of communist family education, the year 1936 witnessed a fundamentally new assessment of the family as the source of education, and of the application of Soviet pedagogy to questions of family education. That same year also saw the announcement of the policy and legislation for the strengthening of the family. Until then pedagogical literature did "not devote sufficient attention to questions of family education; pedagogical theorists hardly considered these questions" (Medynskij and Petruchin 1955, p. 5).

The new pedagogical interest in the family is especially connected with the name and writings of A. S. Makarenko who turned his attention to this question in 1936. His *Lectures on the Raising of Children* and his *A Book for Parents,* which appeared in 1937, still constitute the foundation of Soviet family pedagogy.

In the youth colonies he himself directed, Makarenko was confronted with one of the burning social and pedagogical problems of his time—juvenile delinquency—and with the material and moral misery of a growing number of young people from disintegrated and incomplete families. Based upon this experience, he felt that a crucial way to eliminate the causes of neglect would be to arouse a sense of responsibility among all parents for the rearing of their children. His works on family education were not based on a psychological theory of the child and his development, as was the case with "pedology." Rather, his was a theory of the family as a "friendship collective" that mediated between the child and society, and an appeal to all parents for exemplary behavior and corresponding concrete instructions. This is not the place to discuss Makarenko's theory of family education in detail; it has already been sufficiently done in Western literature.[21] More important for this study is the fact that, according to Makarenko, the family as a whole should be treated as the legitimate, necessary, and suitable source of education for the "new man" of communist society.

The high estimate of the family as the source of communist education presupposes various considerations. In the first place, Makarenko established no dichotomy between "individualistic family education" and "societal education," as did early Soviet pedagogues. Instead, the family itself was considered a "collective." In addition, as in the legal definitions of the "strengthening of the family," both the parents' educational activity and their exemplary behavior as a prerequisite for it were defined as a "social duty." For Makarenko, the parents' authority and the family's ability to fulfill an important educational role were based on the fact that parents represent models of society and its values. The strong emotional tie between parents and children provide Makarenko with an opportunity to realize, particularly in family education, a basic principle of his pedagogy, namely, the combining of high demands upon the child with love and respect for him.[22] Since parents, in their role as educators, should represent society, the demands they make upon themselves and their children, and the values upon which they themselves are oriented and which direct their children's consciences, should correspond to the demands and values of society. In this connection, the concepts of "work," "discipline," "comradely solidarity," and "citizenship" are most important. In those cases where the individual family does not represent these values, Makarenko regards external intervention as justified and necessary, including indirect influences on the child through education in school and through its effect upon the family. In his essay "My Work Experience," Makarenko explains:

> I mean that the question about the types of influence upon the family must be solved with the following logic: the school is a state organization; the family, however, is an organization determined by everyday life; consequently the influencing of the family is best achieved through the students (Works V, pp. 334-335).

At the time when legislation and Party propaganda were declaring family education a "public affair," Makarenko's publications were the first to offer a systematic description of the Soviet family as an "education collective" and an "economic collective." All these materials contributed not only to the increasing frequency with which, since 1936, questions of family education were dealt with by Soviet pedagogy but also to their increasing popularity as a subject of public debates, organized demonstrations of public opinion, and pedagogical propaganda among the people.

Between 1939 and 1941 several pedagogical conferences were held to discuss the family's role in the education of children and methods of family education. Two volumes of collected papers dealing with "the family and the school," as well as a series of brochures about various questions of family education, were published, all reflecting Makarenko's pedagogy.[23]

The Society for the Dissemination of Political and Scientific Knowledge,[24] founded in 1947, furthered the cause of pedagogical propaganda. Through popular science brochures and organized lecture series, as well as through the establishment of parents' universities in schools and factories, it reached wide audiences and included questions of family education in its programs.

The Academy of Pedagogical Sciences (APN), founded in 1943, became the center of pedagogical research, not only in the field of family pedagogy but in other fields as well. Before discussing the family pedagogical research of the APN, it should be mentioned that both the Academy and the Society for the Dissemination of Political and Scientific Knowledge engaged in pedagogical propaganda. Since 1946, *Family and School,* a popular scientific monthly, has been systematically distributed to parents and teachers. The task of the journal is:

> To provide support for parents in the raising of their children, for the school and teachers in organizing close cooperation with families, and for the propagation of pedagogical knowledge among the people. The journal publishes essays about pedagogy and pedagogical psychology, letters from parents and teachers illustrating experiences of family education and the connections between the school and the students' families, critical bibliographical book reviews on pedagogical themes, advice on concrete educational questions, hygiene and health care for children, and, in addition, materials for children's reading, games, entertainment, and work activities in the family (*Pedagogičeskij slovar'* 1960, II, pp. 336-337).

An APN Division for the Upbringing of the Child in the Family, independent of the Division for Preschool Education, was founded. It was dissolved in 1967 and incorporated into the Institute for Preschool Education of the APN. Since the mid-1940s this research department has offered a steadily growing number of publications about family education, devoted mainly to such topics as education for work or the moral, atheistic, physical, and esthetic upbringing of children in the family (primarily those of preschool ages). Only two of these publications deserve closer attention here, since they represent the only comprehensive contributions toward the further development of Makarenko's theory of family education.

The first standard work on family pedagogy to come out of the APN was by the physician, psychologist, and pedagogue E. A. Arkin, *For Parents on Education: The Raising of the Child in the Family from His First Year to Maturity,* published in 1949. Starting with the decisive eduational importance of early childhood, Arkin sees the parents as the child's prime educators and opposes the view that, in light of the growing number of public educational institutions, parents could transfer their children's education to the state:

> Such a view is not only incorrect, it is also harmful. It is not right because

a significant minority of children spend a large part of their time at home; also because, especially under the conditions of our system, which places the same educational goals upon the family as upon the kindergarten and school—namely, the training of a generation of solid and steeled builders of a new, correct, and happy life unconditionally devoted to the socialist fatherland—the closest cooperation between the family and societal educational institutions is not only possible but absolutely necessary. This view is harmful because it deadens the parents' feeling of duty not only toward their children but toward the Soviet state, which is most interested that the creature to which the parents have given life should grow into a useful, well-rounded member of socialist society (Arkin 1949, p. 10).

Although, like Makarenko, Arkin primarily emphasizes the societal character and goal of family education and calls upon the societal duty of the parents, whom he considers the prime source of education, and although, like Makarenko, he attributes "enormous significance to the living model which, in the case of education, is second to none" (p. 12), his theory of family education nevertheless contains features that go beyond Makarenko. As a physician and psychologist, Arkin proceeds more strongly from the child himself and from his needs in various developmental stages. His work is arranged according to age groups: he presents a psychophysical "characteristic of the . . . age group" at the beginning of every chapter; and he emphasizes the applicability of educational measures to each age group—hygiene and health care, play, work, daily routine, an appropriate system of reward and punishment, etc. This approach revives certain trends of developmental psychology presented by the earlier pedologists. In 1919, soon after the October Revolution, Arkin assumed the leadership of a Special Preschool Center for Child Study.[25] Arkin hardly advocates the child's individual and "spontaneous" development as being central to his family pedagogy; like Makarenko, he strongly emphasizes discipline and order, for he feels that the family must be given the task of raising children toward ideological-political conformity with the Soviet regime:

The goal is clear—it remains constant in the whole course of the child's growth and development. . . . Education should develop all those potentialities present in the child, it should arm him with all those traits and abilities which enable him to become a fighter for the cause of Lenin and Stalin, a well-rounded member of communist society. This is the goal, and all reasonable parents are striving toward it (Arkin 1949, p. 49).

After 1949, a large number of papers on individual questions of family education appeared, but only the writings of Flerina (1950), Krasnogorskaja (1952), Dragynova (1955), Volkova (1956), and Markova (1956) will be mentioned here. Their essays are more often examples of concrete pedagogical advice or guidelines for parents rather than scientific analyses. The same is also true for the second standard work on Soviet family pedagogy to come out of the

APN's Department for the Education of the Child in the Family, a volume of collected papers entitled *Parents and Children: The Raising of Children in the Family,* edited by E. I. Volkova and published in 1961. Guidelines for the child's training toward a fixed daily routine, and for discipline and work, are the nucleus of this book. Numerous inserted leaflets provide parents with references about children's games, gymnastic exercises, arts and crafts activities, etc. Programs issued by parents' committees in kindergartens and schools, and the text of student and Pioneer regulations, inform parents about the goals of societal education. On the other hand, Volkova devotes less attention than Arkin to a description and discussion of problems concerning psychophysical development; and questions of sexuality and sex education, which Arkin treated in detail, are hardly considered.

Like Makarenko's and Arkin's writings, *Parents and Children* emphasizes the important educational function of the family and underscores its special character. Father and mother are characterized as "the child's first educators" (*Roditeli i deti* 1961, p. 44). The results of family disintegration and of the lack of family education for the child are considered "unusually problematic" (p. 5). The special nature of family education is seen in the close emotional tie between parents and children; the strength of the parents as educators is exemplified in their "daily contact with the children and in direct influence upon them" on the strength of personal example (p. 4). Like Makarenko and Arkin, Volkova considers the education of children as the "fundamental duty of the Soviet family" (p. 5). Parental responsibility for the social behavior of children is juxtaposed against the educational duty of the parents:

> The undisciplined behavior of young people is a very frequent thing, and difficulties in educational work are caused by parental mistakes which were committed in the early years of the child's upbringing (p. 263).

The volume considers the following factors of family education as especially important: the emotional and moral quality of familial relations, primarily its marital aspects; the uniformity of educational demands; the exemplary nature of parental behavior; the maintenance of a fixed daily routine; and the requirement that children participate responsibly in the household with a view toward their systematic education for work. These factors are not subjected to sociopsychological analysis, with references to problems of marriage, divorce, incomplete families, the parents' time budget, etc.; instead, they are treated exclusively in a normative manner.

The orientation of family pedagogy with respect to societal norms is most clearly reflected in the specific determination of the goal of education: "well-rounded development of the personality."[26] This personality is characterized by "love of work," "discipline," and "cultured behavior," and above all, conforms to the ideological-political value system.

Only since the beginning of the 1960s have several new elements been introduced into the debate on the goals of education. They signify a new trend in Soviet pedagogy of giving serious attention to the values of the personality—both within and outside the framework of the collective. There has also been a move toward establishing family pedagogy on a better scientific basis and expanding the normative behavior theory in Makarenko's tradition into a program of family pedagogical research. This theory, which essentially carries the principles of societal education over to family education, and its related research, should result in practical suggestions for family education. This possibility prompted the pedagogue L. A. Levšin to outline the following program in the *Pedagogical Encyclopedia* (the program has not yet been implemented):

> The further perfection of the practice of family education greatly depends upon the elaboration of family pedagogy as one of the important areas of the pedagogical sciences. Pedagogical science is confronted with the task of elaborating a theory and methodology of family education which will apply the most recent research methods for this purpose, primarily sociological and sociopsychological, and will permit in-depth analysis of the many-sided connections between family and school, environmental milieu and society as a whole, and family relations and their influence upon the growing generation (Levšin 1966, p. 828).

SOCIETY, FAMILY, AND THE INDIVIDUAL—
EMERGING CONCEPTS

In addition to its concern with a special family pedagogy, Soviet pedagogy has in recent years dealt with problems of family education in communist society. The family's role in the upbringing of the younger generation and the future goals of education have been debated in official textbooks on pedagogy, in encyclopedia articles, and in the press. Several examples follow.

The idea of an exclusively societal, extrafamilial education for children, which had a certain importance in early Soviet pedagogy, has now been completely abandoned. Of course, "societal communist education" is assigned the leading role on principle, but at the same time it emphasizes that the family "exercises an important educational function" (*The Foundations of Communist Education* [hereafter *The Foundations*] 1964, p. 301). In 1960 Academician S. G. Strumilin published an article in *Novy mir* (New World), in which he introduced his idea about the dying off of the family and its educational functions under communism. His arguments met with uniform protest, not only from readers but from pedagogical circles as well. The editorial board of the journal *Family and School*, in declaring Strumilin's theory to be harmful, stated:

> We are creating an entire system of societal education not to abolish but to support the family. . . . The family must be strengthened in every respect so that it can become one of the basic elements of communist society and an effective organ of communist education. . . . The children's collective,

with all its undeniable importance, should not be looked upon as the only form of education for the younger generation ("Stroitel'stvo kommunizma i sem'ja" 1961, pp. 6ff.).

Despite a certain distrust against the remnants of individualistic, apolitical, and bourgeois views in many Soviet families, current Soviet pedagogy still feels that the family's potential and customary individual care of the child forms a necessary counterbalance to education in the children's collective. Levšin's statement clearly reflects this view:

> Does it make any sense to replace family education as a whole with societal education? . . . The children's collective undoubtedly constitutes a great [educational] power. It plays an enormous role in the children's lives and education . . . in the formation of their personality. But it has its limitations; and if they are overstepped, the collective will not only not serve the correct education but will directly hinder it. . . . Exclusive education in a children's collective is limited to a certain amount of potential adult influence. The leader of the collective can devote only little time to each child, and there is always the danger that the individual child, with his unique development, will be lost in the mass of children and will not receive the necessary "dose" of direct adult attention. . . . Societal education cannot exist without the familial, nor can family education exist without the societal (Levšin 1964, pp. 291-292).

Recognition of the various and mutually complementary influence potentials of the family and the children's collective has given rise to consideration of a division of tasks between the family and the school in the raising of children.

> In school the teacher teaches and educates; the father and mother, however, not only raise but live with children. They have more points of contact and greater possibilities of influence over the children in many life situations. . . . The parents' love for each other and for their children, the ties of affection, respect, and trust, shape the child's feelings, his moral qualities (Pedagogika 1966, pp. 630ff.).
>
> A whole series of character traits are very important for the formation of communist awareness, feelings, and characteristics, and only the family can impart them. The family is that social organization which is based upon love and which alone can foster this feeling ("Stroitel'stvo kommunizma i sem'ja" 1961, p. 8).
>
> If the school plays the main role in questions of the quality of our children's knowledge, then in questions of personality development the family is destined to fulfill a hardly less fundamental function, and its role will undoubtedly grow (Zuev 1967).

These statements recognize and acknowledge the family as a specific, independent, and irreplaceable educational field. According to Soviet pedagogy, the family's most important functions are the emotional upbringing of children, the "channeling of their needs" (*The Foundations* 1964, pp. 313ff.), and their moral upbringing, including sex education.

Current Soviet pedagogy differentiates between its conception of the family as an educational factor not only with respect to its tasks and fields of education, but also its changing role at every age level of the child. During infancy, the family is the main source of education. Since it is particularly well suited for the fostering of trust and love, it is essential for this phase of the child's development. . . . For the preschool child, the family and the kindergarten are seen as equally important educational factors (although kindergarten teachers do enjoy a certain authority beyond that of parents[27]), but the children's and youth collective is clearly the child's main source of education after he enters school.[28] Soviet pedagogy assigns top priority to the tasks of transmitting knowledge and educating for work, discipline, and ideological commitment, tasks which could doubtless be more effectively fulfilled by a collective than by the family. Although the family continues to be considered an important supplementary educational factor, the school is given the "leading role" and is enabled through its teachers "to direct the educational influence of the family" (*The Foundations* 1964, p. 317).

The Young Pioneers and the Komsomol, both of which are state youth organizations, are a part of the leading role of the children's and youth collective. Although there is little evidence, in current Soviet pedagogy, with respect to a priority between the family and youth organizations, the latter are seen as "more reliable" in the field of ideological-political education because they are completely Party-controlled. Like the school, these organizations are utilized whenever there is a campaign against the "remnants of the past" in the family:

> The majority of Soviet families actively help the school and the Pioneer organization in raising the younger generation in the spirit of communist morality. However, not all parents understand and fulfill their duty well enough. Sometimes the children's conflict with their parents leads to a complete break with the family. Of course we have ways of educating every such child, but we should be thinking of means to increase the effectiveness of the Soviet public and the Komsomol in the future in order to eradicate these negative phenomena in the family ("Obščestvennost', sem'ja, i pionerskaja organizacija" 1963, p. 60).

Soviet pedagogy sets the same goals for family education as it does for societal education. The "most important" educational goal is the "well-rounded development of the personality" (*The Foundations* 1964, p. 308). As with Marx and Lenin, this idea envisions a personality characterized not by "unbridled individualism" and the restriction of interests to the "small world of one's own ego and family" (ibid., p. 34-35), as is the case in "bourgeois" society, but by societal activity and "collectivism" (ibid., pp. 206ff.). The most important tasks of education, therefore, are: formation of the communist world view, education for proletarian internationalism and socialist patriotism, and education for a communist attitude toward work and societal property.[29]

There is some concern today with a deeper examination of the concept of the "well-rounded development of the personality." Well-known pedagogues such as V. A. Suchomlinskij and L. A. Levšin have questioned the absolute priority of the collectivist personality ideal as educational goal. As early as the beginning of the 1960s, Suchomlinskij stated:

> The idea of the personality is becoming more important even outside the collective. . . . All the characteristics of the new man are affecting the younger generation, but the greatest educational effect comes from his individual moral traits. . . . We not only have to train workers with great skill; we must educate persons with a soul (Suchomlinskij 1963, pp. 17, 154-155).

This trend toward a higher estimation of individual personality values has found expression in some areas of educational and economic practice—in demands to individualize instruction by didactic differentiation and optional courses in the school and in suggestions to provide monetary rewards for excellent work performance in production. In a wider framework, however, this trend is part of a still inconclusive philosophical dispute on the relation between the personality and the collective.[30] Strumilin's essay (1960) is also relevant in this connection, for it not only propagates a collectivist life style within the framework of "house communes" and a far-reaching dissolution of the individual family group, but also points to the Soviet public's overwhelming rejection of this program. Unlike Strumilin, the Leningrad sociologist A. G. Charčev has established the social necessity to "individualize" life:

> Along with the increasing satisfaction of material needs and the growth of cultural pursuits, the individual's inclinations, tastes, and moral and esthetic traditions will gain ever greater significance. All this means that one should not try to shape people into a uniform mould but that possibilities of free choice should be granted. (Charčev 1967, p. 18).

The present state of the discussion on the goals of education and on the relation between the personality and the collective can be further illustrated: In 1967, when Suchomlinskij accentuated his earlier statement by placing the values of the individual personality in the center of his theory[31], he was sharply attacked for his neglect of collectivist values of communist education.[32] In the course of these polemics Suchomlinskij had the support of only a few pedagogues, including L. A. Levšin.[33]

These disagreements demonstrate that present-day Soviet pedagogy is increasingly recognizing the values of the personality without, however, abandoning the undisputed priority position of the values of collectivism. As for the determination of the family's role, Soviet pedagogy on the one hand accepts the guarantee of "personal happiness" for the individual in marriage and family ties as an important goal of life and education,[34] and it considers the family as an irreplaceable source of education for the individual personality. On the other hand, the link of the personality and of the family itself, with the collective and its values is seen as crucially important. One should not overlook the fact that, unlike in the Stalin era, controversies over the goals of communist education can be openly debated in the Soviet Union today.

2

Socioeconomic Conditions of the Family and the Role of Women

The abolition of private ownership of land, the collectivization of agriculture and the nationalization of the means of production, the general integration of women into the national economy, the civil marriage law and the campaign against all religious traditions, the abolition of illiteracy and the raising of the general educational level—all these measures have introduced planned social change. While these changes have inevitably led to a radical transformation of prerevolutionary forms of marriage and family, they have not yet transferred the family's traditional household and educational functions to society, in line with the views of Marx and Engels. On the contrary, the Soviet Union's current legislative and policy goal of strengthening the family reinforces its economic and educational functions. At the same time there is an attempt to influence the family in the sense of communist morality and to implement those principles in marital and family life which are considered essential for the "spiritual reproduction" of communist society: a marriage based upon love, equality between husband and wife, and responsible fulfillment of educational functions in conformity with the ideological values of society.

Successful implementation of these principles presupposes, if not a dissolution, then a transformation of the traditional economic and social foundations of the family—for example, not only the elimination of the wife's financial dependence upon her husband, but also a transformation of human consciousness, such as the husband's patriarchal attitude toward his wife. Only under these conditions can the "new communist family" come into being and in its way contribute to the education of the "new communist man."

Objective data on the family's economic and social foundations, its size, structure, and functions can only be provided by empirical social research. In the USSR, such research developed within narrow limits, so that our knowledge about the Soviet family is as yet very sparse. Before presenting the available data, it seems advisable to briefly review and discuss the history of Soviet research on marriage and the family.

THE DEVELOPMENT OF SOVIET FAMILY RESEARCH

During the decades before the October Revolution and in the early Soviet period, all areas of art and science were influenced by Western European and American intellectual trends. Empirical social research, which had its beginnings in prerevolutionary Russia, continued to develop in the early Soviet period,[1] and in the first postrevolutionary years the party leadership officially supported social science research. In 1918, while considering the establishment of a Socialist Academy of Social Sciences, Lenin wrote that it was "one of the top priority tasks to set up a series of social research projects." During discussions on the role of labor unions in 1920, he suggested setting up surveys and combining these with statistical data to develop practical plans for the future. In so doing he supported the view that "the more factual knowledge" there was, "the less disputes which feign loyalty to communist principles" (quoted in Sociologija 1966, I, p. 3).

In addition to the organization of social collectives and collective work processes, questions regarding the organization of the private household also came within the purview of social science research. Among the numerous studies on the structural change in marriage and the family, only Volfson's *Sociology of Marriage and Family* (1929), Jaroslavskij's *Morality and Everyday Life of the Proletariat in the Time of Transition* (1927), and Strumilin's time budget research among workers' and collective farm peasant families will be mentioned here. Despite the application of empirical research methods, the polemics over the fundamental function of the family in communist society impaired the scientific objectivity of these studies. As a result of one-sided research into the restriction of the family's traditional economic and educational functions, scientists like Volfson and Strumilin arrived at the thesis that the family would gradually "die away" under communism.

The publication, in 1936, of the policy and legislation for the strengthening of the family finally put an end to the basic discussion about the family's role in communist society, but at the same time all scientific research came under the dogmatic ideological control of the party, and the rudiments of Soviet family research could not be further developed. A resolution of July 4, 1936,[2] condemned "pedology" and the application of empirical and quantitative research methods in science. Stalin's party wanted no concrete data about the problems of marital and family life, among other reasons because they would have illuminated all too clearly the numerous discrepancies between ideology and reality. In a critical retrospect on scientific policy during the Stalin era, a new volume of collected papers had the following to say about Soviet sociology:

Under the influence of the conditions which developed during the time of the personality cult, scientific thought was directed less toward the actual study of reality than toward operating with general concepts, which, while correct in themselves, frequently lacked a practical sense, since they were detached from practical life. . . . The personality cult had negative effects upon the social sciences (*Sociologija* 1966, I, p. 4).

A weak revival of concrete scientific research (e.g., in the field of developmental psychology) connected with the gradually growing importance of the Academy of Pedagogical Sciences, founded in 1943, could still be observed in the final years of the Stalin era. E. A. Arkin's book about family education grew out of the work of the APN and was published in 1949; it deserves repeated mention here as a contribution to a psychologically oriented family research.[3]

The social sciences, and especially ethnology, developed during the early years of the Khrushchev era. In an attempt to document the social change in the country in light of the collectivization of agriculture, and with the aid of sample questionnaires and direct observation, scientists studied the way of life and the structure of many collective farm families in various Soviet republics. For the first time since the 1920s, Kušner (1956) and others again did empirical research on the family. These studies have shown the great differences in societal and family structure between the urban and rural milieus, the stubborn survival of patriarchal authority in the rural area, the discrepancy between formal and actual female equality, and the retarding educational effects of the low economic and cultural level in rural areas in comparison to those of the city. The findings of these studies have made clear the need for further reforms.

The actual turning point in the emancipation of all scientific research, and of the social sciences in particular, occurred in 1958 when the de-Stalinization, launched two years earlier, began to be evident in all areas of culture. Khrushchev's school reform program of 1958 was based in part on factual studies on the effectiveness of instruction, particularly with respect to young people's preparation for working life. As the title of the school reform law indicated, these studies showed the need for a stronger "connection between school and life."[4] The view, supported by Lenin, that rational planning and state control over societal and economic processes could be accomplished only on the basis of precise information about reality also gained acceptance outside the area of organized school instruction. Establishment of the USSR Association for Sociology (1958) and *Komsomol'skaja pravda's* formation of an Institute for the Study of Public Opinion (1960) symbolize the official rehabilitation of the social sciences.

A differentiated family research has developed since the end of the 1950s—if not as an isolated and independent area of research, then at least as an area of common interest for the various social sciences, e.g., sociology, education, and economics. The research results available so far hardly provide a complete picture of Soviet marriage and family. While many problems have still not been investigated for one reason or another, the main drawback is that the state-controlled statistics make no data available. In addition to a series of individual studies about the Soviet family's time budget, the family background of delinquent youngsters, etc., only one large and comprehensive work on family research exists today: *Marriage and Family in the USSR* (1964), by A. G. Charčev, senior Professor of Philosophy at the Leningrad Academy of Sciences. Charčev, who has written extensively since 1952 on the philosophical and sociological problems of marriage ethics and on the development of the family in communist society, can be considered the most important exponent of Soviet sociological family research.

Charčev's book is based upon empirical material gathered from statistical data and written testimony, as well as upon the results of written questionnaires and interviews in Leningrad. In it he analyzes the following aspects of marriage and the family: the length of acquaintanceship before marriage, the motives for marriage, the age differences between the couple and the age at marriage, the reasons for divorce and the the age at divorce, the size of the family, its structure and social functions. According to Charčev the family is

> a small social group with a historically determined organization whose members are united by marital or relationship ties, by the commonality of a household and mutual moral responsibility, and whose social necessity is based in society's need for the physical and spiritual reproduction of the population (Charčev 1964, p. 57).

This definition indicates that biological ("physical") and educational ("spiritual") reproduction are considered the family's most important social functions (p. 261). He also gives special attention to the effects of the inadequate education of children resulting from disintegration of the family, divorce, etc.

In his sociological analyses, Charčev applies internationally recognized concepts primarily taken from American social research: "structure," "organization," "function," "role," "nuclear family," etc. The use of such concepts, however, does not also mean the adoption of the research methods originally associated with them, such as structural-functional analysis as understood by Parsons. On the contrary, these methods are criticized for their "formalism"; the main objection is that their exclusive application leads to an abstraction of social groups and processes and to a neglect of the societal, particularly the economic, reference system. Charčev argues in favor of the combined application of various methods. Furthermore, as a representative of "Marxist sociology," he regards Marxist social theory as the basis for the "objectivity" of scientific analysis:

> The objectivity of sociological results is guaranteed only when a sociological method is applied and controlled by a correct methodology based upon a theory of social development corroborated by practice (p. 16).

In the light of Marxist theory, the very abolition of private property alone guarantees a new type of marriage and family in Soviet society, while the actual democratization of marital and family ties in the capitalist West is an exception, since they remain characterized by "material concerns." On the other hand, undemocratic and immoral relations in Soviet marital and family life are considered "remnants of the past" in the minds of people. These remnants are based for the most part upon "subjective" factors and represent a deviation from the norm determined by social and economic development.

Another characteristic of Soviet science, especially of family research, must be mentioned in addition to the philosophical-ideological definition of scientific "objectivity": its orientation on "reality." Charčev emphasizes: "The goal of all social research, including family research, is reality" (p. 21). The ideal of a prospective, applied science directed toward reality cannot be neutrality of values:

> Marxist sociology affects the practice of marital-family ties in that it primarily supports such social processes as implementation of a real and actual equality between men and women, improvement of household conditions as well as of marriage and family legislation and the methods of its application, etc., . . . it does not avoid moral valuations, but uses them as a means toward the strengthening of progressive ethical ideals (p. 25).

The ideological orientation regarding reality and values reflected in Soviet family research contains both pitfalls and positive potentials. The pitfalls include mandatory "social commitments," i.e., the ruling party's control over the goal, methods, and publication of research projects, the tendency to avoid an analysis of the social motivation behind "negative" phenomena, and the tendentious interpretation of research results. For example, several questions were omitted in a controlled Soviet examination of a French study on workers' attitudes toward the factory and work. One such question was: "Do you feel it right for a married woman to work in a factory?" The authors justified the omission of this question in the Soviet study in the following manner:

> In socialist society it goes without saying that the woman can work in the factory, just as she can work in all other areas of social production. For this reason the question under debate would sound strange under Soviet conditions (Naumova 1966, p. 142).

On the other hand, in addition to the above-mentioned pitfalls of suppressing questions that touch upon ideological "foregone conclusions," the reality orientation of social science research offers positive possibilities for stimulating social reforms. Concrete investigations of people's time budgets, the alarming data about the decrease in birthrate, and the negative results of early institutionalization of children have contributed to the debate in the Soviet

Union over shortening the workweek for women with small children. Legal provisions were enacted to obligate a husband to support his wife during the child's first year. If social policy planning based on such research results is not nipped in the bud by a revival of dogmatism, as occurred in the Stalin era, there is a chance that Soviet social science will assume an "enlightening" function.

In describing the current state of Soviet family research and its subject matter, the All-Union Symposium of Sociologists held in Vilnius in 1967, and devoted exclusively to marriage and family problems,[5] is noteworthy. The newly founded Committee for the Study of the Family in the USSR Association for Sociology, headed by Charčev, organized the meeting. This area of social science research, obviously highly regarded, now includes an organizational center for family research.

Among the topics presented at the symposium were: the role of family law in strengthening the family and raising the younger generation; results of the ethnological study of the family; family and city planning; motives for marriage; the growth of ethnically mixed marriages; divorce as the object of social research; problems of familial equality between husband and wife; the rural family; marriage and family among students; the connection between mistakes in family education and juvenile delinquency; the woman's productive employment and its effects upon family life.

Several plans for future work were drawn up: a series of family sociological studies; a symposium on "the working woman"; the Central State Institute for Statistics is to be assigned to gather and publish statistical data on the marriage and divorce age, on the ethnic origin and social position of the married couple, on the number of children and the social position of divorced spouses, etc.

In summary, Soviet family research has been given a great impetus and has oriented itself on international research; however, as in the case of all social science research, it must be understood as a normative science, and as such, should be subjected to the principle of political commitment and to direct Party control. Despite this restriction, the study of marriage and family problems based upon quantitative research methods, and the publication of the results—including cases where instances of backwardness and contradictions in social development are revealed—lead to a valuable expansion of our knowledge.

FAMILY SIZE AND THE DECLINING BIRTHRATE

Physical reproduction of the population represents the family's first and, for the survival of any society, most important function. Moreover, its educational function is established by the presence of children and modified by the number of children and generations living together as a family group.

Population growth varies in different societies: according to UN statistics, this growth is twice as high in the developing countries as in the developed industrial nations. Between 1960 and 1965 the world average amounted to about 34 births per 1,000 inhabitants, but for the same population base there were 40 births in the developing nations and 20 in the developed industrial nations.[6] Despite its relatively strong agricultural orientation,[7] the USSR matches the average of the industrialized nations with 18.4 births per 1,000 people (1965); since 1950 the birthrate has steadily declined and after 1965, has shown a regressive trend.[8]

Soviet demographers have determined that even with an average of two children in every family, "no stabilization of the population figure is taking place," mainly because not all women of the next generation are marrying and not all married couples have children. "For the simple renewal of the generation," therefore, "every couple" must "have 2.5 children" (Urlanis 1968)—hence, average family size would have to be 4.5. By 1959, the Soviet family included an average of only 3.7 members,[9] and, as mentioned above, the birthrate has declined since then.

The following table cites figures for 1959, the year of the latest census statistics available in the Soviet Union; 27.1% of the urban and 24.9% of the rural families were childless. The most important social strata of families with children broke down as follows:

No. of children	Workers	Salaried employees	Collective farm peasants
1 child	48%	52%	43%
2 children	38%	38%	32%
3 children	11%	8%	17%
4 and more	3%	2%	8%

These statistics presented by Charčev (1964, pp. 218, 272) prove that, like other industrial societies, the small family with one to two children, and primarily the "single child system," is most popular in the Soviet Union. As in other industrial societies, certain strata-specific differences can be determined: there are less single-child families among the rural population than among the urban (43% as compared to 48% or 52%) and more families with many children (8% as compared to 3% or 2%), while urban working families have on the average more children than urban salaried employees. The most recent statistical data of September 1967 confirm Charčev's findings: of all Soviet families with children, 50.1% have only one child; 34.5% have two; 9.5% have three; 3.5% have four; and 2.6% have five and more children (*Zenščiny i deti v SSSR* 1969, p. 112).

This development contradicts not only the objective demographic needs of Soviet society, but the goals of Soviet family policy and the state's population policy measures that were due primarily to the huge loss of life in World War II. The 1944 family legislation, still in operation today, includes a "childless tax" of 6% of total income for families with less than three children, and families with many children are supported and honored by bonus payments and decorations. Information on the number of families with many children which received state allowances in 1944-1949 and 1950-1963, however, show the small effect of these measures. From 1944 to 1949, 1.4 million mothers were awarded the "Motherhood Medal" for five children and 754,000 mothers received it for six children. From 1950 to 1963, 2.7 million were awarded this medal for five children and 1.5 million received it for six children. From 1944 to 1949, 468,000 women received the "Glory of Motherhood" medal for seven children, 193,000 for eight children, and 67,000 for nine children. The corresponding numbers for the period between 1950 and 1963 were 729,000 for seven children, 312,000 for eight, and 122,000 for nine. From 1944 to 1949, 31,000 women were designated as "Mother Heroines" for ten and more children, and from 1950 to 1963, 46,000 were thus honored.[10]

These data demonstrate that the number of state-supported families with many children did not double in any category, although more than twice the time span—14 years as compared to 6—is involved. Despite the aims of Soviet population policy, the number of families having many children is constantly declining. The social and financial incentives of premiums and decorations for families with many children, which had a positive effect upon the birthrate during the first postwar years, is no longer sufficient to compensate for the burdens of rearing many children. One of the most widespread means of birth control is abortion, which became legal again in 1955. In many urban areas, abortions seem to exceed births.[11]

The overwhelming trend toward the single-child family contradicts not only the need of Soviet society for "physical reproduction" but also its need for "spiritual reproduction" of the population. The single-child family is generally considered relatively "educationally weak." Soviet pedagogy has expressed this view repeatedly since Makarenko; the family should be a collective where not only the parents and one child, but several children, should be mutually involved in a group in order to learn collective behavior. A recent dictionary of education states the following about the single-child family: "Several difficulties in education turn up in families which have only a single child upon whom the parents' love and care are concentrated. This often leads to spoiling the child, to the development of selfishness and other character weaknesses" (*Pedagogičeskij slovar'* 1960, II, p. 332). Recent empirical investigations seem to confirm this statement: "Our special observation carried out under a particular program . . . has shown that social attitudes are more easily formed in children from large families" (Titarenko 1967, p. 12).

Among the many factors contributing to the decline in the birthrate in all industrial societies, three predominate in the Soviet Union: the general lack of living space, the low standard of living of wide population strata, and the general full-day employment of women. These factors have been analyzed with a view toward the dynamics of the birthrate, but at the same time they illustrate the socioeconomic conditions under which children's education in the family takes place.

Despite considerable housing construction, partly due to widespread destruction during the war and partly as a result of the demands of increasing urbanization, very confining housing conditions still prevail. The officially cited average per capital living space of ten square meters[1][2] is often not met in urban areas and among the poorer strata.

While no direct connection can be made between the housing shortage and the low birthrate, there is no doubt a high birthrate, conjoined with inadequate housing, can cause asocial relations and high infant mortality or influence many parents to consciously limit the number of their children. Both effects can be seen in the Soviet Union. Stepped-up housing construction indirectly serves to encourage the birthrate and to deter delinquency and child neglect.

The most comprehensive research available about the living conditions of Soviet families (Slesarev 1965) included 8,468 married women working in large factories in Gorky; the study dealt with the connections between the working conditions, the family living conditions, and birthrate. Slesarev came to the following conclusions:

> Living conditions seriously influence the character of the natural population movement. Since the Soviets came to power, housing capacity has greatly increased. Our data show that in the past few years alone the number of those who received separate apartments has doubled. . . . Nevertheless, a considerable lack of living space still exists and exerts negative effects upon the average levels of the birthrate and infant mortality. Research results show that the birthrate is directly dependent upon the amount of living space, whereas infant mortality stands in an inverted relation to it (Slesarev 1965, pp. 159-160).

The study showed that about 57% of the married working women lived in an apartment or room of less than 20 square meters, about 27% in an apartment of 20 to 29 square meters, and about 16% in an apartment of more than 30 square meters. The constant living together in an apartment of less than 20 square meters—usually one room and a common kitchen for several tenants—is confining for even a childless couple (data on the living conditions of couples seeking divorce demonstrate[13] that such confinement can lead to psychosocial disruption of the marriage). Where children are involved, these conditions lead to considerable hardships for both generations. It is not surprising, therefore, that in that large group of working families surveyed, where the living space was less than 20 square meters, the number of children averaged 0.9 to 1.5 per family, and the average infant mortality rate was 137 to 154 per 1,000 births. Only the small group of working families whose living space exceeded 30 square meters had more than 2.0 children per family, and the infant mortality rate sharply declined.

On the whole, Slesarev's study shows that most urban working families today live in very confining housing, and that these conditions deter a woman's desire for children.

A general causal connection between the overall living standard of the population and the birthrate can no more be established than between living conditions and birthrate. On the contrary, based on the cited international data on population growth in various societies, a decline in birthrate can be detected with an increase in the general standard of living that accompanies industrialization. Just as the birthrate in developing countries is significantly higher than in industrial nations, the birthrate of the economically less developed Asiatic republics exceeds that of the European part of the USSR; conversely, the birthrate of highly developed urban areas—for example, Moscow, with 11 births per 1,000 inhabitants in 1965—is far below the total national average: 18.4 births per 1,000 inhabitants in 1965.[14]

Nevertheless, given the dynamics of a growing industrialization which leads to the integration of women into production, to a higher standard of living, and to a decline in the birthrate, women who are contemplating having children must take the added work and costs into consideration. High living costs and the low level of household mechanization thus assume some importance for the development of the birthrate.

Although real wages in the Soviet Union have steadily risen since the end of the war, the general standard of living increased only slightly because consumer goods prices have generally kept pace with wage increases. In the light of increasing social differentiation,[15] the upper social strata of the population have primarily benefited from economic growth. Monthly food costs for one adult amount to almost 60 rubles,[16] which was officially set as the 1967 minimum wage for a large number of the working population. According to Charčev (1964), food costs make up about 50% of the household budget of a family of three to four; this includes the wife's earnings.[17] In addition, clothing and shoes are very costly and require about 20% of the family budget. Therefore, since a childless couple frequently depend on the wife's earnings to make ends meet, every child represents a real financial burden for those with an average income. This burden could certainly be offset by a wage increase and thereby contribute to an increase in the birthrate. One Soviet demographer found that "one-third of those surveyed stated they would want more children if the mothers' earnings were increased by 10 to 15 rubles. In the event of continuing material support, two-thirds of the women will certainly express a desire for a larger family" (Urlanis 1968).

The low levels of household mechanization, the lack of finished products, and the paucity of public service industries are further evidence of the low standard of living in the Soviet Union. According to available data, with a population of 231 million, only 1.9 million refrigerators, 3.5 million washing machines, and 0.7 million vacuum cleaners were sold in 1966 (the figures represent the then highest annual rate of sale of these household machines).[18] Soviet economists report that such public facilities as laundromats, cafeterias, etc.,[19] on the average relieve the Soviet woman of only 5% of her household chores. All these factors indicate that the Soviet woman has an extremely heavy work load in a household without children, and that it is all the more difficult if she has children to raise. Slesarev's (1965) studies have shown that childless women spend 28.1 hours a week on housework, women with one child 43.8 hours; and women with four children, 51.9 hours.

The results of a sociological study suggest that an increased availability of household machines through mass production at cheap prices, together with other measures, could bring significant relief for women (and indirectly also increase the birthrate). To the question, "What would you do to improve the position of the working woman?" about 70% of the 427 working women questioned said it would be necessary "to increase the number of household machines, the places where one could rent them, and the sale of partially prepared and conserved foods." About 50% favored "shortening the workday, but maintaining wages"; about 30% wanted "to increase the number of ironing establishments, cafeterias, and other household institutions" (Slesarev and Jankova 1967).

The section on family structure will discuss in greater detail the woman's full-time employment and the resulting work overload, but these factors must also be seen as leading causes of the decline in the Soviet birthrate.

According to Strumilin's research results in the 1930s, the birthrate among working women was only half as high as that among nonworking women.[20] This trend has been confirmed by more recent studies. In his investigation of the connections between the factory, the family, and the birthrate, Slesarev noted that the working woman "consciously limits the number of children she wants" (Slesarev 1965, p. 159). However, since outside employment for the woman is the rule in the USSR (according to 1959 census data, only about 10 million women, that is, about 20% of all women of working age, were exclusively engaged in housework[21]), this also exerts a general influence on the birthrate.

Not only is a larger number of the female population employed in the Soviet Union than in all other industrial societies, but the women concerned usually put in full-day employment under often difficult conditions. Among other things, the high costs of living do not allow most Soviet women to interrupt their employment for many years—perhaps to care for several children born one after the other. According to Yanowitch (1963), the mothers in almost 70% of the families (including incomplete families) with children under 16 years of age are employed. Furthermore, there is hardly any part-time work in the Soviet economy, and it would hardly suffice to sufficiently supplement the husband's earnings to support a family with children. Moreover, Soviet women perform difficult physical labor at work more frequently than women in other societies, and they are responsible for almost all the household chores under similarly difficult conditions (little mechanization, etc.).

A growing number of Soviet demographers and economists have been making recommendations aimed at facilitating and shortening the production work of mothers. Slesarev proposes to "free them from excessive physical burdens and from contact with chemicals which have harmful effects upon the female organism." He also suggests a four-hour workday for mothers until the fifth month after childbirth, and a five-hour day until the infant is one year old.

In addition, he advocates "shortening the workday for women who are raising two, three, or more children" while at the same time paying them full wages (Slesarev 1965, p. 161).[22]

The Soviet leadership has done little until now to implement suggestions of this kind, possibly because the data on the regressive birthrate are still not considered alarming. It is more likely that women's full employment is seen not only as an economic necessity but as one of the "foregone conclusions" of ideology. In the teachings of Marx, Engels, and Lenin, however, these ideological "foregone conclusions" originally presumed a "socialized" household that would completely liberate the woman from housework.

For the most part, a large number of children was as characteristic of the rural Russian family as the fact that three and more generations lived together under one roof and worked on the family farm. In contrast, the two-generation family is the rule today, both in rural areas, where the collectivization of agriculture has greatly reduced family farming, and in urban areas. In the early 1960s, 60% of the families in a representative RSFSR village, 55% of the families in a representative SSR Kirghiz village, and 53% of the workers' families in Leningrad consisted of two generations: parents with one or more children; 17-19% included only one generation, that is, a childless couple; and between 20% (RSFSR village) and 30% (Leningrad) of the families consisted of three generations.[23]

The housing shortage primarily accounts for the relatively high percentage of three-generation families.[24] Three-generation families are unexpectedly more numerous in Leningrad than in rural areas, probably because the housing shortage is more visible in the metropolitan areas, where many young couples are forced to spend the first years of married life in their parents' apartment.[25] Furthermore, women's full-day employment and the lack of preschool institutions usually make it necessary for grandparents—for the most part, grandmothers—to fulfill the important functions of supervising, caring for, and raising the children as well as running the household. Since the possibility of passing on a large share of these chores to the grandmother might have a positive effect upon the desire of working mothers to have more children, the Soviet regime has a certain interest in maintaining this living arrangement.

Although grandparents play a vital role in supporting young housewives and mothers in the three-generation family group, their very presence increases the likelihood of marital and family conflicts that arise under crowded living conditions.[26] It is not surprising, therefore, that the trend toward limiting the family to the "nuclear unit" is steadily growing; both the young couple and their parents prefer to combine human closeness with spatial distance.[27]

WOMEN'S FUNCTIONS AND FAMILY STRUCTURE

Our discussion of the structure of the Soviet family refers predominantly to those societal, economic, and psychological correlations found within the nuclear family and between the nuclear family and society, because these correlations are essential for the education of children in the family. The distribution of authority and functions between husband and wife in providing a living, running a household, bringing up children, and guarding their interest vis-á-vis societal institutions will all be treated as aspects of family structure.

Women's Position in Economic and Public Life

The position of women in Soviet society is determined by three main factors: legal equality with men, equality of educational opportunities, and equal employment opportunities.

A woman's legal equality has been a general principle of Soviet legislation since 1917. She has the right to retain her maiden name after marriage and to sue for divorce; she has the right to vote and run for office; and she can accept employment and change her residence without her husband's consent. Possessions acquired during marriage are the common property of both spouses. The woman has an equal voice in decisions about the education and rearing of their children and, in the case of disagreement with her husband, can appeal to the "comrades' courts" or to other societal institutions.

Woman's equality also involves the right to an education and to training. The widespread illiteracy among women that prevailed until the October Revolution has been almost completely eliminated.[28] Since the end of the 1950s the proportion of males and females in schools and universities has been almost equal. According to the 1959 data, 53% of secondary school graduates were women[29]; in 1966, 63% of the graduates of secondary specialized schools and 52% of the university graduates were women.[30] Yet, the opportunities for women to enter a career that corresponds to their educational level are definitely limited because of the double burden of maternal and household functions.

The woman's participation in a career probably represents the most important aspect of her changing position in society. Let us recall that only about 10 million Soviet women devote themselves exclusively to housework; about four-fifths of the women of working age pursue some outside employment. According to the 1966 data (which embrace about 54% of the population at that time), women constituted 50% of all workers and salaried employees and 54% of the total working force on collective farms.[31] They also formed the overwhelming proportion of the personnel in public health and education and in several public service organizations.

Legal and job equality, together with integration into educational institutions, has undoubtedly led to a far-reaching emancipation for Soviet women. But, there are many contradictions. "Equality" in employment does not yet compensate for a mere three-month maternity leave, and for the burdens of childbearing, child care, and housework, plus the expectation that she is still expected to perform the same amount of work and frequently the same physical exertion as the man. Lenin maintained that women's integration into production did not mean they had to exactly equal men in productivity or in the amount, length, and conditions of work.[32] But the fact remains, at least since the Stalin era, that the needs of the planned economy have been given priority consideration over those of women. For example, women work in road construction and trucking and are even found in mining. A. Šelepin, the then First Secretary of the Komsomol, reported to the Thirteenth Komsomol Congress in April 1958 that "upon orders from the Komsomol more than 40,000 boys and girls went to work underground in the mining areas of the Donbass, Kusbas, Kuznetsk, and Karaganda, and in the coal mines near Moscow" (Hindus 1963, p. 282). The obligation of men and women to work hard and to put in the same number of hours necessarily results in the overburdening of many women, and in health hazards, as demonstrated by Slesarev (1965).

Another contradiction in women's emancipation is the fact that highly qualified careers and leading positions in the economy, in science, and in politics still remain a male domain. No women are currently members of the highest party bodies—for example, the Politburo—and women are gravely underrepresented in higher governmental agencies. Only 28.9% of the deputies to the Supreme Soviet of the USSR are women.[33] And in 1966, when women constituted about 58% of secondary school and university graduates, only 38% of the "scientific workers" and 27% of the "scientific trainees" were women.[34] Every third man, but only every seventh woman, attained the rank of a "candidate of sciences" (comparable to a master's degree), and one man among 28, but only one woman among 250 university graduates, earned the rank of "doctor of sciences."[35] According to Kuznecova (1967), women are predominant in unqualified or semiskilled and difficult manual labor in many areas of the national economy, while men dominate the skilled and mechanized work processes.

These discrepancies in the emancipation movement (which, by the way, are characteristic not only of Soviet society but of the West as well) must be understood in the light of deep-rooted male prejudices against women. Women, on the other hand, because of maternal and household duties, devote less time to their careers and to continuing their education. Under these circumstances the emancipation of Soviet women has essentially been a low-level adjustment to the social roles of men.

Formal Equality and Traditional Family Roles

Utilizing Marxist social theory, Charčev outlined the following picture of the change in Soviet family structure: in contrast to the hierarchal-patriarchal family structure based on an economic foundation and supported by religious tradition which predominated in prerevolutionary Russian society, the USSR has "created the objective conditions for a genuine democratization of family structure. These include the abolition of private property; unlike bourgeois democracies, a more consistent implementation of the principle of equality between the sexes; and the predominance of communist morality which is permeated by the ideals of collectivism and humanism . . ." (Charčev 1964, p. 222). In describing the elimination of the husband's economic predominance as one of the essential foundations of women's equality, Charčev cites an analysis of the household budget of 300 families where both spouses were employed; "In 146 families the husband's earnings exceeded those of the wife by 10 and more rubles; in 54 families the wife's earnings exceeded her husband's; and in 100 families the earnings of both were about the same" (ibid., p. 223).

Concrete sociological family research results have only partially confirmed the theory of the social change of family structure. While Charčev could demonstrate that "democratic" structures were widespread in the 300 workers' families he studied, in a large number of these families the husband has maintained his formal and actual authority over his wife. In more than 60% of the families surveyed "an actual equality between the spouses in deciding basic familial questions was hidden behind the husband's formal predominance. For this reason this equality is frequently combined with an equal distribution of spheres of "priority influence" in one or another area of family life. For example, the husband usually does not interfere with the family's daily household expenses, but he does insist on the last word when it comes to the purchase of large items. Sometimes one spouse enjoys a relatively comfortable priority position in deciding such questions as leisure time, family vacation, control over children's behavior and learning, choice of future career plans, etc." (ibid., p. 224). He also learned that in about 36% of the families studied the husband has maintained his "personal authority"; this authority, however, no longer rests on "coercion" but—in 80% of the cases—on his "moral authority and the more or less willing subordination on the part of other family members to this authority" (ibid.).

Despite all these qualifications, Charčev's research data give the impression that a far-reaching "democratic" structure is characteristic of most Soviet families. A comparison with other studies in urban and rural milieus shows, however, that his conclusion cannot be considered as universally representative.

Slesarev and Jankova worked with categories similar to the old hierarchal and the new democratic family type as defined by Charčev. Their study of 427 workers' families in Moscow (1967) concluded that only about 20% of the families questioned could be counted among the "new" family type, one in which "mutual help, mutual support, and cooperation in family tasks" predominated.

Ethnological studies on the collective farm family have demonstrated that more kolkhoz women than urban women are gainfully employed, and that they have obtained the right to share in family decisions—for example, in questions pertaining to household budget. However, in these rural families and especially in the Asiatic part of the Soviet Union, patriarchal structures seem to be so strongly rooted that "despite the fundamental transformations in the family, elements of the old way of life which retard the collective development of people remain here more strongly than in any other collective" (Selivanov 1966, p. 461).

Disregarding basic differences (which are due to various economic and sociocultural backgrounds) between the traditionally fixed authority structure of rural families, especially in Central Asia, and the loosened authority structure of urban families, particularly in the European part of the Soviet Union, hierarchal family structures seem to have persisted to a great degree in all social strata. It is remarkable that no positive correlation apparently exists between the married couple's educational level and the degree of democratization in their marital and family relations. Charčev indicates that "the past few years have uncovered many cases where scientific workers, trainees, engineers, government officials, and even teachers turned out to be the initiators and protectors of patriarchal-despotic conditions in the family" (Charčev 1964, p. 227). The lack of sufficient empirical data makes it difficult to determine how closely hierarchal structures in middle- and upper-strata families are connected with a lower employment rate among their own women. Charčev's 10 million "only housewives" undoubtedly includes an above-average number of women from families of the middle and upper strata where there is no economic need for both spouses to earn a living. On the other hand, the data cited about Leningrad and Moscow workers' families do not substantiate the Marxist belief that there will be no male domination in the proletarian family where women's employment is taken for granted.

Obviously, not only are subjective psychological factors at work here but objective, social, and economic factors are also pressing in the direction of a reduction of male domination in the family. These subjective factors stand in the way of a change in husbands' attitude toward their wives and in wives' assessment of their own roles—as Charčev emphasizes, the latter frequently "willingly" subordinate themselves to their husbands. To illustrate the problems involved, two aspects of family structure will be discussed in more detail: the distribution of household duties—that is, the extent of the husband's participation in housework and the wife's participation in decisions pertaining to the household budget—and the couple's distribution of educational tasks and authority.

As regards the husband's helping around the house, numerous studies by Soviet sociologists have shown that nothing even resembling equality exists in this area of family life.

Their 1967 study of 427 workers' families led Slesarev and Jankova to the following conclusion:

> Seventy to 75% of the women in our study group bear the full burden of household chores (3.5 to 4 hours a day). They shop every day for food,

prepare breakfast, lunch, and supper, wash the dishes, tidy up and clean, wash and iron periodically, make sure that the clothes are mended, and keep the apartment generally in order. Only in 20 to 25% of the families does the husband help with shopping, prepare his own breakfast or supper, and assist in tidying up, cleaning, and washing with the help of household machines.

Moreover, the authors point out, the few families in which the husband does help with housework generally belong to a definite age group: the youngest, those between 23 and 30. To the question, "Do you feel your husband helps enough?" almost all the older working women answered with a categorical "no," and almost all of them felt that their husbands should definitely do more housework.

Data on the time spent on housework in Soviet families clearly illustrate how unevenly household chores are distributed. A comparison of research dealing with time budgets in the 1920s and 1960s shows how little the situation has changed. Strumilin's 1922 data indicate that women spent an average of 34.7 hours a week on family chores and in child care, while men spent an average of only 10.3 hours per week on these chores.[36] Zemcov's report[37] on the 1963 data, which were gathered with the same methods, showed that women spent 27.9 hours per week on the same activities while men spent only 7.8 hours. After four decades, the Soviet woman still had to spend more than three times the amount of time men spent on housework.[38] The unduly heavy load of housework necessarily leads to a lack of leisure time for women and, Zemcov points out, to a situation where "working women over the age of 30 have almost no time to develop their personality" (Zemcov 1965, p. 65).

Numerous articles in the Soviet press reflect these very same facts. Four working women wrote a letter to *Sovetskaja Rossija* (March 16, 1960), and complained about the discriminatory attitude toward household work as being "women's work":

> We work in the factory just like our husbands, often in the same factory. But the chores are unequally distributed at home . . . shopping for food in the evening after work, preparing lunch and supper, washing, ironing, mending—these are not men's work. And if you ask a man for help, the answer is always the same: "Do you want me to do a woman's work? The neighbors would make fun of me!"

Testimony such as this and the empirical time budget research indicate that women, despite full-time employment, are branded in everyday living and in the minds of most men as "housewives." Yet according to classical Marxism-Leninism, social production work and general emancipation were supposed to free her from this role.

The woman's equal contribution in earning a living for the family has shaken the patriarchal control over the household budget. Her growing authority in matters pertaining to family finances perhaps most directly expresses the significance of her outside employment and underscores emancipation in this area. The earlier-cited poll of 427 women factory workers in Moscow gave evidence of "women's growing independence in the control and use of the family budget." "In 70 to 75% of the families, the woman usually makes the purchases alone; in the rest, either alone or together with her husband. In 45 to 50% of the families, the woman also makes major domestic purchases independently; in the remaining 45 to 50% major expenditures are determined jointly by husband and wife" (Slesarev and Jankova 1967). The growing independence of women in the control of the household budget has also been observed in rural collective families.[39] This development must be interpreted as a necessary and natural consequence of the fact that the working woman contributes just as much as her husband to the budget. Her growing control also involves greater responsibility for the intelligent running of household affairs, which, in turn, relieves the husband of at least some responsibility in this area. The catering to the family's needs and wishes, once expected of her in the patriarchal family structure, has indeed been eliminated; but the working woman's role as housewife has been further emphasized while the husband's remoteness from household chores has been given additional justification.

As regards child care and rearing, the working Soviet woman also seems to have to fulfill her traditional functions (without her husband's help), but she does seem to be gaining some influence and authority in this area. The study of 427 Moscow workers' families showed the following:

> Only in 20 to 25% of the families surveyed did the husband help take care of the children (washing, dressing, walking to nursery school or kindergarten). It bears repeating that most wives not only fulfill the functions of caring for the family, but also those that used to be performed mainly by the husband in connection with educating the children, and they do so with or without his help. They attend parents' meetings, check homework, etc. (Slesarev and Jankova 1967).

In addition to that of public institutions, the mother's role in raising her children has generally been established as "very important." A spot check in a Moscow factory showed the following:

> About 65% of the women working in this factory regularly visit their children's school, check their homework, train their children in work habits of all types, and guide their value orientations. The remaining 35% share educational functions with their husbands. These data coincide with materials gathered in factories in other areas. For example, Sverdlovsk mothers are significantly more concerned with the education of their preschool and school-aged children. On an average, 27.4% of the fathers attend parents' meetings, while 48% visit the kindergartens (ibid.).

Charčev mentions other studies pointing to the father's greater participation in the care and raising of children, without in any way contradicting the impression that child-rearing continues to be the woman's domain or is increasingly becoming so. He found that the husbands in workers' families at the Kirov Works of Leningrad spend "about two hours a week on things that relate to the raising of children; wives spend even a little less." Studies in Siberia have shown that "men spend about 15 minutes, and women spend about 28 minutes, every day in caring for their children (bathing, walks). . . . However, the time spent in supervising the children's learning and in individual conversation with them is about the same for husbands and wives: 22 or 24 minutes a day" (Charčev 1963, p. 71).

If, as in those families studied by Charčev, the husband spends almost as much time as his wife on educational activities, this in itself must be seen in perspective. Because of his avoidance of housework, the man has much more leisure time than the woman (who has hardly any); he can therefore more easily devote some of that free time to the children. And even if he does spend more time with them, this says little about his educational role. The data show that his educational activities generally involve fewer educational areas than those of the woman; he is more likely to be concerned with such "informal" activities as games, walks, hobbies, and talks. On the other hand, the mother has been assuming more importance as the controlling agent and authority with respect to her children; more than the father, she supervises their learning and watches over their interests in school. Even the youngsters' education for work, which includes training them to help with housework which the father avoids and the mother must perform, belongs primarily to the mother's sphere of influence.[40]

The increase in the woman's authority in the field of education is undoubtedly connected with her emancipation, that is, her integration into educational institutions and social production. But this emancipation remains problematic as long as she has to spend 40 hours a week at work, plus 30 to 40 hours a week on housework.

WOMEN'S WORK OVERLOAD AND ROLE CONFLICTS

As has been shown, there are numerous contradictions between the ideological conception and formal legal foundation of women's equality and her actual situation. According to Marxist-Leninist ideology, the woman's integration into social production is an important prerequisite for her emancipation; her employment outside of the home should lead to liberation from household and educational duties. To this day the Congresses of the CPSU propagate the socialization of household services and children's education as the best solution to "the woman question." Nevertheless, reality demonstrates that the Soviet woman, fifty years after the founding of the Soviet state, still performs the functions of housewife and educator almost completely and almost without the help of her husband, in addition to putting in a full workday in production. A family structure based upon partnership remains incomplete where the partnership does not extend to the sharing of household duties.

It would be inaccurate to say that the Soviet public is unaware of how difficult the situation is for the woman. Her production work is glorified, and her liberation from household and educational duties is propagated as compensation, even though the prerequisites for such liberation are not present and only a small number of women seem to want to forego these very duties.

The combination of production work with household and educational functions leads to a constant role conflict for the woman. She consciously limits the number of children and/or decides on a low degree of work skills, so that neither role—mother nor worker—affords complete satisfaction. Only a small number of women successfully avoid this conflict by not having children or by devoting themselves exclusively to housework and to the education of their children. For most women, however, job employment is an economic necessity, a personal need, and a matter of social prestige. Then, too, an intensive family life with one to two children is considered to be the foundation of lifelong happiness. Thus, 86% of the 427 workers' families surveyed said that the woman had two equally important "main tasks": societal activity, as well as the raising of children and the organization of a household. The study goes on to state:

> A large number of women realized beyond this that these tasks are interconnected and mutually dependent: "The working woman has a wider horizon than the nonworking woman and therefore enjoys greater authority with her husband and children." ... Nevertheless, as the materials show, the modern woman simultaneously continues to play those new and old roles which are directly connected with serving the family. ... As a rule, even these traditional duties create special burdens, and a role conflict arises—here comes the new contradiction, which is most in need of an immediate solution with all the means of social regulation.
>
> To the interview question, "Do you find it difficult to combine family duties with work in the factory?" 25% reported it to be "very difficult"; 31%, "difficult"; and 44%, "bearable." To the question, "What do you find most tiring: work, the household, the children, your husband, shopping?" the most frequent reply was "all of them" or "the household and shopping" (Slesarev and Jankova 1967).

These materials demonstrate the overburdening of the woman and the role conflict connected with it. They also show that she basically wants to identify with both roles. The available research data also show that, despite their work overload, most women prefer meals at home to those prepared at places of work,[41] that they consider greater mechanization of the private household more desirable then the impersonal socialization of household services,[42] and that they prefer the education of children within the family to a comprehensive societal education. About 80% of the 427 women in the above study felt that "the woman should not work during the first two to three years after childbirth and as long as she has small children."

Apparently, while most women do not want to be liberated from their traditional roles, they generally prefer a temporary extension that favors the family when it comes to a decision about their priority involvement in the family or at work.

In addition to those women who basically advocate a combination of family and career life, there are many Soviet women in the older and younger generations who identify more or less exclusively with their traditional roles as mother and housewife. Their role conflict consists in the fact that they are forced to work, thereby neglecting family life. Surveys dealing with women's motives for their career activity, as well as numerous articles in the Soviet press, document this role conflict. According to the Slesarev and Jankova data (1967), 53% of the women workers gave as the overwhelming or exclusive motivation for their career the "necessity of the additional income for the family."[43] Many of them find no satisfaction in their work and would prefer to devote themselves completely to family duties. Yet they express this view not only for selfish reasons, but because they believe that fulfillment of these duties is an important service for their husbands and children and thus indirectly for all of society. A teachers' college instructor expressed his opinion in the Komsomol newspaper in response to a discussion in 1966 about the woman's role in society:

> It seems to me that the ideal family is one in which the husband works but the wife is busy with the household and with raising the children. . . . Is the education and upbringing of the younger generation a less important task than the woman's work as a locksmith . . . or even an engineer? In the current situation the woman can neither work completely in production nor completely educate her children. She either works with less than her total energy, or she devotes little attention to the house and to matters of education.
>
> It seems that the conviction that only the woman's work in production or in an institution is socially useful is altogether wrong. My view obviously displeases many, but I think it also has many supporters (Mel'nikova 1966).

Such testimony indicates that many Soviet women still do not consider their emancipation as liberation; their status is a burden to them because they want to identify primarily with their traditional role as mother and housewife. As long as these burdens continue, burdens imposed by the multiple functions of women, one can assume that genuine emancipation and a change in the self-conception of women will not take place in the Soviet Union.

MARRIAGE, DIVORCE, AND INCOMPLETE FAMILIES

The internal family structure is largely determined by the relationships between husband and wife, and especially by the wife's position in society and in the family. The classical interpreters of the Marxist-Leninist design of a new social order focused their attention on the sex question much more than on the problems of the relationship between parents and children. Their main goal was the emancipation of the woman and the realization of "individual sexual love" (Engels) brought about by the elimination of financial dependency relations in the individual family. This should be accomplished through the nationalization of the means of production, the integration of the woman into production, and the taking over of familial educational functions by state institutions. According to Engels, monogamy and the communist marriage based on love should be freed from those traits "originating in property relationships, and these are: first, the husband's overriding authority; second, the unsolvability" (Engels 1946, p. 59). Marx and Engels wanted to see a change in marriage forms and in family structure brought about by a radical change in the production relations, which would ultimately bring greater freedom for the individual and, above all, for the woman. The Soviet Union is attempting to realize the Marxist program through the nationalization of the means of production, through women's integration into production, and through the guarantee of freedom of divorce. The first phase of the social experiment in the USSR (1917-1936) resulted in the radical realization of freedom of divorce—at the expense of the family and especially of the children—but this development has demonstrated two things:

In the first place, alteration of the economic base does not lead, at the same rate and in the same degree, to a change in marriage forms and relations between the sexes, as Marx and Engels had assumed. By the 1960s, Soviet marriages still exhibited traditional characteristics in many respects—among other things, the distribution of authority and household duties between the husband and wife. On the other hand, phenomena such as the free choice of partner and the spreading of partnership marriages based on love, which Charčev and others describe as indicative of such changes, are seen not only in the socialist Soviet society but in all modern industrial societies. For this reason a causal connection between such phenomena and the nationalization of the means of production cannot be established.

In the second place, Marx and Engels neglected some problems. The minute the state takes a serious interest in the physical and spiritual reproduction of the population (i.e., the next generation and its integration into society), and as long as it is unwilling or cannot completely realize the care and education of the next generation in state institutions, it must consider a consolidation of marriage and family relations. This means that the state must (1) restrict the freedom of sexual ties and the freedom of divorce for the sake of the care and educational relationships between parents and children, and (2) press for the social stability of marriage. In contrast to the principles established by Marx and Engels, then, since 1936 the Soviet Union has increasingly subjected marriage to legal regulations and reduced the freedom of divorce. At the same time it has increased the individual family's legal protection as an economic and educational unit, and emphasized the legal stipulation of mutual dependency relationships in marriage and family.

As our analysis of marriage, family legislation, and family policy has shown, it is now considered a citizen's social duty to see his marriage as a lifelong union and to take full responsibility for the care and upbringing of his children.[44] There is not only legal opposition to divorce, but a social one as well: the pressure of public opinion, particularly when children are involved. The husband's moral and financial responsibility for illegitimate children and for children of a divorced marriage has been increased. The introduction of such legal and social controls indicates that the USSR has recognized the existence of legally sanctioned and socially stable marriage ties as important for the growth of the population and the development and education of children. Moreover, the need to introduce such controls substantiates our previous statement that the change in marriage forms cannot be considered a spontaneous result of the change in production relations. Rather, this change is due mainly to the development and formation of the moral awareness of the people and seems to be only partially dependent upon the economic base of society. Despite the socialist transformation of production relations, marriages in the Soviet Union today are fully comparable to those in Western societies: built upon an inadequate foundation of mutual love, respect, and moral responsibility, they tend toward dissolution.

Despite the state campaign for strengthening the family, the divorce rate in the Soviet Union has steadily increased in recent decades. According to data derived by N. Ja. Solov'ëv (1968), divorce rates doubled between 1956 and 1960. Official statistics indicate that in 1960 there were 12.1 marriages and 1.3 divorces per 1,000 people. In comparison, in 1959 the United States had 8.5 marriages and 2.2 divorces per 1,000 people, and the Federal Republic of Germany had 9.4 marriages and 0.8 divorce per 1,000 people.[45] Divorce rates have steadily increased since 1960, while marriage rates, at least until 1964, have steadily declined. In 1964 there were 8.5 marriages compared to 1.5 divorces.[46] Between 1965 and 1966 the divorce rates once again almost doubled (in 1966 there were 9.0 marriages and 2.8 divorces for every 1,000 people[47]), probably in connection with the simplified legal divorce proceedings enacted in December 1965. As Solov'ëv (1968) pointed out, this proves that the number of couples willing to divorce is still significantly higher—or, at least before 1966, was significantly higher—than the number of actually divorced marriages.

In their totality the data cited indicate that marriage in the Soviet Union shows a relatively weak—and in the past years a steadily sinking—stability. This negative phenomenon can be evaluated only by an examination of the reasons for marriage and the reasons and causes for divorce. The very limited research material available on this complex of questions seems to confirm our previous analysis of family structure and the fact that marriage in the USSR is far from that ideal partnership based upon love which Marx and Engels envisioned. For example, 26.6% of the women in a survey group of 500 Leningrad couples wanting divorce advanced "the husband's coarseness and cruelty"[48] as their motivation for divorce—clear evidence of widespread patriarchal relationships. The same survey showed that not only were love (45%) and "congeniality" (14.5%) given as motives for marriage, but the "attractive appearance" of the partner (13.5%), the approaching birth of a child (7%), the attractiveness of the partner's financial and living conditions (7%), and "common sense" (6%)—all of which have nothing to do with the ideal of the love marriage. Furthermore, in listing the qualities they found especially attractive in their wives, most husbands named "domesticity" next to "sociability" (15%) and "goodness" (12%); at the time of the divorce application, in listing the qualities they missed most in their wives, they again emphasized "domesticity" (14%) in addition to "a caring attitude" (about 18%) and "honesty" (about 17%). These statistics illustrate that many husbands still judge their wives, despite the employment of the latter, according to the traditional value standards of "the caring housewife." Under present-day conditions, the Soviet woman cannot live up to this.

In noting an "irresponsible attitude toward marriage," "infidelity," and "alcoholism" as the main reasons for divorce, Solov'ëv (1968) is referring to phenomena that socialism claims to have eliminated. Considering the widespread nature of these negative behavior patterns by husbands, patterns that are destructive for a marriage, it is clear that the traditional male psychology has not significantly changed under the conditions of Soviet communism.

Objective factors, primarily societal and financial, must be added to the psychological factors. In this connection, the acute housing shortage is noteworthy. In a survey of 1,000 Leningrad couples wanting divorce, only 5.1% had an apartment of their own.[49] The need to live with parents or in-laws frequently leads to intergeneration tensions that are destructive for a marriage; 41% of 500 Leningrad couples mentioned such tensions.[50]

Data on the divorce rates and its causes are informative in analyzing not only marriage forms but the educational situation in the family. Next to illegitimate birth, divorce is the most important factor resulting in incomplete families, usually consisting of a mother and one child. Considering the high divorce rates and the fact that every ninth child is illegitimate,[51] it follows that about one-fifth of all children grow up in incomplete families.

While divorce leads to the breakup of an existing family group, illegitimacy involves a one-sided relationship between mother and child from the very beginning and seems to have some significance for the fate of the child. Children from divorced marriages seem psychologically more endangered than illegitimate children, frequently because they consciously experience the internal breakdown of their parents' marriage as well as the loss of a parent. Divorce in this sense is only the formal conclusion of an internal breakdown. The temporary or indefinite maintenance of a broken marriage can have just as negative, or even more negative, effects upon children than its dissolution and life in an incomplete family. Titarenko (1967) pointed out that the overwhelming majority of children from "discordant" marriages exhibit "negative moral traits." Therefore, when determining the influence of marital relations on the child's development, it is not only a question of the mere presence or absence of this relation, or the completeness or incompleteness of the family; the inner quality of the existing marital ties is also relevant.

Although illegitimate children have not experienced the breakdown and dissolution of their parents' marriage, a number of psychological and socioeconomic factors make their fate almost as difficult as that of children from divorced marriages. Illegitimate children depend just as much as do children from divorced marriages upon a spiritual identification with only one parent, generally the mother, and they miss the example of a harmonious relationship between husband and wife. A study of juvenile delinquency has shown that the absence of a father figure often has a disastrous impact, mostly upon male adolescents.[52] In addition, some factors influence the fate of both illegitimate children and those from divorced marriages: as only children, there is no interaction with siblings; their economic conditions are poor; and they are frequently raised in social institutions. Most children in incomplete families have no brothers or sisters; of all the unmarried mothers living in the USSR in 1960, 2.4 million had only one child, 0.3 million had two children, and only 73,000 had three or more.[53] Furthermore, most divorces involved couples with no children or only one child.[54]

The situation of the incomplete family suffers further because of its poor economic resources. If the unmarried mother receives no alimony—only the 1968 law made alimony mandatory—and has no opportunity for additional training, she must depend on her own meager earnings and on a small state allowance;[55] in the case of divorce, which is especially high among families with a low standard of living, the family's financial situation is adversely affected too.

Finally, data on the composition of students enrolled in state boarding schools indicate that children from incomplete families are more frequently sent to societal educational institutions than other children.[56] Similar facts are presumably also true for day nurseries or children's homes, since an unmarried (or divorced) mother depends upon full-time employment and cannot devote herself to child care.

All these psychological and socioeconomic factors characterize the fundamental educational weakness of the incomplete family. The increase in incomplete families, chiefly due to higher divorce rates in recent years, poses serious social and pedagogical problems. Legislative and educational measures that were promulgated as far back as 1936 to combat irresponsible attitudes by younger people toward marriage and the family have been intensified. However, this campaign cannot be fully understood without a consideration of the lessons learned in connection with family breakups and its impact on the education of children.

3

The Family
and Preschool Education

In the Soviet Union, as elsewhere, the education of children is one of the family's most important functions. At the same time, however, it is not the Soviet family, but society and its educational institutions, which can claim a leading role. The Soviet state is more intent than the pluralistic democracies of the West upon achieving maximum nationalization of the educational process, upon guaranteeing the transmission of its uniform ideological-political value system to the younger generation, and upon effectuating the general integration of women into the social production process.

However, despite the generally widespread integration of women into production, both Soviet women and the Soviet family retain their traditional household and educational functions. In view of the fact that considerable education takes place within the family and is not nationalized, the state seeks to influence the family in the direction of the Soviet value system and to control educational activity within the family. . . .

NEW EMPHASIS ON THE FAMILY'S IMPORTANCE
IN EARLY EDUCATION

Soviet educational policy aims toward the realization of a comprehensive system of "societal preschool education" that will still not fully supplant the family as an educational factor.[1] Moreover, "societal preschool education" today generally does not involve children under the age of three; rather, it concerns the full-day (but not full-time) upbringing of children from the age of three until they enter school. An official textbook on preschool education notes that in the education of the preschooler, "the kindergarten is assigned the leading and organizing role because as a state institution it implements the policy of the socialist state." The "preschool age" is differentiated from the "nursery school age"; for the former category, the family remains the primary educational factor: "Until the age of three, children are raised in the family and in nurseries" (Sorokina 1962, pp. 244, 264). Finally, it is noteworthy that attendance in Soviet preschool institutions has never been obligatory; compulsory schooling begins in the child's seventh year. Presumably, the insufficient time to establish a full network of preschool institutions has mitigated against making attendance mandatory.

An examination of educational policy for a comprehensive preschool societal education and its comparison with the actual situation shows that the quantitative development of these institutions has lagged behind the program. Another factor, based upon scientific research results, is that Soviet pedagogy is acquiring a greater appreciation of the family as the decisive source of preschool education and especially of early childhood training.

Quantitatively speaking, there can be no talk, now or in the near future, of assigning to preschool institutional education a priority over family education. Despite the intensive development of preschool facilities in the last four decades, most Soviet children still remain untouched by public preschool education: in 1927, 2,100 institutions cared for 0.107 million children; in 1937, 24,500 institutions served 1.05 million; in 1958, 35,800 institutions had an enrollment of 2.35 million; in 1965 there were 67,500 institutions with 6.21 million children;[2] and in 1967 about 8.5 million children were being cared for in year-round or seasonal preschool facilities.[3] If one considers that in 1960 there were already more than 34 million children between the ages of one and seven,[4] societal preschool education has apparently been realized for only about one-fourth of the children. The official 1962 figure for the number of preschoolers attending institutions of any type was 28%.[5] This represents a rough statistical average value—i.e., the number of children cared for by preschool institutions is very variable, depending upon the different age levels and the families' geographic location in urban or rural areas. The one- to three-year-olds clearly present an exception: in 1960 their number amounted to more than 15 million;[6] but in 1965 only about 1.5 million of this group attended year-round nurseries and less than one million attended combined day nurseries and kindergartens.[7] Urban and rural differences can be gathered from the following official data: while "70% of the children in a number of cities attend preschool institutions" (Prokov'ev 1968, p. 15), the network of rural kindergartens is growing "significantly more slowly than that of urban kindergartens. Our country has more than 36,000 collective farms, but only 4,200 kindergartens [on them] " ("O Vsesojuznom seminare po doskol'nomu vospitaniju" 1968, p. 85). Further evidence of the lack of preschool facilities in rural and urban areas is the overcrowding of existing institutions: in 1960 an average of 30 to 40 preschool children were assigned to one teacher.[8]

The Twenty-third Congress of the CPSU set a 1970 target of 12.2 million children in state preschool institutions, noting that this expansion will allow the institutions to "substantially satisfy the urban population's need for such institutions and to improve the provision of these institutions for the rural population" ("Dlja samych malen'kich" 1967). Obviously no one is thinking about including all children in such institutions in the near future.

A quantitative examination of Soviet preschool societal education indicates that most children presently attending state educational institutions were not previously enrolled in preschool facilities. This phenomenon, together with the fact that the large majority (80%) of working mothers with preschool-aged children are also confronted with household burdens, means that neither the collective nor the family principle of preschool education is currently being fully realized. There are an insufficient number of good nurseries and combined kindergartens and nurseries to accommodate the small groups that could guarantee an effective supplement to family education. The full-time employment and housework of mothers with small children leave no time for effective family education even if it is only a supplement to institutional education. Since, unlike Poland,[9] mothers of small children in the Soviet Union have to put in a full work day and, unlike Hungary,[10] they do not receive any financial allowances which could make extensive interruption of their outside employment possible, mothers often have no choice but to call upon grandparents, relatives, or neighbors to help care for their children, or they resort to organizing alternating work shifts for parents and other such measures. In this way the Soviet family, while statistically defined as the main educational factor for the young child, can fulfill its educational function only to an extremely limited degree.[11]

The leading role assigned to preschool societal education vis-à-vis the family is being questioned not only quantitatively in the light of current educational conditions, but also "normatively" by the most recent Soviet psychological, pedagogical, and sociological research findings. These findings can be summarized as follows: in the family, preschool children can receive a quality education without the aid of social institutions, but this cannot be done in social institutions without the help of the family;[12] the family represents the decisive educational factor and the ideal medium of educating children up to the age of three; the combination of family and kindergarten education is most suitable for guaranteeing the maximum development of three- to seven-year-olds.

Soviet educational science had for a long time (since the denunciation of pedology in 1936) neglected questions of developmental psychology, especially those pertaining to early childhood. The late 1950s saw the beginnings of lively research activity in this area. The crucial importance of the first years of life for the development of the personality is gaining recognition, although it has still not achieved complete acceptance everywhere.

Professor Kol'cova, director of the laboratory for higher nervous activity of children at the Pavlov Institute for Physiology, summarized the research results in this area:

The facts discovered by specialists in various scientific fields—psychologists, sociologists and physiologists—attest to the fact that, up until the age of three, the child needs individual attention; but from the third year on he can adjust well to the conditions of a collective education (Šeremet'eva 1968).

Most researchers do not doubt that desirable individual education for the child in his first years can best be guaranteed through family education. A manual on handling family questions in Party schools, presumably written by A. G. Charčev, notes: "One can say that a child, especially at an early age, tends to be influenced by the family more than by any other factor" ("Šem'ja i ee rol' v stroitel'stve Kommunizma" 1966, p. 114). In replying to the question, "But where do the specifics and, in this sense, the necessity of family education lie?" Charčev explains:

> Chiefly in the fact that the nature of family education is more emotional than any other education, since its "leaders" are the parents' love for the children and the reciprocal feelings of the young toward their parents. . . . If one imagines a small group, a "microcosm" in its own way, then the family corresponds most to the child's need for step-by-step integration into societal life and to the gradual expansion of his horizon and experience (Charčev 1964, p. 268).

Charčev refers in positive terms not only to the fundamental necessity of family education for the preschool child but also to the dangers of a one-sided model of extrafamilial education[13], to the dependency of educational institutions on imitating family patterns of interaction[14] and cooperation.

Besides Kol'cova and Charčev, numerous Soviet researchers have emphasized the family's decisive significance in the child's upbringing during the first years of life and its crucial importance for the entire preschool period. For example, I. S. Kon in his *Sociology of the Personality* describes the family as "the primary cell of the child's socialization" and substantiates this as follows:

> Only direct parental tenderness and care can guarantee the emotional warmth which the child needs, especially in the first years of life. The family represents a primary group where there is intimate contact, not only between children and parents but also between children of different age levels. It is in the family that children gradually become accustomed to the complicated world of adults. This is extremely essential. There are data that pupils, even from the best preschool children's homes, lag in several aspects of their development behind their peers who are raised in the family . . . (Kon 1967, pp. 125ff.).

These findings demonstrate the similarity between the Soviet experiences and those in the West: the family has proven to be the most effective societal medium for a child's initial socialization and emotional foundations. This hardly means that a child must necessarily be educated exclusively in the family and spend all his time there in order to achieve a normal development. The kibbutz experiment has shown that the combination of family and collective education can succeed even with the very young—of course, under certain conditions: the children's groups must be small, the educational institutions must be of the highest quality, and the parents must have daily and intensive contact with their child.[15] Several studies describe similar experiences in the Soviet Union.[16] However, it must be noted that the prerequisites are frequently absent in the Soviet Union: the groups are too large, and the busy mother can give only a few minutes a day to the education of her child.[17]

It is important to note that there are contradictions not only between children's need for family care and parents' possibilities, between the need for supplementary institutional care and the factual quality of institutions, but also between the economic necessity of women's work activity outside the home and their fundamental motivation to concentrate on the care of their children in their first years of life:

Recent research using questionnaires with working mothers points to the fact that most mothers would like to devote themselves exclusively to the care and education of their babies and toddlers and to interrupt productive work during this period. Non-interruption of work is seen as renunciation of interaction with the child, regardless of to whom child care is transferred—societal institutions, grandparents, relatives, or neighbors. For example, 80% of 427 working mothers expressed their opinion that "women, during the first two to three years after childbirth, should not work" (Slesarev and Jankova 1967).

Family-centered early child care seems, in summary, to be the best solution, not only with regard to the developmental needs of children, but to the emotional needs of most Soviet women, too. On the other hand, there are some factors in present-day Soviet society working against an official consideration of these needs—the demand of the economy for women's participation in productive work and the ideological fixation of women's role in society.

THE EFFECTS OF INSTITUTIONAL CARE OF CHILDREN

Developmental retardations and disturbances in the child can be traced to conditions of both family and institutional education, depending upon which was predominant. Although the family can be the ideal basic medium of primary socialization and, only under atypical conditions, harm the child's development, the children's institution, at least as an isolated educational factor, often fails to meet the child's emotional, spiritual, and social needs. Psychological studies in the Soviet Union have shown that "poverty, uniformity, and monotony of the early childhood emotional experience stamp a person's character for life. Many psychologists directly connect the inhibition, immature adjustment to reality, and the intellectual poverty of many people with a childhood spent without parents or with indifferent, intellectually limited or backward parents" (Lavrov and Lavrova 1967, p. 13). L. A. Levšin's reference to the general dangers of a one-sided collective education bears repeating:

> The children's collective is undoubtedly a great power. It plays an enormous role in children's lives and education. . . . But it has its limitations, and if they are overstepped the collective will not only not serve the correct education but, on the contrary, will directly hinder it. . . . Exclusive education in a children's collective is limited to a certain amount of potential adult influencing. The leader of the collective can devote only little time to each child. And there is always the danger that the individual child with his unique development will be lost in the general mass of children and will not receive the necessary "dose" of direct adult attention. . . . This can easily be avoided if life in the children's collective is combined with life in the family (Levšin 1964, p. 291).

Actual research into the harmful effects of institutional preschool education is difficult because of the many considerations involved: first, whether it is a predominantly or completely extrafamilial education; second, the qualitative and quantitative conditions under which the children's institutions operate; and third, how the family fulfills its particular educational task.

Clearly detrimental effects upon personality development could be determined in those institutions where children were educated full-time outside the family. After visiting several of these children's homes, a child psychologist reported as follows:

> What is the situation in the children's houses? Two adults, a nurse, and a governess take care of a group of 15 to 18 children. The "procedures" evolve in an uninterrupted chain: changing diapers, feeding, washing, taking them outside, washing them again and changing them, feeding, performing various odd tasks. Conversation with the child is very brief, negligible—it can't be otherwise: there are many children, all demand attention, all should be fed and neatly dressed. One talks more with the older children during games and walks, but each individual child receives infinitely little. Activities are set up with the older children, but not for more than ten minutes a day. . . . A child's language does not develop in planned "activities," but in conversations with adults and older children during the entire day (Kotovščika 1960).

Kotovščika says that these requirements are normally met in the family: the mother pays constant attention to the child, accompanies her care with words, and thus every day often "converses" with the small child. "In the children's homes, on the other hand, there is extremely little conversation; and what little there is for the most part has no individual character, but a group character. There are no older children there, and contact with the outer world is very limited. . . ." (ibid.).

In summary, under the prevailing conditions in children's homes, Kotovščika found clear indications of developmental retardation. In the early school grades, children from these homes "couldn't cope with many very simple things already understandable to an ordinary child of four or five" (Kotovščika 1961).

A completely extrafamilial education in children's homes, therefore, cannot guarantee normal development and education, all the more so when the usual size of the groups is 15 and more. Charčev called this extreme form of institutional education a "convincing sociological experiment" and concluded:

> [Although the children's home] completely replaced the family in caring for children and providing for their material needs, it could not replace the family in an intellectual and psychological respect. . . . It follows that, due to its uniqueness for each child, the family is an obligatory factor in normal education. Children who are raised without the family's participation are more greatly exposed to the danger of one-sided or retarded development than those who are members of family collectives. . . . Not a single one of these institutions can do without the help of parents. This help includes the utilization of the parents' educational influence over the child (as long as he is in the family) equally as much as their direct participation in the work of the children's institution (Charčev 1964, pp. 269-275).

The type of nursery-boarding home described above has never been widespread in the Soviet Union and has not been officially proclaimed as a recommended form of preschool education.[18] Even though the exact number is undeterminable, only a minimal number of preschool children are currently living in these institutions, presumably all with unstable family backgrounds. In determining the fundamental problem in full-time boarding home education, therefore, contemporary Soviet research does not oppose the goals of Soviet educational policy, which recommends active family participation in matters of education.

A more difficult question is whether children suffer harmful effects from the planned and already partially implemented combination of institutional and family preschool education. Little research has been done about this, possibly because it touches upon the taboos of previous family policy, and the few available studies have advanced contradictory information. Whether the combination of institutional and family education succeeds or has a detrimental effect depends upon two vital factors: the quality of the children's institution and the actual educational potentials of the family. Under the conditions now prevailing in the USSR, that is, in light of the overcrowding in children's institutions and the overburdening of the mothers, one cannot rule out harmful effects. There is a possibility that neither the institution nor the family can give the child the "necessary" dose of direct adult attention (Levšin), especially during his first years. V. Kondratova confirms this assumption in her research report:

> The practice of preschool education probably does not eliminate the

contact "deficiency" between children and adults. The study on the moral character of the preschool child demonstrates the negative results of this: children show a negative or indifferent relation to their environment as early as their fifth year. According to several test results, indifference turns out to be characteristic for almost 60% of the children. Such a situation demands (1) deeper research into the foundations of the contact and collaboration between adults and children, and (2) the introduction of various forms of common activities (Kondratova 1968, p. 83).

Kondratova attributes the negative educational results less to the actual lack of preschool institutions than to the general lack of family educational influence. In so doing she cites not only the experiences in Soviet children's homes, but those in Czechoslovakia as well:

Comprehensive Czechoslovakian studies involving the joint strengths of sociologists, pedagogues, psychologists, and physicians indicate that material care, which the children's homes and institutions guarantee with the long workday, far from solves all the tasks of education (ibid.).

Kondratova warns against overestimating the kindergarten's potentials and underscores the family's great importance in preschool education:

The child takes everything in through the prism of family education; the family and the domestic environment exert the main influence. In the children's institution the child finds it very difficult to create lasting and mutually fixed emotional ties with people, something which is entirely natural for a child raised in the family. Children need the family, the mother's training, her love and attention. In families where parents fulfill their duty conscientiously, children adopt a basically positive relation to their environment (ibid.).

If, therefore, in the combination of institutional and family preschool education the family remains crucial, then the success of education depends primarily upon its educational potentials. In this connection Kondratova refers again to the working mother's lack of time and to the negative results it can have for the education of the child:

Investigation results show that, if 63% of the families are stable, only 43% of the children adopt a positive relation to their environment. The remaining 20% of the families guarantee no positive educational influence over their children. The parents' lack of time for education turns out to be an essential reason for this. Sociological data from the industrial area around Rostov attest to the fact that, in working families here, the husband spends 1.3 hours a week on the education of his children; the wife, 0.7 hours. . . .

Sociological data about women's activity in societal work show that several occupations are totally incompatible with properly ordered motherhood. The lives of a large number of women are constantly divided between occupational and maternal duties (ibid.).

The working mother's role conflict has already been discussed as one of the Soviet woman's essential problems.[19] It is also a societal problem, for this role conflict has been recognized as one of the important causes for the regressive birthrate.[20] Moreover, as regards the education of the preschool child, the working mother's conflict proves to be a difficult pedagogical problem, actually the child's problem. It has been shown that not only the total lack of family educational influence, but its extreme limitations, can cause developmental disturbances in the child's earliest years. Under current conditions, the detrimental effects of the system of societal preschool education are due to its constant expansion in order to make the woman's full-time occupational activity possible. Her full-time employment, however, so strongly restricts the potentials of educational contact with the child that his needs for parental love and attention are often unfulfilled.

While more and more professional and lay voices in the USSR have in recent years called for more release time and material support for the tasks of educating the small child in the family, leading representatives of preschool pedagogy have defended the social necessity and pedagogical effectiveness of nursery school education for one- to three-year-olds for two reasons: to improve the education of children and to increase the desire to have children. Thus, A. Zaporožec, director of the APN's Scientific Research Institute for Preschool Education, said that good results could be achieved through scientific organization of educational work in the nurseries and close cooperation between children's institutions and families. In reporting on a study of a large group of one- to two-and-a-half-year-olds who were raised in 25 children's institutions in various cities, Zaporožec points out:

> The results showed that, thanks to the application of the suggested programs for games and activities, excellent results in the physical and mental development of the small children were achieved. It turned out that children who attended nursery schools were more independent, more active, and more organized. They sleep and eat better and have stronger life and health habits than their "domestic" contemporaries (Zaporožec 1969).

Zaporožec's research results contradict somewhat those of Kondratova. Of course, he does not go into emotional and moral development; he enumerates traits which primarily serve the children's adjustment to life in a collective. Still, his data have to be taken as proof of the fact that children do not necessarily have to lag in physical and mental development if they are simultaneously brought up in good children's institutions and in the family. Zaporožec concedes that, particularly with respect to the quality of children's institutions, numerous deficiencies still remain, especially "many cases of violating the existing requirements for the number of children in one group"; but he basically persists in the conviction that in day nurseries "there is every possibility of creating conditions for small children that approximate domestic [conditions]" (ibid.). Like those of Kondratova and others, Zaporožec's statements should represent objective information, but they lose their value when combined with strongly ideologically colored arguments. He justifies the need for day nurseries chiefly with the questionable traditional reference to the woman's social role, that is, she must be guaranteed societal activity and equal rights with the man. Such an argumentation ignores the fact that the woman can lose her equal rights through the double burden of employment and household duties, which adds up to an excessive amount of work. This argumentation also ignores the fact that the education of children during the crucial years of their lives must also be recognized as a necessary and socially useful activity by the woman. Above all, however, such an argumentation does not consider that even with the fundamental affirmation of the usefulness of day nurseries, a temporary release from work or, at least, a shortened workday for mothers of small children must be created in order to balance out her greater household burdens and meet her own needs as well as those of her children for intensive contact with each other.

The situation just described, and the attitudes of mothers toward it, obviously lead to cries for both maintaining and rejecting day nursery education. Some parents have a positive evaluation of their children's development in day nurseries; others, however, observe retardation.[21] The crucial problem for mothers, therefore, does not lie in recognizing or rejecting the actual potentials of day nursery education, but in identifying with their own role as mothers. The available research shows that the large majority of Soviet women do not want to leave the education of their small children, those between the ages of one and three, to social institutions or to others—even close friends and relatives; they prefer to do this on their own. The impossibility of realizing this intention, and the burdens of the woman's role conflict, necessarily engender frustrations that also burden her relation to the child and can lead to wrong attitudes in education or discourage her from having more children, or even none at all. One author observed:

> The ever-growing number of kindergartens and nurseries in no way stimulates the desire to have children. "Have a baby to give it to others?" Indeed, this probably not only relieves the mother of many cares about the child, but of many of the joys of motherhood (Nikitina 1968).

PLANNING FOR FAMILY-TYPE PATTERNS
IN PRESCHOOL INSTITUTIONS

Since 1958 Soviet preschool pedagogy has not only increasingly emphasized the importance of the family for the education of the child and intensified the cooperation between the children's institution and the family, but the institutions themselves are striving toward forms of interaction—between younger and older children, and between educators and children—which approximate the interaction structure of a family with several children.

Where children have to grow up without parents, direct replacement of the family influence is attempted by assigning adoptive parents and/or by "imitating" familial relations in the children's institutions. In connection with the widespread use of adoption, I. S. Kon observes:

> It is no accident that the development of a system of societal education is connected with attempts to imitate family life for children who have been deprived of their parents (adoption or the child's regular Sunday visits with the family of a friend) (Kon 1967, p. 127).

In criticizing full-time children's homes, A. Kotovščika reported the following about the usefulness of imitating familial sibling ties:

> Preschool children are significantly better developed in those children's homes which also include school sectors than in children's homes where only preschool children are raised. The cause of this phenomenon is obvious: in a common garden, and also often in groups, the schoolchildren play with the little ones and include them in their activities. Naturally, they talk to each other during play, and "older siblings" are on hand (Kotovščika 1960).

Based on these experiences Charčev concluded that "even in those cases where children necessarily have to be raised outside the family, they cannot do without some 'imitation' of familial relations" (Charčev 1964, p. 270).

The trend "to create conditions for small children which approximate domestic [conditions]" (Zaporožec 1969) is actually extended to the entire realm of societal preschool education. Three elements of reform should be mentioned in this connection: creation of uniform institutions for children of all age levels, efforts for continuity of educators during the preschool phase, and reduction in the size of children's groups.

The May 21, 1959, decree "On Measures toward the Further Development of Children's Preschool Institutions" promulgated the introduction of combined day nurseries and kindergartens where children should be raised from infancy (two months) until their entry into school (at age seven). By 1965, already 953,800 children up to the age of three were being taken care of in combined nursery-kindergartens, while 1.5 million children of the same age group were still in the traditional nurseries.[22] The consolidation of nurseries and kindergartens into one uniform preschool institution should enable regular contact between younger and older children as well as the combining of children of different ages into stable groups. Measures were taken to form mixed age groups in institutions with more than 50 children.[23] These new organizational forms should offer the younger children stimuli from the older ones, and also instill a sense of responsibility in the older children toward the younger ones.

The new institutions also emphasize the sought-after imitation of "sibling ties" by keeping the group composition fundamentally the same during the whole preschool phase. Thus the transition from nursery to kindergarten involves no change of locale or group. At the same time the establishment of combined day nurseries and kindergartens ensures the maximum continuity of teacher figures, thereby approximating the continuity of the mother as the educator in the family. Since the same teachers can take care of the same group until the children enter school, maximum continuity and uniformity of educational influences are assured.[24]

Finally, the efforts to keep children's groups as small as possible in the uniform preschool institutions illustrate the trend of emulating the educational conditions in the family. The 1962 Educational Program of the Kindergarten fixed the standard size of children's groups at 15 in the youngest age groups, 20 in the middle age groups, and 25 in the oldest ones.[25] This has undoubtedly still not achieved an ideal norm; but where these norms are realized, one already notes significant progress as compared to the hitherto widespread overcrowding of groups with 30 to 40 children, an overcrowding due chiefly to the general lack of institutions. Only a further restriction of group size can prevent the negative results of institutionalization and create conditions of interaction between the children and between them and adults. Such conditions make the children's collective a positive educational factor that supplements family education or replaces lacking or negative family education.

The system of cooperation between the children's institutions and the family has also given rise to a certain shift of emphasis in favor of the family: in addition to the material and organizational support expected of parents, their inclusion into the children's group activities and the acknowledgment, encouragement, and intensification of their educational activity have become increasingly important. This is due mainly to the growing recognition that the family must remain the most important factor in the education of the preschool child and that a complete, well-rounded education cannot be accomplished by children's institutions alone.

PARENT EDUCATION AND COOPERATION
BETWEEN KINDERGARTEN AND HOME

Next to the family, societal institutions are becoming an important educational factor for a growing number of preschool children. These circumstances gave rise to the pedagogical goal of "attaining a uniform influence over the children through the kindergarten and the family in order to guarantee the continuity of education" (Sorokina 1962, p. 252). The task of preschool educational institutions—not only in the Soviet Union but, since Pestalozzi and Froebel, all over the world—is considered to be to educate not only the children but the parents too, to be not only a children's institution but a "mothers' school" as well. Various forms of cooperation, of both mutual and one-sided influencing, suggest themselves. It is characteristic of the USSR that societal educational institutions are granted more authority than the family. On the other hand, as discussed earlier, since 1958-1959 the prevailing trend is for societal preschool education to adjust to the principles of family education and for parents to participate in the educational work of the kindergarten and support its educational authority. Of course, numerous possibilities exist for the public to directly intervene in family life, but their application in the post-Stalin period should not be overestimated. T. A. Markova's textbook for kindergarten teachers probably gives a realistic picture:

> The adult family members are inseparably bound up with the life of the society. . . . The majority of parents are naturally more or less aware of the family's role in preparing the young person for life. And yet private conditions determine a great deal of the education of children and all of family life (Markova 1964, p. 16).

Although the family is recognized and encouraged as an independent and irreplaceable source of education, this can lead to increasing self-isolation by the family with respect to the public. Collectivist values, however, are preeminent in Soviet society, a fact which makes all the more necessary the pedagogical enlightenment of parents aimed at maintaining the collectivist, society-oriented education of children in the family. The expansion of a system of cooperation between preschool institutions and the family certainly serves this goal.

The basic principles, contents, and forms of educational cooperation between kindergarten (or nursery school) and family, which are based on the preschool pedagogy of Krupskaja and others, have been worked out by the RSFSR Ministry of Education and the APN's RSFSR Institute for Preschool Education. They were written down in an official Program of Kindergarten Education (1962) and in the July 10, 1963, Decree on the Parents' Committee in Kindergarten,[26] and can be summarized as follows:

> 1. Uniformity in the work of the kindergarten and the family in the education of children will be achieved where teachers and parents understand the goals and tasks of education, and where the parents know and to a certain degree master the fundamental contents, forms, and methods of teaching small children.
> 2. Mutual trust in the reciprocal ties between teachers and parents, a good-will relationship toward one another, appreciation of the needs and interests of the child and of one's own duties as educator; increased authority of the teachers in the family and of the parents in kindergarten in the education of children.
> 3. The common work of the kindergarten and the family is based upon mutual help, a principle that is characteristic of the reciprocal ties of the Soviet people as a whole.

4. Learning from the best experiences of family education and their dissemination in a wide circle of parents; utilization of positive methods of family education in the work of the kindergarten.

5. The system's main forms of cooperation between the kindergarten and the family are: group and general parent meetings; learning about the child's life in his parental home; pedagogical conversations with parents and other members of the family; consultations, open days, and activities in kindergarten; various forms of observable pedagogical propaganda (Parents' Corners, exhibits, etc.).

6. The kindergarten's work with parents must be carried out systematically according to a definite plan and on a year-round basis. . . . Individual and collective forms of work must be coordinated and supplement each other.

7. Positive mutual criticism as well as self-criticism is indicative of correct ties between kindergarten teachers and parents; this serves the self-education of both and supports the improvement of children's education in the family and in kindergarten.

8. In working with parents, the kindergarten relies upon the parents' committee and the public (Markova 1964, pp. 9ff.).

These principles illustrate the efforts being made to harmoniously link familial with institutional education, and individual attention to a child or his parents with the collectivist orientation of education. The same effort is also reflected in the organization of the leading forms of educational cooperation, which will now be briefly discussed.

Family Visits and Conversations Between Parents and Teachers. These activities very clearly demonstrate the individualizing nature of the cooperation between the kindergarten and the family. Teachers' visits should take place at least once a year in every family—not just in the case of "problem" children. It is recommended that families of newcomers be visited before the child enters kindergarten. The informal character of the meeting is emphasized by the shift from the kindergarten to the parental home. Family visits should chiefly serve to inform the teacher. His or her "understanding of the child and the successful education of the child are impossible without a knowledge of the family's living conditions" (ibid., p. 31). The informal talk serves to establish a personal tie between the parents and the teacher. The child should not be criticized, nor should notes be taken. The educational counseling given to parents by the teacher is another function of the family visit—indeed, of repeated visits in the course of which objectivity and "pedagogical tact" must predominate. Teachers should "see something positive in the education of the children in every family and help the parents to overcome mistakes by referring to this positive aspect" (ibid., p. 33). Finally, family visits should afford the teachers an opportunity to get to know typical forms of family education and to share these experiences with others.

Individual parent-teacher talks at the kindergarten itself are a complementary source of communication; they can come about spontaneously or be scheduled in connection with definite problems. Parents should visit the kindergarten daily if possible and get to know the child's behavior in the group and the teacher's methodology.

Planned family visits and group conversations differ from informal routine visits and talks, and they chiefly concern "problem" families. In such cases it is not only a question of mutual information and individualized counseling and aid, but of direct intervention, on the part of the educator or the "parent collective," over families who deviate from the norm, i.e., who neglect the education of their children and fail to cooperate in the pedagogical process. Because of their priority role over that of the family, societal educational institutions are able to intervene in family education even where criminal or antisocial behavior by parents is involved. Finally, it is not only the personnel of state educational institutions who call upon individual parents to fulfill their societal educational duties, but any chosen representative of the kindergartern's "parents' collective" can do so:

> Teachers are aware . . . of the great force in the influence exerted by the parents' collective over individual parents. That which the educator sometimes cannot achieve by his or her work with "problem" families is accomplished by the parents' collective (ibid., p. 29).

This right to intervention, which can also assume the form of summoning individual parents before the "parents' collective," is expressly granted to the parents' committee of the kindergarten.[27] Recent textbooks on preschool pedagogy warn against coarse forms of intervention, since their ultimate pedagogical success is questionable.[28] Charčev feels that "the family does not need to be told what to do and to be regulated if it is morally sound. If, however, 'degeneration' of the family unit sets in, the public does not have the moral right to stand aside" (Charčev 1964, p. 228).

Viewed in this light, the existing system of cooperation between kindergarten and family represents an effective social corrective for the maintenance of the principles of communist education in the families of children attending preschool institutions.

Parent Meetings and Parents' Committees. Participation of Parents in the Work of the Kindergarten. Parents' meetings include either the parents of a children's group or the parents of the entire kindergarten. Meetings for parents of individual groups are convened once every quarter by the teacher; their main business includes reports and lectures by pedagogical and medical personnel, and their tasks are described as follows:

> Group-parent meetings are an effective form of work with the parent collective, a means of acquainting the parents in an organized manner with the tasks, content, and methods of educating the child in kindergarten and in the family. The teacher uses group-parent meetings to discuss the best experiences of family education and to make the paths toward their implementation known in solving some organizational problems (Markova 1964, p. 43).

Every meeting should have a definite theme and take the respective age level of the children into consideration—for example, "The Education of Children for Societal Attitudes in Play and in Appropriate Work" (ibid., p. 46). Parents are given the opportunity to ask questions and to discuss them, and individual parents should, in agreement with the teacher, report on positive educational experiences. The meetings alternate: one is devoted to the teacher's report, which should have something to say about the development of every child; a written characterization of each child and his family should be worked out; and, according to T. A. Markova's suggestions, the names of parents should never be given when discussing negative examples of family education. Participation is, of course, not formally obligatory, but socially expected:

> [the pedagogues] ascertain who did not show up and tactfully try to find out why. This type of control encourages the more active participation of parents in the kindergarten's activities. It is especially important to urge those parents who do not devote enough attention to the education of their children to participate [in these meetings] (ibid., p. 50).

"General parents' meetings" include the parents of all the children in the institution, and are convened every quarter by the kindergarten leader. Their purpose is to acquaint parents with the work of the kindergarten as a whole, to solve general organizational problems (such as meals and group vacation outings in the country), and to serve to propagate pedagogical knowledge.

The parents' committee not only affords formal representation for the parents, but is an important factor in the solution of the kindergarten's financial, organizational, and educational problems and in the establishment and care of the ties between the kindergarten and the families. Its tasks and rights have been set down in the RSFSR Ministry of Education decree On the Parents' Committee in the Kindergarten (1963). An annual plan, decided upon together with the kindergarten teacher, outlines the actual activities of this committee. A progress report must be given at the general parents' meeting.

The tasks of the parents' committee, which is composed of at least one parent representative from every children's group and meets at least once every two months, include: support of the kindergarten by assigning constant or temporary "parent activists" to help in organizing pedagogical propaganda[29]; establishing a tie between the kindergarten and individual families through family visits, etc.; [aid] in the health care of the children and in strengthening the kindergarten's financial and material base (repairs, the setting up of teaching aids, etc.). Every member of the parents' committee has definite duties; every parent representative, for example, must contribute two days of services a month to the kindergarten, visit families after consulting with the teachers, etc.[30]

The duties of the parents' committees are paralleled by the following rights: to make suggestions concerning actual educational work; to systematically check the quality of the food being served; to contact trade unions, the factory leadership, and other organizations for the kindergarten's support; to take measures toward the improvement of family education in cases where parents neglect their educational duties, and in certain circumstances to also arrange for the employer of such parents to intervene.[31]

In addition to these forms of parents' meetings and the systematic appointment of several parent activists in the parents' committee and in commissions for the work of the kindergarten, there are other, less formal forms of parental participation. These include "open door days" (held every two to three months), organized individual visits during children's activities, and exhibits and showcases which give all parents the opportunity to get to know the everyday educational reality of the kindergarten or of their child's group. In this way the kindergarten should lose the aura of a "closed" institution.

Because of the semi-obligatory nature of many activities and due to the mutual controls in the parents' collective, parental participation in meetings and activities is greater on the kindergarten level than on other school levels. Conversely, the public has a considerable influence on the families of preschool children. As a result, neither the family nor the kindergarten remains an isolated educational factor. The Soviet Union has also learned that the degree of parental participation in the educational work of societal institutions depends upon general educational awareness. In other words, it is precisely those parents who most need pedagogical stimuli and controls who are the most difficult to win over for cooperation.[32] Of course, the Soviet system offers more possibilities than other national systems to call upon even passive and negative parents for cooperation. The slight educational activity of fathers is balanced by the generally strong participation of mothers in the work of the kindergarten.[33]

"Pedagogical Propaganda" among Parents as a Main Task of the Kindergarten. Our description of the various forms of cooperation between kindergarten and family has made it clear that the Soviet Union looks upon the kindergarten not only as a daytime home for the children of working mothers, but also as a place of stimulation, direction, and control over parents' educational activity.

There are various forms of pedagogical propaganda in the kindergarten. In addition to those mentioned, many kindergartens have set up consulting services to counsel parents. Adult education departments, the "Znanie" [Knowledge] Society, and the Pedagogical Society arrange forums and lecture series in cooperation with individual factories and institutions, and direct them to a wider public. In recent years parents' universities have sprung up at different higher educational institutions and in large factories; in them, parents can take two-year courses in aspects of education. Kindergarten teachers also participate and take an active part in parents' conferences which are organized by the adult education departments and serve to exchange experiences in the field of family education and to spread pedagogical knowledge.

Pedagogical propaganda should especially reach those parents who have a low level of education and who either fail to handle educational problems or do not solve them in conformity with the principles of communist education. The practice of pedagogical propaganda, however, shows that participation in lectures, discussions, and courses on pedagogical themes increases with the educational standard of the parents. For example, the most recent reports on the activity of parents' universities stated that "few workers and collective farm peasants were found among the students" (V prezidiume APN SSSR 1968). The endeavor to impart broader pedagogical training to families of the lower educational strata partly explains the intensification of the pedagogical propaganda seen in recent years. However, it also represents a reaction by the state against the trend of many families to emphasize their private life and individualistic and material values, and to renounce a specific society-oriented education toward love of work, etc.[34]

The outline of a "Minimal Program of Pedagogical Knowledge for the Self-Education of Parents"[35] will be mentioned as a final example of pedagogical propaganda. Proposed by the USSR Academy of Pedagogical Sciences in 1968, this program about the goals, contents, and methods of communist family education should receive maximum dissemination and become a basic source of information for all, including those parents who take little part in the usual pedagogical propaganda events or whose children do not attend preschool institutions.

The purpose of this system of pedagogical propaganda is to indoctrinate and instruct parents. Planned family visits and measures against individual parents represent undue interference into people's private lives, and the parents' integration into the work of the kindergarten represents an exploitation of the parents' working capacity. Nevertheless, the fact that the kindergarten activities offer a great pedagogical potential that in many cases supplements and enriches family education, that individual children from antisocial families are freed from the exclusive influence of the family, and that the kindergarten attempts to balance the "institutionalization" of children through close contacts with the families should not be ignored. The kindergarten's overall educational activity can be credited with positive educational results for it provides parents with numerous stimuli for games and activities, for health care, arts and crafts, and for many other things.[36] Of course, kindergarten education and pedagogical propaganda cannot undo the fundamental lack of familial educational influence, which, as has been shown, is due mainly to the Soviet woman's work overload and lack of time.

FAMILY UPBRINGING: PRINCIPLES AND PRACTICES IN CONFLICT

Theoretical Concepts of Family Education

To this day the works of Krupskaja and Makarenko provide the foundation of Soviet preschool pedagogy. The teachings of these educators and quotations from their works are regularly found in official textbooks on preschool pedagogy and in numerous brochures for parents and teachers concerning questions of preschool education, especially those published by the Academy of Pedagogical Sciences. Krupskaja's essays and lectures and Makarenko's *A Book for Parents* as well as his *Lectures on the Raising of Children* are the most frequently used pedagogical texts[37] in the training institutions for kindergarten teachers and in lectures and book clubs for parents.

Krupskaja's and Makarenko's fundamental ideas about the education of the preschool child in the family can be briefly summarized:[38]

The early years of life are crucial for the development and formation of the personality. During those years, when a child is particularly susceptible to any kind of molding through his environment, every adult influence has a great effect, even if it does not occur as a conscious educational act. A lack of conscious educational influence, of love and authority, or else negative (unconscious) influences result in inadequate or nonexistent education of the child. It then becomes necessary to reeducate him, a process that is considerably more difficult than the initial correct training. Due to his plasticity and his drive to imitate others, the small child depends in his orientation upon the example of his parents' behavior as well as upon the concrete family relations and conditions. As his first and natural educators, therefore, parents must endeavor above all to set an example through their own behavior, which should reflect the principles of communist education because their educational responsibility is a social duty. The parents' love, which the child needs, and their respect for his developing personality must be combined with clear and consistent demands upon him. Without consistent demands regarding obedience, discipline, increasing self-control, and cooperation in the family household, there is a chance that the child will become an egoist, a danger that is particularly great in families with an only child whose parents concentrate their love on him. These demands must reflect the goal that the child develops the realization that he is a member of a collective built upon mutual help; yet, they must also be appropriate to his developmental stage and take his age into consideration.

While distance of authority should be maintained between parents and small children, extreme forms of authoritarianism (despotism, etc.) must be avoided; authority rests, above all, upon a social foundation and must be expressed through the socially oriented behavior of parents. Punishments are to be prudently meted out and should be the exception rather than the rule in education. Physical punishment is to be completely rejected. At the center of communist education is work education, which is closely related to moral and patriotic indoctrination. Parents should allow their children to participate in their work and societal life and encourage them to take increasing care of themselves and to assume responsibilities within the household. A stable family life style, modeled on the principles of a communist society and organized in a regular daily routine, should prepare the child for life in that society.

The following passages on the application and further development of the fundamental thoughts of Krupskaja and Makarenko in the current conceptions of preschool education in the family are not intended to provide a complete picture of Soviet preschool pedagogy. Rather, a few selected examples will highlight some tendencies.

Bringing education into line with the values and needs of society must be considered the most characteristic feature of Soviet preschool pedagogy. The child's preschool education is looked upon as direct preparation for entrance into the school collective and into communist society:

> Soviet parents are currently confronted with a clear program: the education of children from infancy on toward the personality attributes which a builder of communism must possess (Markova 1964, p. 17).

Work education forms the nucleus of socially oriented family education, just as it does in the works of Makarenko:

> Communist education is primarily work education. People must be trained for work from early years on (O vospitanii doškol'nikov v sem'e 1963, pp. 33-34).

Education for work is the most amply treated subject in textbooks and brochures on preschool education. With respect to very young children, the work education program is aimed primarily at the early mastery of simple activities, at self-control, and at maintenance of a definite routine:

> By the time he is about two years old, a child can eat by himself, push his chair in its place following the meal, take his own shoes off, etc. (ibid., p. 34).

Parents should assign three-year-olds some fixed and regular household duties which correspond to the abilities of that age; in this way the child develops fixed habits and the awareness that through his work he becomes a useful member of the collective.[39] A regular daily routine should be the basis not only of work education but also of the child's whole life within the family. All pedagogical advisors place great emphasis on strict observance of this routine because it "strengthens the child's health and trains him in organization from early years on" (Markova 1964, p. 85). The systematic preparation for school also falls under work education: both in the family and in the kindergarten the child should be trained in the ability to concentrate, in efficiency, and in the basics of reading and writing, so that he may be prepared for the demands made by the school.[40]

The strong emphasis, in the education of the child, upon adjustment to life in a collective is not restricted to work education and its central position in pedagogical theory. It is also apparent in the stressing of such characteristics or goals of moral education as "organization," "discipline," "order," and "obedience."[41] Parents should curb spontaneous outbursts like obstinacy, naughtiness, and moodiness "through strict adherence to order, resolute sternness, and fulfillment of the child's reasonable wishes" (Programma-minimum 1968). Finally, the pedagogical demand to raise the child from his early years toward membership in the communist society finds expression in the propagation of patriotic and atheistic education, which parents should begin with their children as early as the preschool period.[42]

Compared to this collectivist trend of preschool pedagogy, the second trend—the fostering of individual personality formation—is clearly of secondary importance. To be sure, recent works on preschool or family pedagogy advocate, more strongly than did Makarenko, the demand for education that is suitable to the age group and to individual differences, and more information is provided about the child's psychophysical development.[43] There are even indications that the child is not shaped solely by his environment and education, but that he is also pre-formed by individual, inherited factors which must be developed.[44] On the whole, however, it remains characteristic of Soviet educational theory that the individual uniqueness of personality is considered less as an independent factor than as a function of collective social life. While the main chapters of leading works and numerous brochures are dedicated to the development of such traits as obedience, discipline, and love of work, systematic observations about education for spontaneity, initiative, creative growth, the ability to solve conflicts, etc., are nowhere to be found. Only in connection with play, the importance of which is currently receiving increasing emphasis in preschool education, is the development of imagination and creative activity appreciated. It is significant that, even with reference to a child's play, the predominant direction of thought tends toward categories of adaptation and avoidance of conflicts. One should make the most of a child's play drive by directing it toward the establishment of interpersonal contacts, toward preparation for work activities, and toward his first encounters with conceptual learning (language development, etc.). Parents should direct the child's play intelligently and prevent him from taking on negative roles with which he could identify.[45]

To sum up, Soviet preschool pedagogy assigns to the family the task of providing the child with an education oriented toward those values and needs of Soviet society which primarily enable him to take his place as a useful member in a collective—the family, school, society. The consistent demand toward a socially oriented value system for the child, and the emphasis on his adjustment to life in a collective, are not to be equated with renunciation of child-centered education; with its demands, however, current Soviet preschool pedagogy places itself in conscious opposition to the "free education" principles that were extensively practiced in the early years in conformity with international trends. In the very rejection of free education and in its orientation on Makarenko, the position of present-day Soviet preschool pedagogy is well defined:

Until the end of the 1950s the ideas of free education enjoyed a certain popularity in the theory and practice of Soviet preschool education. . . . The educational process was spontaneous and undirected, the effectiveness of activities [in kindergarten] was extremely diminished. . . . The untenability of the views held by representatives of free education has become evident today. . . . (*Narodnoe obrazovanie SSSR* 1967, pp. 42, 48-49).

The rejection of free education primarily concerns educational planning in state preschool institutions. According to the reference just cited, free education enjoyed a "certain popularity" in the USSR until the end of the 1950s, even though an offical rejection was issued as early as 1936, when pedology was condemned. It has meanwhile become clear that Soviet pedagogy places the same demands upon parents as it does upon professional educators: parents should not educate their children spontaneously but lead them deliberately and purposefully so as to contribute to their effective preparation for the learning achievements and social skills demanded in school.

Educational Practices in the Family

The lack of studies and scientific observations concerning families with small children presents difficulties in making well-founded statements about the educational practices of Soviet parents. The following comments are based upon several social factors, alluded to in previous chapters, which restrict the educational potential of Soviet families:

1. The double burden of employment and household duties leaves the majority of Soviet mothers only minimal time to perform their educational functions. For this reason, many children cannot be guaranteed a fixed daily routine in the family. The limited parent-child interaction seems to assume more of an informal, leisurely character than that of a demanding educational activity, since after a full day of separation both parents and children need to confirm their mutual emotional ties.

2. The extremely confined living conditions of many families impede education in cleanliness and order, often prevent the child from having his own play area, and increase the possibilities of conflict within the family.

3. In most families the father's share of household chores is minimal. Together with other factors, this makes it difficult for many children to perceive the family as a work collective with common duties, and an effective program of work education for the child is not guaranteed through parental example.

4. Half of all Soviet families limit themselves to a single child. Based on experience, there is a good chance that these families will take their educational responsibilities lightly and that the parents will focus their emotional concentration on the child and tend to spoil him.

5. A considerable number of children, about 20%, grow up in incomplete families, either because of illegitimacy or divorce (most cases concern the only

child), and in disharmonious families. Such families are for the most part unable to utilize the specific educational potential of family life; the impact of this potential more frequently appears as a negative factor.

In light of all this, one can presume that family education practices in many cases and in many respects do not meet the demands made upon them by society and pedagogical theory.

The discrepancy between theory and practice is particularly evident in the area of work education. Work education, in the sense of introducing children to a routine of household duties and acquainting them with their parents' occupations, holds a central position in Soviet family pedagogy. Empirical investigations, however, demonstrate a low realization of these demands in actual practice. Among 647 families questioned, "the children in 17.1% [of the families] were totally exempt from work obligations, and in 30.2% these duties bore a casual character" (Titarenko 1967, p. 18). A survey of 139 pupils in grades one through four proved that 89.5% of the beginners did indeed know where their parents worked. Only 50%, however, knew what their parents' occupation was; only 43% knew what their parents did at work; and only 10.7% knew "what the value of their parents' work was for other people" (Burštejn 1961). The data in these two studies show that, in almost half the families involved, no systematic program of work education for the child was taking place. Statements by official representatives of preschool pedagogy also confirm this fact (although without any quantitative analyses). T. A. Markova criticizes the mistakes of many parents in these words:

> Even if they do train their children in work, they do it sporadically. Children have no fixed duties at home; adults devote little attention to teaching their children to work intelligently and cooperatively, and they do not examine the results of the children's work. An attitude which considers a child's work as little more than a pastime will not foster his preparation for work, the formation of a love of work, or the habit of working (Markova 1964, p. 22).

The discrepancy between the theory and practice of family education is also seen in the child's education regarding a regular daily routine. Titarenko's study indicated that "children in more than half of the families [involved] have no definite and constant daily routine" (Titarenko 1967, p. 18).

Second to a program of work education, atheistic education, one of the essential foundations of communist education, can be cited as a special indicator of the degree to which family education is socially oriented. Empirical studies show that a large number of families, particularly in rural areas, do not fulfill the societal demands of atheistic education; religious traditions are cultivated in many families. In 1963-1964, even in several industrial centers of the RSFSR, 25-50% of the families in the district of Vyborg in Leningrad and in two districts around Odessa had their children baptised.[46]

The following research results show that the family's religious influence is not solely confined to the observance of external rites: of the 150 atheists polled, 61.3% said they got their early faith in God through the family, and 25% of the second graders in Moscow's elementary school No. 540 went to church on Sundays during their stay in the countryside.[47] These data demonstrate that a considerable number of preschool children receive a certain religious education, presumably frequently from the influence of tradition-conscious grandparents who take over their care and education while the mothers work.

In addition to the question of the parents' value orientation in their educational activity (which should be discussed in more detail in connection with the education of adolescents), there is the problem of how basic their feeling of educational responsibility is, what educational authority they have over their children, and how they express it. One can infer from the data about the low realization of work education that many parents dispense with systematic educational activity and tend to spoil or neglect their children. A study by V. Kondratova, which included 200 families with children who were being brought up both at home and in kindergarten, confirms this supposition. Its findings show that many parents exert no educational authority over their children. As Kondratova pointed out, there is a particularly good chance of this in cases where an only child is the center of attention and everyone is "at his beck and call." Specifically, the investigation yielded the following results:

> A positive influence over their children is exerted by 140 out of 200 families. These children adapt themselves to the other children in their group, are helpful to others, and carry over to their teachers the respect they show for their parents. The remaining 60 children have to be reeducated; they demonstrate a clear contrast between their behavior at home and their behavior in kindergarten (Kondratova 1966, p. 47).

A closer analysis of the 60 educationally weak families led Kondratova to set up various categories of parents who fail in the education of their children. Some parents (for the most part, the younger ones) leave it up to a grandmother or to relatives; for some this neglect stems from insufficient parental love; other parents feel they are too busy and that the education of children falls under the responsibility of social institutions; and the final category consists of parents whose families are incomplete or whose marriages are discordant.[48]

Kondratova's observations show that a certain number of parents—generally working mothers—pay little or no attention to their children and to their children's education. The remaining parents, who Kondratova feels exert a negative influence over their children, do in fact seem child-oriented, but they are not education-oriented in the sense of societal demands: they love and support their children, but do not make any demands upon them and do not control their own behavior, which serves as an example for the child. The spread of institutional preschool education could, in certain cases, encourage such attitudes on the part of parents toward the education of their children, inasmuch as parents can transfer the main responsibility for their children's education to social institutions.

Kondratova's study does not say which forms of educational relationships between parents and children—aside from neglect and indulgence—are characteristic of the Soviet family. Based upon Soviet pedagogical literature and personal observations, the attempt by the psychologist A. G. Kovalëv to arrive at a typology of family education offers some information on this question.

Proceeding from the hypothesis that "the family gives the child not only its physical but its moral life" (Kovalëv 1965, p. 255) and that the nature of family life, the quality of parental authority, and the "system of demands" decisively impress the preschool child, Kovalëv distinguishes three types of family education and three personality types which can be looked upon as the "result" of the corresponding education:

1. Indulgence prevails in the first type of family education, just as it did in a large part of the group with a negative educational influence in Kondratova's study. In these families the child appears "as the object of his parents' tenderness and admiration. They use diminutive words when speaking to him and often imitate his speech. Everything the child wants is granted. . . . The child is not used to taking care of himself and is of little help to his parents. Until his sixth year someone else dresses him, and until his seventh year he is spoon-fed. . . ." According to Kovalëv, this type of education leads to the formation of an "emotional and impulsive character type," a person who is unable to overcome any obstacles or difficulties in life and who comes into conflict with his contemporaries and teachers when they do not fulfill his wishes (ibid., p. 256).

2. In contrast, the second type of family education is characterized by authoritarianism. The child "becomes from his earliest years the object of drill and a pedantic system aimed at training in obedience. Constant rough yelling, moralizing and continual rebukes that such-and-such is not allowed—all diminish the child's activity. . . . A strict daily routine rules in the house, one that favors order but not initiative. . . . Every form of learning begins at a very early age. . . ." According to Kovalëv, these families produce "passive, apathetic people" (ibid., p. 257).

3. This type of family education, the only one which corresponds to Soviet pedagogical demands, affords "the necessary degree of activity and restraint. Parents arouse the child's activity by every possible means, and guide it in the necessary direction; at the same time, they curb his impulsiveness and bring him up with definite habits and behavior patterns." According to Kovalëv, the characteristics of a personality brought up in this manner include, among others, "confidence in one's own abilities," "initiative," "sociability," and "collectivism" (ibid., pp. 257-258).

These types of family education and personality are certainly found in every society. It is doubtful whether the Soviet family realizes one type of education—for example, the third type, as Kovalëv assumes—more than the others. In our final chapter we shall again discuss the educational goals and means of Soviet parents, and will show that a very large proportion of families currently apply authoritarian educational practices (the tendency of many parents to spoil their children has already been discussed). Kovalëv and other authors do not deny the widespread existence of these extreme types of education, all of which deviate from the norms of Soviet pedagogy. Their survival seems to be explained not only by the insufficient pedagogical awareness of parents, but it also seems to be connected with the family's actual living conditions. One must assume, for example, that the mother's work overload and the nervous stress accompanying it, the confined living space, and the short time available for parent-child interaction can create numerous family conflicts or at least intensify such conflicts, and that these are then solved in an authoritarian manner through suppression of the child's willfulness and impulsiveness, or are glossed over by the parents with complete indulgence, noninterference, and pampering.

The effect of all these social factors of family life on the educational potential of the family seems at times to be so strong that, as Kondratova could ascertain from the time factor, even given a responsible parental attitude toward the child and his education and under the conditions of a happy marriage, a "positive" education for the child is often not guaranteed:

> Among 63% of the families considered stable, only 43% of the children develop a positive relation to their surroundings; the remaining 20% of the families do not guarantee a positive educational influence over their children. The parents' lack of time for education proves to be an essential cause (Kondratova 1968, p. 83).

The variety of actual forms and goals of family education presents a specific problem for the pedagogical situation in Soviet society, for it is confronted by a uniform pedagogical theory which, in turn, is based upon an integrated system of officially sanctioned social values.... The discrepancies, noted earlier, between pedagogical theory and the everyday actualization of family education are not simply accepted in the Soviet Union; the fact that, in educating their children, only some parents—about 30 to 50%—lay the foundations for the formation of that type of collective personality which is viewed as the ideal personality under communism, and that a great number of children must therefore be reeducated (as far as is still possible) in societal educational institutions, has moved official representatives of preschool pedagogy to consider measures that will more effectively achieve society's educational goals. There are, e.g., individuals who feel that preschool education in the family could be improved if mothers were freed to a certain extent from employment in favor of their educational functions. Opponents of this view point out that a strengthening of the family potential in child education will not necessarily lead to a strengthening of the accepted value orientation of society.

The Family's Role
in the Education
of School-Age Children

The family generally loses its role as the exclusive source of education by the time the child enters school. It has been shown that, although most women go to work, the majority of Soviet preschool-age children are still brought up within the family and in the neighborhood. However, the child's school entry marks the transition to an educational spectrum in which the family represents only one of several educational factors. Next to the family, the school and the children's or youth organizations appear to be important sources of education. In view of this fact, which is characteristic of all societies to a certain extent, the question arises as to just what importance the family still retains, under the specific social and pedagogical conditions of Soviet society, as an influence factor in the education and social integration of the young. The balance of this study will be devoted to answering this many-sided question. The research material currently available necessarily limits this discussion to several selected problems.

First of all, the family's position within the educational field must be described in more detail. This position is based upon the family's potential temporal and psychological influences and upon the tendency of Soviet educational policy to strengthen the educational influence of society over young people and to make the family itself, including the parents, the object of this influence. We shall offer several examples to illustrate the importance of the family as an educational factor. Thus, the school achievements and school careers of young people will indicate how far the educational chances of adolescents, even within the Soviet comprehensive school system, are determined by the social position, the standard of living, the educational level, and the educational milieu of their families. Similarly, a discussion of juvenile delinquency will point out the influence which the family's internal structure, its educational milieu, and its social position can exert on the moral education and social integration or, on the other hand, on the development of antisocial behavior patterns among young people. The following section will then attempt to determine the importance of the family and family education in imparting specific social values. The role exerted by the goals and ideals of communist education with respect to family education or to the awareness of the adolescent will be examined through the example of work education in the family—the adolescents' attitude toward work—as well as through the example of the ideological education within the family—the ideological awareness and ideological-political activity of adolescents. The final section deals with the educational goals and practices of Soviet parents.

This discussion will be restricted with respect to the age levels under consideration and to certain selected problem areas, and we will deal with the relationship between family and society, between family education and extrafamilial—that is, collective—education. Since, next to problems of preschool education, the majority of Soviet research concerns problems of adolescent education, we will not cover the elementary school age (grades one through four).[1]

We will focus upon an analysis of the family's educational influence over fifth through tenth graders and upon adolescents who have completed their school education.

THE FAMILY IN THE EDUCATIONAL FIELD

In an industrial society which has displaced the family as a production unit and a permanent living community, the adolescent years represent a developmental stage of the growing independence of the personality, a gradual detachment from the family, and the adolescent's entrance into peer groups at school, on the job, and in other spheres. It is also true of Soviet society that young people are not left to the influence of spontaneous and informal peer-groups, but are directed to comprehensive political youth organizations within and beyond the scope of the school and the job, so that they can be educated toward the goals of society. As has been noted, under communism the school, as the administrative center of societal education, is accorded a leading role vis-à-vis the family and is assigned the task and the capacity to direct the family's educational influence. In actual practice there is a tendency to realize the extrafamilial education of adolescents as completely as possible within the scope of state educational institutions and youth organizations, while at the same time placing family education under a certain control. The view, often emphasized in Soviet pedagogy and psychology, that "the organizing of demands on young people in a collective represents the most important path to the formation of a complete personality," that "through active participation in the life and activities of a collective made up of his contemporaries" the adolescent is taught "to live for the interests of the collective, and to let them direct his behavior"—this view demonstrates the state's intention to systematically realize the collective education of youth: "to carry out educational work with young people by organizing a uniform, healthy, strong, and purposeful collective" (Kruteckij and Lukin 1959, pp.70-71).

Time Budget and Family Interaction

The Soviet adolescent is by no means under the exclusive or even predominant influence of an organized collective education, and this must be kept in mind when attempting to assess the hold of ideology on educational reality. The potential educational influences of the Soviet school should not be overestimated. The great majority of schools function only for a half-day instructional period. Because it imparts only formal instruction, this standard school maintains a traditional structure of teacher-directed lessons and attempts to impart an excessive amount of learning material. For this reason it can devote little time to the education of the individual youngster and to the formation of an effective pedagogical collective. This does not deny the educational effects of classroom instruction or the possibility of the gradual formation of "public opinion" within the class. Nevertheless, the article in *Pravda* already referred to (Zuev 1967) seems to correspond to the facts when it says that the school plays "the leading role with respect to the quality of our children's knowledge," but the family is called upon "to exercise a hardly less important function with respect to the student's personality development."

The educational influence of the Pioneer and Komsomol organizations is also, at least time-wise, quite limited. Apart from school-supported activities, youngsters are occupied for short periods of time in sports events, club work, and "socially useful work" on some weekdays and weekends, and for longer periods of time in youth camps and work activities during vacations.

Even if the effect of individual educational factors on the youngsters can hardly be evaluated by their time dimensions, it is certainly interesting, for the intensity and priority aspects in education, to analyze the quantity and continuity in time of these various educational factors.[2]

Time budget studies have shown that adolescents spend a large part of the day in an unorganized manner outside of school and youth organizations. An analysis of the time budgets of 537 pupils in the fifth through tenth grades of 15 schools in various cities showed that on the average two-thirds of their 24-hour time budget was determined by home environment; even the tenth graders spent an average of 16 hours and 16 minutes at home. The domestic time budget consisted of various categories: the time necessary for sleeping, eating, and daily needs amounted to an average of 11 hours; about two to three hours was spent on homework; household chores took an average of about 50 minutes; and "free time" accounted for three to four hours.[3]

Aside from actual time spent in school instruction, outside activities, both organized and unorganized, seem to occupy a subordinate position within the adolescents' time budget. A survey of 500 upper-graders in and around Sverdlovsk yielded the following results: only 10% of the youngsters participated daily in "societal activity"; 27%, several times a week; and 25%, several times a month. 14% of the adolescents took part daily in sports; 56%, several times a week; 5% attended lectures several times a week, and 34% attended several times a month; 5% reported they went to the movies, the theater, or concerts every day; 38% went several times a week, and 37% went several times a month. In contrast, extensive domestic leisure time activities belong in the daily time budget of most young people: 94% of those questioned read newspapers and books on a daily basis, and 87% listened to or watched radio or television programs every day.[4]

These data prove that the young person spends most of his time outside the frame of an organized collective. Neither his school nor the youth organizations exert a continuous influence during extracurricular hours. Not only the completion of homework assignments, which, next to actual time spent in lessons, fills up the adolescents' exceedingly long "workday," but the spare-time activities also remain predominantly a matter of the private sphere—last but not least because of the mass media available at home. Under these conditions the home environment takes on a crucial significance for the education of adolescents. This is true not only for control of the learning process, but also for general "social control" over youngsters, for the formation of their spare-time interests, for their choice and judgment of programs offered by the mass media, and for moral education as exemplified by family life.

Of course, the parents' potential educational influences should be no more overestimated than those of the school and of youth organizations. Although it has been repeatedly stated that an adolescent spends his extracurricular time predominantly "in the family," this does not mean that he spends it with his parents or under their supervision. Rather, the problem is that most young people remain without any supervision for many daytime hours, doing homework and filling their free time on their own, because both parents generally work and at the end of the day are busy with shopping, household duties, societal activities, etc. Hence the time available for parent-child interaction is extremely limited, as has been shown to be the case with the education of the preschool child. Although a family's life style can have a functional educational effect even without the constant presence of parents or during the limited time devoted to common household chores in the evening and to leisure-time activities, nevertheless, the fact that youngsters spend many hours a day alone or under the influence of informal groups and the "street" necessarily diminishes the educational importance of the parents. If one disregards for the moment the not uncommon cases in which parents themselves are poor models for their children or pay very little attention to their education, then, given the extreme restriction of time available for interaction (conversations, etc.), even exemplary parents cannot always offer their youngsters sufficient psychological support.[5]

The lack of any educational control during many hours of the day leads, among other things, to the fact that youngsters cannot be guaranteed a fixed daily routine. The previously cited study by Davydov and Pelipenko (1967) indicated that only 10.5% of the pupils questioned had a fixed daily routine and observed it systematically; 49.5% did not systematically observe the routine set by their parents because there was no parental supervision; and 40% had absolutely no fixed daily routine, which had a negative impact not only upon the youngsters' school achievements but also upon their social behavior. Davydov and Pelipenko considered the "nonsupervision" of adolescents a great pedagogical danger, "one of the main contributing factors in delinquency."[6] The only solution to this situation seems to be the assumption of a greater degree of responsibility on the part of societal educational institutions for the education of adolescents during nonschool hours. Rather than abandoning young people to the uncontrollable influences of the home, the community, and the street, forms of school-directed full-day education represent a trend to supplement the "spare" education of youngsters from an educationally weak school and an educationally weak family.[7]

Children's View of Parents as Educators

Despite the limited time available for parent-child interaction, and despite the growing importance of informal peer-groups and organized educational collectives during adolescence, the family generally seems to remain the most important social reference group and the most important psychological support for young people. Surveys show that adolescents consider their parents their most influential educators: a study of 1,241 students in grades 5 through 11 in 57 schools in and around Lugansk regarding what they felt were the "sources of their moral influence" indicated that 94% considered their mother and 67% considered their father as the main educator. Teachers were named as important factors by 62.3% of the students; the school by 52.4%; their friends by 19.9%. These young people felt that the mother played a particularly important role in their education.[8] Even students in the highest grades put her in first place—for example, 104 of the 120 tenth graders—while only 45% of the 11th graders named their father.[9]

A 1966 survey of 15,000 boys and girls undertaken by a research team of the Central Committee of the All-Union Komsomol Organization arrived at a similar result: "Among other things the survey asked the following question: 'What has had the greatest effect upon the development of your character—school, family, Komsomol, friends, radio, television, etc.?' The overwhelming majority ranked the family in first place. In the process the following characteristic was discovered: the higher the family's cultural level, the more meaningful and fruitful its influence" (Gurova 1968, p. 8).

These uniform survey results are particularly noteworthy because the youngsters were asked these questions within the framework of the school or youth organization, societal institutions which claim the leading position in the educational process. The order of precedence included in setting the questions in the second survey—school, family, Komsomol—also seems to have anticipated a result in favor of social educational institutions. The fact that young people ascribe the greatest significance in the development of their personality to their parents, and not to teachers, the class collective, or the youth group, can be explained in various ways. It is the family, and not any social group, that accompanies a person from birth to maturity. The emotional ties between parents and children, with their foundations in early childhood, are therefore deeply rooted and continue during adolescence in a stronger or weaker degree, depending on the educational understanding of the parents; the emotional ties to other persons must be formed from school age on and are less continuous (due to teacher change, etc.). As has been shown, the parents' educational influence can indeed be diminished during the adolescent stage, but the foundations of education were already laid in the family before the child entered a social educational institution. The family, as Gurova observes, is "the child's first educator. The foundations of his character are being laid before the age of six or seven. . . . It is not without good reason that the saying goes: the first grader 'brings his parents to school with him.' Then the school becomes his leading educator. But the family influences the growing person in the future as it did in the past" (Gurova 1968, p. 8). The degree to which the family remains a controlling educational factor during adolescence depends a great deal upon the individual parents' intellectual and moral authority, upon "the cultural level of the family."

There are indications that youngsters feel more emotional about endorsing the family and informal groups of friends rather than organized collectives. The need for intimacy, for emotional support, and for individual attention seems better able to be satisfied in the small family group, trusted from childhood on, than in organized youth collectives which impose a greater demand for adaptation and discipline upon the individual personality. Since the latter are often characterized by a certain formalism in assigning societal tasks, their ideologically doctrinaire influencing can in certain cases "turn the youngster off." In a survey of 1,500 Leningrad Komsomol members, it was found that "the overwhelming majority of those questioned did not want to spend their free time in school. They preferred the limited circle of friends, sports activities, theater presentations, and their own home because they assume that even at evening affairs they would not be able to relax naturally and informally in school" (Mal'kovskaja 1968).

On the other hand, the fact that most young people named their parents as their main educators should not be overestimated. The first of the above-mentioned surveys shows that, in the minds of the youngsters, the school and their teachers are very significant factors of educational influence; upper-grade students rated them even more highly than they did their own fathers. But the surveys contain no statements about the youngsters' relations to their parents at the time of the study, about their preferred free-time associations, etc. . . . During adolescence, in particular, conflicts between parents and children can arise which, as the sociologist I.S. Kon pointed out, are connected, on the one hand, with the adolescents' general drive toward independence and, on the other, with the inability of many parents "to turn away from authoritarian educational methods that provoke a feeling of protest on the part of the youngster" (Kon 1968, p. 10). In a study of 123 families in which many conflict-ridden relations between parents and adolescent children existed, it could be demonstrated that in 49 cases the parents excessively bossed the youngsters, in 32 cases they "did not enter into the adolescent's inner world," in 28 cases they showed excessive strictness and at times resorted to physical punishments, and in 17 cases the parents displayed an indifferent attitude toward education.[10] Many young people do not find in the family that emotional support and individual encouragement which theoretically is thought of as being more family-rooted when compared to the situation in organized youth collectives; these youngsters will more likely be inclined toward alienation from the family, toward giving themselves over to the influence of informal age groups and the "street," than would those youngsters whose parents prove to be conscientious and understanding educators. One may, however, assume that the cases of parental failure described above are the exception. Even in such cases Soviet pedagogues do not advocate the replacement of family education by social institutions; they do recommend pedagogical enlightenment of the parents. This indicates that Soviet pedagogues increasingly recognize the family's significance for the individual and societal education of the adolescent and, contrariwise, the dangers that loss of family ties can pose for the personality development of the young. Dunaeva emphasizes that one of the essential causes of the alienation of individual adolescents from the family is the "parents' lack of pedagogical knowledge," and that it is therefore necessary to transmit to them, through pedagogical propaganda, the knowledge necessary to make them good educators of their growing children.[11]

ALTERNATIVES TO FAMILY EDUCATION: THE DEBATE ON BOARDING AND ALL-DAY SCHOOLS

Because instruction in the regular school is limited to the morning hours, and parent-child interaction to the evening hours, youngsters remain without educational supervision for many hours each day. Neither the regular school nor the family can guarantee them an effective leisure-time education and a consistent supervision of their learning activity. In light of the pedagogical dangers which can result from insufficient educational control over youth, the organization of full-day education for all youngsters has become a top-priority problem in Soviet educational policy. Even apart from the day-to-day questions of the campaign against child neglect, etc., the idea of comprehensive societal education in children's homes and full-day or boarding schools finds solid support in Soviet pedagogy. This concept was advanced in the early Soviet pedagogy, among others, Krupskaja, in the 1920 Ukrainian program of "Societal Education," and in the school reform draft of 1930;[1][2] but it was only in the Khrushchev era that this idea was realized on a larger scale.

During the Khrushchev years, just as in the early Soviet period, there was never any doubt that the school represented the single administrative center of full-day education. The leading role in the education of the younger generation was relegated to societal education, and the integration of women into social production was not only not to be revoked, but in fact was to be fostered and facilitated by society's assumption of educational functions. However, while the thinking during the Khrushchev era was first focused on the realization of a completely extrafamilial boarding school education, the idea of limited extrafamilial all-day or full-day school education has in the meantime found stronger support. This development has particular significance for analyzing the family's position in the educational spectrum.

Following Khrushchev's recommendation at the Twentieth Congress of the Communist Party, in February 1956, to initiate the construction of boarding schools, and following the publication of a September 15, 1956, directive by the Central Committee of the Communist Party and the USSR Council of Ministers, "On the Organization of Boarding Schools,"[1][3] the boarding school was propagated as the model for the communist school of the future. The RSFSR Ministry of Education announced that dormitory schools "were called upon to become the model educational institutions which will establish and implement the most complete methods of communist education for the younger generation." The dormitory school would, of course, confer with parents, but it would bear "the full responsibility for the education of the child" ("Škola-internat" 1958, pp. 16, 20). After the development of a network of boarding schools, the establishment of full-day schools began after publication of a directive by the Central Committee of the CPSU and the USSR Council of Ministers on March 15, 1960.[1][4] Until the end of the Khrushchev era, however, less attention was paid to full-day schools than to boarding schools, which were designated as "instructional and educational institutions of a higher level."

Since the beginning of the 1960s, especially after the fall of Khrushchev, a shift in emphasis from the boarding school to the full-day school clearly took place. This became evident as early as the autumn of 1964 in discussions held at an international conference in Rostock concerning daytime education. Werner Lindner, the representative of the German Democratic Republic at the conference, stated in his report on the Soviet system of full-day education that the boarding school "could not maintain the extensive claims attributed to it by many during its early phase" (Lindner 1966, p. 348). The following years saw the publication of reports in the Soviet Union showing "how difficult some children found their stay in boarding school groups" and noting that "these groups were good only in certain cases" (Kondratova 1968, p. 83). The reports also concluded that, economically speaking, boarding schools are significantly less profitable than full-day schools. E. G. Kostjaškin, the most prominent advocate of Soviet full-day school pedagogy, presented calculations which showed that a student in a full-day school costs the state annually only 40 to 50 rubles more than a student in the regular school, but a student in a boarding school costs 500 to 600 rubles more.[15] Furthermore, even in the Khrushchev era the boarding school proved to be unpopular. Only a few parents decided to send their children off to a full-time institutional education which generally also involved tuition costs; apparently, in the main they were parents who could not offer their children normal conditions for positive family education, a fact that is easily demonstrated by the composition of the student body in boarding schools. Charčev considers it characteristic that "the majority of the student body in the existing boarding schools is composed mainly of children from incomplete or 'unstable' families": "325 of the 422 pupils in boarding school No. 36 in Leningrad have only their mother; 15 have only their father; 16 are orphans; and only 66 have both parents, many of whom lead an abnormal life. According to data obtained in 1961, the parents of 100 out of 330 children in boarding school No. 9 were under psychiatric care" (Charčev 1964, p. 275).

The disillusioning experiences with the boarding school have led in practice to a change of positions in pedagogical theory and educational policy. At the international conference in Rostock the question of the connection between boarding school and family was a "central problem, heatedly discussed and disputed, which significantly advanced the operational change then taking shape . . . ; the occasional tendency to underestimate the family as a pedagogical institution was rejected . . ." (Lindner 1966, p. 347). *Škola-internat*, the pedagogical magazine which proclaimed the boarding school as the prototype for all children, suspended publication late in 1965.[16] The boarding school lost its comprehensive claim to importance, and from then on was mainly considered a kind of special school for socially underprivileged children. It is in this sense that the Academy of Pedagogical Sciences, in its *Pedagogical Encyclopedia,* character-ized the boarding school as an educational institution which enrolls "primarily orphans, children of disabled veterans or whose parents were disabled on the job, children of single mothers and retired people, as well as children whose parents need state aid for various reasons (employment responsibilities of both parents, inadequate living conditions, etc.)" (*Pedagogičeskaja enciklopedija,* IV, Moscow 1968, pp. 718-719).

At the All-Russian Teachers Congress in July 1968, M. A. Prokof'ev, USSR Minister of Education, stated that boarding schools had to "orient themselves more and more toward the instruction and education of children who need a particular daily routine, and toward the aid of those families in which a normal education for children is, for one reason or another, not possible" (Prokof'ev 1968, p. 16). Within the scope of these goals, the boarding school fulfilled an important function, particularly at the time of its origin, when the war caused many children to grow up in families without a father. It is in this sense that the boarding school will also be able in the future to fulfill a certain "ersatz" function for deficient family education. Furthermore, boarding schools were expanded, on the one hand, as special schools with a particular curriculum emphasis—in 1965 Moscow alone had eight special boarding schools with increased foreign language instruction[17]—and, on the other, as central schools for sparsely populated rural areas[18] where the introduction of a general secondary education was facilitated. On the whole, the boarding school no longer occupies a prominent position in the Party's educational policy program, and was not even mentioned in the directives of the Twenty-third Congress of the CPSU (1966).

In contrast, the importance of the full-day school has grown steadily since its official propagation in 1960, especially since 1964. Much more than the boarding school, the full-day school is currently looked upon as the model for all children: it fundamentally fulfills the same functions as a boarding school with respect to a full-day education but without the disadvantages of complete separation from their families and without such high costs. The introduction of the five-day week in industry (1966) was followed by an increased division of educational functions between the full-day school and the family; as a result, parent-child interaction on workdays was diminished, but a continuous family gathering on the weekends was made possible. As early as 1965, almost twice as many pupils were accommodated in full-day schools and groups than in boarding schools (including children's homes)—about one million as compared to 550,000.[19] In 1968 the USSR Ministry of Education could report that "during the thirteen years of their existence, the schools and groups with full-day instruction have won wide recognition among the people and with the pedagogical public," and embrace about 3.5 million students.[20] These statistics show that the number of pupils in full-day schools and groups increased more than threefold as compared with 1965, and they had just about reached a threefold rise in the student population of boarding and dormitory schools, which in 1968 was cited as 1.3 million.[21] In contrast to boarding schools, full-day schools were mentioned explicitly in the directives of the Twenty-third Congress of the Communist Party (1966): their student contingent ought to be more than doubled within the course of the Five-Year Plan enacted in 1966.[22] If this plan can be met—and the 1968 statistics do not seem to contradict this—in 1970 about five million students, approximately 10% of the school population, will be raised and educated in full-day schools and groups.

The announcement and realization of a program of full-day school education in the USSR corresponds to an international educational development in all industrial societies. In the Soviet Union, however, the choice of a full-day or an all-day school as an organizational form of full-day school education not only marks a step toward lengthening the instruction period and expanding the educational influence of society, but also signifies a turning away from the originally announced utopian program (which goes back to Marxist traditions) of a "completely nationalized" education in boarding schools. This program has proven unrealizable for two reasons: (1) it could not take into account the child's psychological need for individual adult attention or the parents' need for intimacy with their children; and (2) it overburdened the financial capacity of the Soviet educational system.

PARENT EDUCATION AND COOPERATION BETWEEN SCHOOL AND HOME

The system of cooperation between societal educational institutions and the family has already been described in connection with our discussion of preschool education. Even more than the kindergarten, which has to date embraced only a minority of preschool children, the school, as the administrative center of societal education, claims the leading role in the education of the younger generation. The stronger the realization that, next to the school, the family remains a decisive and necessary educational factor, the more efforts there will be to make the parents conscious co-workers of an education that is oriented on society's values and to make family education a "part of the communist system of popular education" (Rostovčeva 1963, p. 70).

This goal is served by the creation of social controls over the family through a "public voice" in schools, industry, and housing organizations as well as through the systematic dissemination of pedagogical knowledge. The attempt is being made to produce a public opinion and to encourage the formation of a collective parental community whose influence should extend to as many parents as possible. While a minority of parent activists make up the organized "parent public," the others become the object of societal educational influence, especially in those cases where they or their children deviate from social norms.

It would be one-sided, however, to consider the system of cooperation between family, school, and public and of pedagogical propaganda merely as an instrument of social control and indoctrination. A large part of the practical work entails concrete aid for individual families or students. This includes not only the youngsters' free-time activity and the campaign against juvenile delinquency, but also individual counseling of parents and adult education in pedagogy. Pedagogical aid for the family in itself leads to a strengthening of society's educational influence on the students and their parents, with an effect similar to that brought about by extending the hours in full-day schools.

The schools' extracurricular functions are supported and supervised by local departments of public education and by Party organizations. In addition, ever since the October Revolution there has been a tendency to organize a public of active citizens who support the state's educational policy. Originally conceived as steering committees of a democratic form of municipal self-government, Councils for Popular Education were founded in 1918 but were superseded one year later by a centralized administration.[23] Out of these councils grew the committees for cooperation, organizations of parent-activists with no managerial powers. Renamed parents' committees in the 1930s, these committees took over, among other things, the task of supervising regular attendance at school, giving financial aid to schools, and campaigning against child neglect,[24] and have steadily gained in importance. Various versions of their statutes published in 1950[25] and 1960[26] by the RSFSR Ministry of Education indicate that their activity has increasingly shifted from the economic-organizational to the pedagogical area. Parents' committees have become the key link between the school and the family, as well as organs of the directed self-control of the parent collective. Their rights, duties, and the specific forms of cooperation with the family and of pedagogical propaganda among parents correspond to those of the parents' committees in kindergartens. In the 1960 statute on parents' committees, a whole list of tasks was outlined: help "in the realization of control over the general direction of education in the students' families, over the students' learning activity at home ... over the calling upon of parents to participate in the realization of various educational measures" (*Roditeli i deti* 1961, pp. 417-418). In addition, they were to aid in enforcing the compulsory education law, in organizing "socially useful work," in giving vocational orientation to students, in carrying out pedagogical propaganda among parents, etc. In exercising the significant influence granted to them, the parents' committees represented the interests of the school more than those of parents or children. Their activity falls under the rubric of the "responsible task of the education of the new man in communist society" (ibid., p. 416). Other tasks included "helping the school" and keeping in touch with housing and workers' organizations, thereby contributing to an influence over parents and students in the spirit of society's educational goals.

The authority of the school-oriented parents association is officially sanctioned by the automatic inclusion of the school principal as its chairman and voting member. The manager of the industrial establishment which has assumed sponsorship of a school is also a member of the parents' committee. Comparable organizations of parent activists have sprung up in large apartment developments and at factories.

In a model statute of April 22, 1955, the RSFSR Ministry of Education defined the rights and duties of parents' committees in housing organizations.[27] These include "support of the schools and the organs of popular education in the prevention of child neglect," "measures of societal influence (with the help of trade unions and social organizations) over parents who do not care about the education of their children," concern for the students' regular learning activity and their leisure-time activities, the organization of pedagogical lectures for parents within the housing complex, etc. Systematic spare-time education and pedagogical propaganda by parents' committees in housing developments are conceived of as a supplement to and a continuation of the school's societal educational influence:

Work with children in housing developments helps to organize their free time in a sensible manner, for it continues the educational line of the school and supports the family in the education of children.

This work must definitely be carried out under the school's guidance. Such cooperation is primarily necessary because it guarantees uniform educational influence over the students during school hours and during their leisure hours (*Roditeli i deti* 1961, p. 408).

Apart from its function of exercising school-directed supervision of parents' educational activity, the work of the housing committee gives a strong priority to practical pedagogical aid. The setting up of children's clubs, "Red Corners," hobby groups, and work activities led by nonworking parents, retired people, and youth organization activists can open a wide horizon of meaningful activity for students and relieve their parents of concern during working hours. The same impact was seen when full-day school instruction was instituted. A survey of 2,100 parents whose housing area provided leisure-time, mixed-age groups for the school-based Pioneer and Komsomol organizations indicated that more than 90% of the parents welcomed the assurance of a regular daily routine for their children, 90% noticed an improvement in their children's school work, and more than 80% felt that their children enjoyed the group activities. Of the 2,100 students questioned, 80 to 90% gave positive opinions about the free-time activities in their apartment developments.[28]

Creation of an organized parent public in agricultural and industrial enterprises was suggested in 1952 by the Secretariat of the Central Council of Trade Unions in a directive, "On the Intensification of Trade Union Work in Supporting the Workers and Employees in the Education of Children."[29] The tasks of these organizations of worker-activists known as Commissions for Educational Work among Children and Adolescents, were stipulated in a statute published on December 8, 1954.[30] They include constant cooperation with the educational councils and parents' committees of schools attended by the workers' children, the influencing of parents "whose children do not adhere to the behavior norms established for them," the organizing of pedagogical lectures, readings, and discussions on pedagogical propaganda among workers and employees, and support for the establishment of industry-sponsorship groups over individual school classes in order to provide industrial instruction and out-of-school free-time activities.

Like that of the parents' committees in housing organizations, the work of these commissions is aimed at supplementing the educational influence of the school, but it is focused more upon adults than upon students, whose time in a factory is devoted solely to industrial instruction. By publishing school achievement lists in the factory, parents are encouraged to be more attentive to their children's learning activity. Those who neglect their children, or whose children stand out because of bad conduct or poor school work, are criticized at Party and parent meetings that are held jointly with the education commissions. The following excerpt from a report gives an idea of a factory's activities in the area of pedagogical propaganda:

A Party meeting was convened in the Obidinian division of Tula Brickworks No. 1. The reason for the meeting was unusual. It had nothing to do with production matters. The Communists assembled to exchange opinions on the state of the education of children in the family. E. I. Nikitina, a teacher, delivered a lecture. With actual examples taken from her own school, she showed how some parents were not educating their children properly, how they were not properly fulfilling their parental obligations. She read out the names of those who can be proud of their children, who bring them up properly and make them active fighters for communism. . . . The participants came to a unanimous conclusion: they had to be more concerned with the education of children in the family, not just to push it off on the school, but to cooperate closely with the school (Vorožejkin 1965, p. 43).

A research report, "New Forms of Cooperation between the School, the Family, and the Public," made similar observations:

Parents' assemblies held directly in the factories are beginning to play an increasingly more significant role, and the participants criticize in a comradely manner those individuals who prove irresponsible with respect to the education of their children. . . . The public takes these families under its control (Rostovčeva 1963, p. 71.)

Other organs of collective mutual control are street committees, parent patrols, and comrades' courts, as well as institutions of pedagogical propaganda—for example, parents' lecture programs and parents' universities in schools, higher institutions, and factories. This brief description of the activity of parents' committees and education commissions suffices to show that family education in the USSR is not treated as a private matter, but is an issue of public concern. Societal educational influence is not restricted to formal educational institutions and to the formal instructional period, but extends to the out-of-school area and to extracurricular time, and it includes both students and parents. Soviet students attend schools whose teachers and parent representatives work together with youth organizations, housing organizations, and industrial concerns to insure a uniform system of societal education; Soviet parents are under the influence of an organized parent public at work and at home. . . . The organized parent public, which, according to 1963 data, included 80,000 activists in Moscow alone,[31] has already become a factor of considerable practical pedagogical and ideological significance. Its influence is to be strengthened even more, as can be seen in a letter entitled "Measures for Improving the Work of the School with the Students' Parents," which the RSFSR Minister of Education sent to all agencies of public education in connection with the June Plenary Session of the Communist Party in 1963.[32]

The intensification of efforts to expand the societal educational influence can be interpreted in various ways. One important motive is the campaign against nonsupervision of many adolescents during extracurricular hours.

Equally important is the ideological struggle, already noted during our discussion of preschool education. The Soviet leadership seems to be confronted with a growing tendency toward sociopolitical passivity and ideological indifference among the population. In view of the great influence of the parental example, it can weaken or even threaten the collectivist value orientation of the younger generation. K. L. Petrova, acting RSFSR Minister of Education, feels strongly about this:

> One occasionally complains about the wrong influence of some parents, which is primarily reflected in the cultivation of parasitism, religion, and a bourgeois spirit. Indeed, such cases do exist. However, it is a point of honor for the school to exert a more effective influence over the students and, through them, to carry the new life style, culture, and communist ethics into the families (Petrova 1965, p. 2).

The campaign for ideological awareness leads to a restriction of the family's autonomous position within the educational field and to a restriction of parental rights. The effectiveness of this campaign is, however, still questionable. It remains to be seen to what extent the younger generation is still influenced by individualistic familial values despite strong societal influence. This alone will allow an objective estimation of the family's position within the educational field and of the ambivalent relation between the family and a collectivistically oriented society.

FAMILY, SOCIAL CLASS, AND SCHOOL CAREER

The quantity and quality of his education significantly determine the adolescent's future position in professional life and, with it, his position in society. The young person's chances of attaining a higher education and a high level of vocational qualification depend upon numerous individual and social factors. Modern psychology and social research are moving more and more away from the traditional idea that individual biological traits are the most important of these factors, and they are increasingly coming around to the conception that the social environment (family, social stratum) and the school structure itself exert a crucial influence on the ability, the school success, and the school career of young people. Empirical investigations in the West have shown that adolescents' ability, school success, and school career show strong differences according to the social level of their families and the educational level, professional status, and income of their parents, and that this fact is closely connected to the selection process of a horizontally structured school system. This selection process solidifies a relation between certain social strata and certain school types.[33]

The following section will examine whether, and in what way, the family's environmental influence and its social level prove to be an important factor in school success and in school career under the social conditions in the USSR and within the Soviet school system. Communism strives, as is well known, for the creation of a classless society, and Soviet educational policy has fundamentally subscribed to this goal. Since the October Revolution it has propagated the organization of a uniform school system for all children and has gradually realized this, especially since the school reform under Khrushchev (1958). The propagation of an egalitarian educational system rests upon the pedagogical conviction that ability is not native to a person, but is developed through the influence of the social environment.[34] Conversely, an important goal of the egalitarian educational policy is to organize, within and outside the school, an environmental influence that is as uniform as possible for all children. In this sense Soviet educational policy is closely connected with social policy and is seen as an important lever for the social transformation of society, for the elimination of differences between physical and intellectual work and between the city and the countryside. A classless society is to be created through the democratization and proletarianization of education, that is, through the guarantee of equal educational opportunities for all and through special support for working-class and peasant children who were traditionally underprivileged but who are supposed to represent the ruling classes of a communist society.

In view of this social and educational policy, as well as of the introduction of eight-year compulsory comprehensive education (1958) and the announcement of the goal of lengthening mandatory school attendance to ten years (1966), one could assume that there is extensive equality of opportunity for all children in attaining an education. It must be remembered, however, that children and adolescents are formed not only by the school but by the family. Families of the parents' generation exhibit considerable class-related differences in their educational level, in vocational qualifications, and in standard of living, largely due to the neglect of a democratic or proletarian educational policy during the Stalin era. In Soviet society, contrary to the intentions of an egalitarian social and educational policy, a strong process of social stratification has taken place. The traditional economic and educational differences between urban and rural populations have hardly diminished, and they restrict the equality of opportunity in attaining an education. It is, therefore, revealing to examine whether the current realization of the goal of a maximum expansion of secondary education offers the guarantee for the equalization of various class-related family influences. To illustrate: in 1967-68, more than 73% of eighth grade graduates continued their education, and 62.4% of those entered the ten-year comprehensive secondary school which leads to university admission.[35]

Social Strata in Soviet Society

Collective farm peasants, who in 1959 made up about one-third of the labor force, represent the lowest social stratum in the USSR. At the beginning of the

1960s, 80 to 85% had no (or only low) vocational qualifications;[36] in 1966, 35% had no more than an elementary or seven-year education.[37] In 1963 the proportion of specialists with a university and secondary specialized training among collective farmers amounted to only 1.1%.[38] Until 1966 they enjoyed no fixed wages[39] and no legally established minimum wage. Even with the introduction of the legal minimum wage, the standard of living on collective farms remains extremely low.

In contrast, industrial workers, who constituted about 47% of the labor force in 1959, represent a well-organized social stratum and occupy a middle position. According to data from 1962, 30 to 40% of the workers possessed low skill qualifications; 40 to 50% had middle-range skills; and 20 to 20% had high vocational qualifications.[40] Wages were based on differing skill levels. Since 1967 the legal minimum wage of 60 rubles a month, which unskilled workers generally earn, has assured the family just enough to live on only when both parents are employed.[41] In 1967, out of a total of 1,000 industrial workers, 500 were graduates of an incomplete or complete secondary, professional, and university education; only 330 such graduates were found among the same number of collective farmers.[42]

Salaried employees, who made up about 20% of the labor force in 1959, occupy a comparatively high social position because their ranks include those in the unskilled and low-paid service occupations, as well as the intelligentsia, who constitute the upper class. In 1967, 928 salaried employees out of 1,000 were graduates of an incomplete or complete secondary, professional, and university education (including 197 university graduates); all the strata combined supplied an average of only 27 university graduates.[43] Above-average income possibilities generally coincide with excellent school education and professional skills of salaried employees, especially of the intelligentsia. The monthly wages of a factory manager, for example, are six times more than that of an unskilled worker: 350 rubles.[44] On the other hand, one finds considerable overlapping between workers and salaried employees, both with respect to educational level and earnings. Highly skilled workers often have a higher education than some salaried employees in service occupations, and they may even earn more than some professionals—for example, teachers and doctors are paid comparatively poorly.[45]

Macrosociological Factors of Educational Inequality

Urban and rural populations, each representing about 50% of the nation, vary greatly with respect to technological-cultural levels. This can be demonstrated by the social structure as well as by the development of the educational system. Nine-tenths of the rural workers are collective farmers (60%) or workers (30%) engaged exclusively in physical labor. Since most of them, especially the collective farm peasants, possess low vocational training or none at all, they draw the lowest wages. Only 10% of the rural population are salaried employees and members of the intelligentsia, but in the urban population 30% belong to this stratum.[46] Rural areas are characterized by a deficient development of the general education school system; many remote rural areas have poorly equipped one-room schools with poorly qualified teachers.[47] Numerous reports attest to the fact that eight-year compulsory schooling and general ten-year secondary schooling in rural areas fall far short of the plans and lag far behind the development of their urban counterparts.[48]

The backward social structure of the rural population and the lag in the development of its school system necessarily restrict the educational opportunities of rural children. Soviet sociologists have stated that "today the chances for young people who live in large cities to enter institutions of higher education are considerably higher than for those in rural areas" (Šubkin 1965, p. 65). Of course, the underprivileged condition of rural children basically concerns all social strata of the rural population, but, as university admission figures demonstrate, it particularly affects the educational opportunities of peasant children, who represent 60% of the rural population.

Family-Related Factors in School Career

In addition to the macrosociological factors mentioned above, a series of strata-related factors exert a demonstrable influence over educational opportunities. The following criteria have been chosen for a correlation between the adolescent's social stratum and his educational opportunities: the characteristics of stratum membership include the family's standard of living and the parents' educational level or occupation; the characteristics of an adolescent's educational opportunities include his school achievements and the attainment of the school's goal, the choice of alternative types of schools, his educational aspirations for a university education, and actual admission to a university.

Limited to these criteria, the factor analysis must be narrowed down with respect to the educational influence of the school as well as to that of the family.

Empirical studies on the social determinants of educational opportunities, such as the investigation of the school success of a representative number of Novosibirsk secondary school graduates in 1963-64, undertaken by the sociologist V. N. Šubkin, have shown that "the parents' educational level exerts a strong influence on the interests and inclinations of children. The standard of living, living conditions, etc., significantly affect a child's grades, his vocational inclinations, and consequently his opportunities for obtaining an education" (Šubkin 1965, p. 65). Correlation calculations based on Subkin's representative data have shown in detail that positive and relevant statistical connections do exist between the degree of the adolescent's general school success, on the one hand, and the per capita income of the family and the parents' education on the other.

If the per capita income of the family—which, among other things, determines the living conditions as a relevant factor influencing school achievement—is divided into various categories and correlated with a five-point evaluation system, it appears that "there is a positive correlation between the factors under consideration, that is, success in school increases with an increase in material income" (*Količestvennye metody* 1966, p. 202). While male adolescents from families with a monthly per capita income of up to 20 rubles show 3.14 achievement points, the school achievement of male adolescents from families with 80 to 100 rubles per capita income is on the average 3.96 points.

It is safe to assume that family income level can influence a youngster's school work not only insofar as it determines the living conditions—the spatial and psychological conditions for home learning activity—but also to the degree that a higher income permits parents to provide tutoring for their children (however, there are no reliable data available concerning the extent of tutoring).[49] Moreover, it must be remembered that adolescents in low-income families are often motivated to prematurely contribute to the family earnings. In this way their learning activity is deprived of an important future perspective: the aspiration toward university study. Finally, one must consider that low family income is directly connected with the parents' low schooling or vocational qualifications, and therefore does not operate as an isolated factor.

The correlation between the parents' educational level (which, among other things, determines the degree of intellectual demands made upon the youngster and the parents' supervision of homework assignments) and the adolescents' overall school success turns out to be statistically positive and relevant. This connection exists especially with respect to the educational level of the mother, who usually supervises the children's learning activity more than the father does, and keeps in touch with the school and teaching staff.[50] For example, while male adolescents in families where the mother has only an elementary school education show 3.32 achievement points, the school achievements of children whose mothers have a university education are, on the average, 3.85 points. The corresponding values for girls are 3.66 points for those whose mothers have an elementary school education, and 4.25 for those whose mothers have a university education.[51]

Of course, the different family educational influence in various social strata cannot be measured solely through the connection between the parents' formal education and the adolescents' formal school achievements. Rather, one must presume that the family's social position influences the speech structure to a definite degree and, with it, the young person's preparation for the intellectual operations demanded in secondary school as well as for his adaptation to the societal values that are also demanded in school. While there are no data available about language socialization and the phenomenon of "speech barriers" among lower-strata children, it can be inferred from Titarenko's study (1967) that the family's educational level and material prosperity "determine to a certain degree (if not directly) the moral orientation and the behavior, and the level of its open-mindedness for the values and demands of society" (Titarenko 1967, pp. 19-20). According to Titarenko, the overwhelming majority of adolescents with deviant behavior come from families with a low standard of living and a low educational level;[52] for the most part, youngsters with deviant behavior are at the same time truants and premature school dropouts.[53]

Finally, the youngster's motivation to learn and his educational aspirations seem to depend upon the school level and educational consciousness of his parents, as well as on their standard of living. This is evident from a topical leading article in a Soviet teachers' newspaper. It demanded that in certain circles of the population the educational consciousness of parents must be strengthened through pedagogical propaganda; it was a question of "overcoming the indolence which rests upon the preconception that eight classes are really complete enough" ("Novyj rubež" 1968).

The social determination of educational opportunities can perhaps best be deomonstrated by the different percentages of secondary school graduations and by the different social composition of the student body in the lower and upper grades of secondary school. As the end result of his Novosibirsk study, Šubkin recorded that "the social structure of first graders varies considerably from that of school graduates, and even more from that of students in higher educational institutions" (Šubkin 1965, p. 65). Data from the city of Gorky on the same problem were cited in the above-mentioned newspaper account, according to which the relation between working-class children and children of salaried employees, which in the lower grades is four to one, radically changes in the upper grades in favor of the children of salaried employees. These undocumented statements from Gorky can be better substantiated with data from Sverdlovsk:

In 1965, using a representative sample, the sociologist Rutkevič studied the social composition of the student body in secondary schools in two districts of Sverdlovsk. It was shown that working-class children in the eighth grades supplied 61.6% or 54.4% of the students—depending upon the district under consideration—while their proportion in the eleventh grades declined to 46.0% or 22.4%, respectively. In contrast, the proportion of salaried employees' children increased from about 11% in the eighth grades to about 19% in the eleventh grades. The proportion of children of the intelligentsia, finally, who were distinguished from the salaried employees' stratum in this study, increased from 21.7% or 25.0% in the eighth grades to 28.9% or 43.5%, respectively, in the eleventh grades.[54]

These survey results prove that working-class children are substantially underrepresented among complete secondary school graduates, not only in relation to their proportion in the student body in the lower grades but also in relation to the proportion of the working-class stratum in the total population. Children of salaried employees and, above all, of the intelligentsia are substantially overrepresented. The social structure of the secondary school graduates of 1965 mirrors, albeit in a diminished form, the educational pyramid within the adult population of Soviet society. This fact is especially evident in the following data, compiled by the sociologist N. A. Aitov, on the average educational level of children from different social strata: while children of collective farmers complete an average of 7.31 grades and working-class children complete 7.66 grades, children of salaried employees (including the intelligentsia) achieve, on the average, a school and university education of 12.22 years.[55] These data verify our previous point that truants and premature school dropouts are generally recruited from socially underprivileged families that are often found among collective farm peasants and the working class, but almost never among salaried employees or the intelligentsia.

Since our discussion has so far focused only on students of the eleven- or ten-year normal type of secondary school, we shall now briefly mention the types of schools which deviate from the regular school and their student body composition. Obviously, specialized secondary schools for the arts, foreign languages, or natural sciences, and especially the few specialized mathematics- and physics-boarding schools sponsored by the Academy of Sciences, enroll predominantly students from well-educated and education-conscious families, even if admission depends upon passing the competitive tests held in regular schools.[56]

Statistical data are available on the social origins of the students in one of these schools, the mathematics and physics special boarding school in Novosibirsk. At the beginning of the 1964-65 school year, 607 students attended this school, including 67 girls. The macrosociological origin of the students is quite revealing: only 62 students, about 10%, came from rural areas. The social origin of the students is not coded according to social stratum, but according to their parents' occupations; nevertheless, a hierarchy of social strata arises. Collective farm peasants were represented by only 12 students, supplying about 2% of the student population. The working class was represented by 83 students—about 14% of the total—whose parents were described as skilled workers. Almost all the remaining students came from families of salaried employees, especially from the intelligentsia. The most important professional groups were engineers and technical personnel—123 students (about 20% of the student population); teachers—61 students (about 9% of the total); military personnel—54; physicians—46; scientific researchers—26; accountants—23; commercial employees—21; and university teachers—19 students.[57]

No other reliable data are available with respect to the social origin of students in specialized schools which lead to preferred university admission. From indications in the press, however, one can infer that the Soviet leadership is concerned about the underrepresentation of working-class and peasant children in these schools, a fact which can be clearly demonstrated by the above-mentioned breakdown in the specialized Novosibirsk school.[58] The discussion as to whether differentiated types of schools should be extended and supported, and whether or not they restrict the equality of educational opportunity, has not yet been finalized.[59] The most one can say is that growing scientific-technological progress is strengthening the tendency to select the gifted in these specialized schools and to train a scientific-technical elite in them, and that this elite is currently recruited predominantly from the social strata of salaried employees and the intelligentsia.

It is not surprising that vocational-technical schools, which replace the upper level of the comprehensive secondary school and train skilled workers for industry without preparing them for university admission, are for the most part attended by children from the worker and peasant strata. According to data gathered by Rutkevič in Sverdlovsk, 82.5% of the student body there consists of workers' and peasants' children, with only 11.5% consisting of children of salaried employees.[60] Students of vocational-technical schools are generally not oriented toward higher education, but rather toward becoming wage earners who engage in industrial labor at an early age. What has been shown here with respect to the social origin of students in vocational-technical schools presumably also applies to evening schools, but there is no statistical information available on the subject.

While children from different social strata have different educational opportunities, one should not overlook the fact that the general secondary school attendance has resulted in an overall raising of the educational level of all children. If, in 1959, only 12%—but in 1967, 26%—of the population possessed a complete secondary school education,[61] then, with further realization of the educational policy program of the Twenty-third Congress of the Communist Party (1966), there is a chance that the overwhelming majority of Soviet youth will complete secondary school and attain potential access to higher education. Young people from all social strata, therefore, will exhibit slight educational differences in their future influence over their own children.

The same trend toward the generalization of secondary school education leads, however, to the fact that university education increasingly becomes the single educational criterion and the most important means of upward social mobility. As soon as most students attain potential access to higher education, the university, which can absorb only a small number of secondary school graduates, is confronted with the need for a strict achievement-based selection process, which only the best students can pass.[62] At the present time, as long as the best students (rated according to their achievements in secondary school) come more often from salaried employees' families than from working-class or peasant families, there is a chance that the universities' achievement-based selection increases the educational opportunities of salaried employees' children and diminishes those of workers' and peasants' children. Preferential admission into universities of workers with industrial experience, together with the universities' heavy program orientation on evening and correspondence courses between 1958 and 1964, increased the proportion of working-class children to 58%.[63] Yet the replacement of the social by the achievement-based selection (brought about by the increase in the number of secondary school graduates) brings with it the danger of a "deproletarianization" of the university.

Šubkin traced this problem in his survey of 10% of Novosibirsk's secondary school graduates. Although his data relate to the last year of the Khrushchev era, they also reflect current relations, as a comparison with more recent data will show.

Šubkin divided his study into two parts. The first had to do with the youngsters' life plans and broke down into three categories: working, working and studying, and studying. The second part was devoted to ascertaining the extent to which the corresponding life plans were realized. In both parts of the study the adolescents involved were subdivided into groups determined by their family's social stratum. This enabled a differentiation to be made between educational aspirations and actual educational chances, corresponding respectively to social origin.

Analysis of the life plans showed that, on the overall average, only 7% of the young people wanted to work in industry directly after completing school and only 10% wanted to work and study at the same time, while 83% planned to take up university study. The desire to study was more strongly expressed by youngsters of the intelligentsia than by children of urban industrial workers—93% as compared to 83%—and this desire was again more strongly expressed by the latter groups than by children of rural workers, only 76% of whom aspired toward university study. On the whole a uniform trend for secondary school graduates from all strata to strive for higher education was clearly expressed.[64]

Another study carried out in 1965-66 in the city of Nižnyj Tagil furnished similar results. The study measured the various degrees of educational aspiration among secondary school graduates, not so much according to their formal social stratum as to the educational level of their parents. Thus, 76.9% of the children whose parents had a university education and 64.9% of those whose parents had a secondary school education aspired toward university study, but only 41.8% of those whose parents had an elementary school education aspired toward higher studies.[65]

Although the analysis of the life plans of the graduates and their educational aspirations shows a certain, albeit relatively weak, correlation with the educational level and social status of their parents, an examination of the actual university admission figures strongly confirms this.

Šubkin's survey results show that only with respect to children from the urban intelligentsia stratum is there an almost complete agreement between educational aspiration and actual educational opportunities: 93% wanted to study, and 82% attended university. The children of rural workers, on the other hand, have by far the poorest chances: 76% wanted to study, but only 10% actually took up higher studies. The remaining groups of students belong midpoint between these two extremes: rural children, irrespective of social stratum, have basically poorer chances than city children to enter a university. On the average barely 50% of the children of workers and lower-skilled employees must enter industrial production against their wishes after completing secondary school, thus foregoing a university education.[66]

The results of the Nižnyj Tagil study can be summarized as follows: in general, the school graduates—about 60% of whom were working-class children, about 15% the children of salaried employees, and about 18% the children of the intelligentsia—in their majority (66.6%) took a job in production, while a minority of 33.3% entered a university or technical school. A division of the students according to social origin showed that working-class children (59.8%) strongly dominated the group of graduates who went on to industrial jobs; salaried employees' children supplied 18.6% of the group; and the children of the intelligentsia, 15.2%. In contrast, the number of working-class children in the group of those studying was considerably less than those from the intelligentsia: working-class children supplied 48.0% of the group; salaried employees' children, 14.4%; and children of the intelligentsia, 32.7%.[67]

Despite its partially deviating results, which are mainly explained by the choice of the research subject—a school in which working-class children made up an unusually high proportion of 60% of the graduates—the study in Nižnyj Tagil confirms Šubkin's statement that children of the intelligentsia have above-average chances of realizing their life plans and being admitted to a university. On the whole, the data presented indicate that the majority of young people continue in the social stratum of their family, although the quota of upward social mobility, by means of higher education—from the working-class stratum into that of the intelligentsia—is significant and is greater than in most Western societies. Of course, no comprehensive statistical data about the social composition of the school and university population have been published in the USSR for decades, a fact which indicates that until now the Soviet leadership has had no satisfactory results of their educational policy of "democratization" and "proletarianization" to which it can refer. According to Rutkevič, the proportion of working-class children is very different among students in various higher educational institutions. In 1965 the proportion of working-class children among students in the Sverdlovsk Technical Institute amounted to 44.9%; among students in the State University, the proportion was only 24.4%. Children of the intelligentsia formed the largest group at the State University: 38.5%; and together with children of salaried employees, the children of the intelligentsia constituted 57.7% of the State University's enrollment and 50.0% of the student body at the Technical Institute.[68] The data cited with respect to the proportion of working-class children among Sverdlovsk's university students, however, appear in their true light only when they are considered in relation to the proportion of the workers' stratum and the other social groups in the total population of that city: in 1959 Sverdlovsk's population consisted of 70% workers, but only 22% salaried employees (including the intelligentsia) and 8% collective farm peasants.[69] In light of this fact, a study carried out in 1964-65 on the social functions of higher institutions with regard to the treatment of Sverdlovsk's higher schools—the State University, the Polytechnical Institute, the Medical Institute, and the Law School—established the following:

Currently the percentage of students from working-class families does not differ considerably from the proportion of students from salaried employees' families [including families of the intelligentsia]. However, if one considers that the proportion of workers in the total population of Sverdlovsk is about three times as great as that of salaried employees, it then becomes clear that, until now, entrance into the group of specialists with highest qualifications still represents a less frequent occurrence among working-class families than among families of salaried employees ("Sistema obrazovanija" 1968, p. 210).

Insofar as the local data from Sverdlovsk can be generalized—and this seems logical since Sverdlovsk is a typical industrial center with an overwhelming working-class population—one can accordingly state that working-class and peasant children are strongly underrepresented in the universities, whereas children of the intelligentsia (as the group of "specialists" with university or professional school educations within the salaried employees' stratum) are greatly overrepresented. Also, among higher educational institutions, technical institutes appear to be relatively more proletarianized than the universities.

In light of the extension of general secondary school education, the growing competition for higher education, which makes the young person's chances largely determined by his family's educational level and standard of living, may have the effect of advancing the process of social differentiation in Soviet society.

Educational sociologists like Šubkin have emphasized the necessity of "taking measures in advance which counteract these trends [of "deproletariani-zation" of the universities] " (Šubkin 1965, p. 66). These measures should not begin at the university level, perhaps through social selection in favor of working-class and peasant children,[70] but should take the form of compensatory education for lower-strata children. The intensified development of preschool and full-day education represents one such measure, in addition to the growing importance of differentiated and individualized instruction.[71] Preschool institutions should guarantee an early balance of variable educational influences in the family and an equal preparation of all children for school;[72] situated in centers, full-day schools and boarding schools should encourage school attendance in thinly populated areas, offer all children supervision over homework assignments independent of the family environment, and make available an effective spare-time education.[73]

For economic reasons, this educational policy program will take decades to be realized. Only 28% of the children are currently being educated in preschool institutions, and less than 10% are enrolled in all-day and boarding schools. Rural children, who are most in need of educational support and compensatory education, are significantly worse off than those in urban areas.

FAMILY CHARACTERISTICS AND JUVENILE DELINQUENCY

Generally speaking, delinquency is considered not only an individual phenomenon, the expression of individual failure, but also a social phenomenon. The spread of juvenile delinquency indicates the growth of societal disintegration tendencies and provides a measure of the young person's degree of integration in society and in its value system, which is conveyed by means of education.[74]

This view is also an element of communist ideology, although in a radical form: according to it, delinquency is directly dependent upon a definite social structure, capitalism. The decrease of delinquency in communist society is interpreted as an intrinsic development, the "necessary result of the elimination of its causes in socialist society" (Min'kovskij 1966, p. 490). The mutual exploitation and the class struggle of capitalist society are described as remnants of the past. For this reason, particularly in Soviet social theory, delinquency is explained as an individual, subjective phenomenon.

Since society makes use of this ideological interpretation to rid itself of any responsibility for negative phenomena in societal life, it undoubtedly becomes more difficult to make an objective analysis of juvenile delinquency in the USSR. Nevertheless, the following section will attempt to describe several aspects of juvenile delinquency in the Soviet Union based upon the results of recent sociological research. We shall give particular attention to those aspects which connect a young person's becoming delinquent with the educational potential or social structure of the family. In Soviet society, too, the family remains the most important social reference group for youngsters. The actual interdependency between the individual-subjective factors—which Soviet ideology overestimates—and the objective socioeconomic factors of juvenile delinquency will also be pointed out.

Research and Information on Juvenile Delinquency

The USSR has long neglected research into delinquency. True, during the early Soviet period a statistical recording and scientific analysis of delinquency was begun: a State Institute for the Investigation of Crime and the Criminal was founded in the RSFSR in the mid-1920s; among others, M. N. Gernet's standard works on *Moral Statistics* (1922) and *Crime and Suicide in the War and Postwar Years* (1927) were published. In the mid-1930s, however, these beginnings of a scientific criminology were nipped in the bud, and until the end of the Stalin era criminology remained taboo. There were serious efforts to combat the rather widespread neglect of children and youth, but its causes were not investigated because objective research data would have contradicted the ideal picture of socialist society then being propagated.

On the other hand, it was not difficult to find a scapegoat for the neglect of many children and adolescents. Whenever talk in the Soviet Union centered on negative social phenomena, the family was generally held up as that social group and pedagogical institution which was the first to be held responsible for deviation from socialist ethics. It is no coincidence, therefore, that at the very time criminological research projects were forbidden, a directive of May 31, 1935,[75] stipulated legal parental responsibility for the antisocial behavior of their children, including definite threats of punishment. The connection between juvenile delinquency and the disintegration of the family was certainly apparent then, as it is today; criminological studies before the 1935 directive showed that 90% of the juvenile delinquents in Leningrad and 88% of those in Moscow spent their free time in an unstructured manner outside the family.[76] However, just how far the social disintegration of the family was socially conditioned was not discussed during the Stalin era.

Unlike the decades of the Stalin era, since the Twentieth Party Congress (1956), juvenile delinquency has been handled in scientific terms and no longer solely as a matter of propaganda. As in the case of other social sciences, criminology has been supported, for example, by the establishment, in 1963, of an All-Union Institute for Research into the Causes of Delinquency and the Development of Countermeasures. Studies carried out since then do not yet convey a complete picture of the causes, extent, and forms of antisocial behavior of young people, but they have at least resulted in a more differentiated approach. The close interrelation between the phenomenon of antisocial behavior and the educational failure of the family could certainly be proven, but at the same time it became clear how strongly objective societal factors determine the structure and educational potential of the family. Moreover, these investigations also exposed deficiencies in the educational work of societal institutions.

Precise data about the quantitative development of juvenile delinquency are not found in the Soviet literature. This lack of information can be explained primarily by the fact that, as a "remnant of the past," juvenile delinquency has remained somewhat taboo. It should be noted that, as a mass phenomenon, juvenile delinquency existed only during political and socioeconomic crises, during the years of the Civil War and famine following the October Revolution, as a result of the forced collectivization in 1929-30, and in the years during and after World War II. According to Min'kovskij (1966, pp. 490ff.), the rate of juvenile delinquency—here the delinquency of minors up to the age of 18 is included under the heading of "juvenile" or "child delinquency"—has steadily decreased since 1946. Min'kovskij indicates that in 1960-1966 only 3 to 4% of the lawbreakers legally brought to court were minors, and petty delinquency—thefts, disturbances of the peace, etc.—predominated. Min'kovskij's data lose in information value when one considers that youngsters in the Soviet Union must be 16 years old before they are brought to court for light crimes and 14 years old in the case of serious crime. It is also important to remember that the number of youths between 18 and 25—an age group which Min'kovskij did not take into account—tends to be significantly higher in the total picture of criminality than those between 16 and 18.

Individual studies in metropolitan areas, where delinquency always tends to appear more strongly than elsewhere, show how misleading such statistical statements about the average rate of juvenile delinquency in the entire area of the Soviet Union can be. For example, a group of sociologists working on studies in Leningrad had to point out that almost every second violation of the law was committed by groups of minors; in 69% of the cases it was a question of theft and robbery, and in 21% a question of rowdyness.[77] Based on such data, as well as on the fact that since 1956 several bills, numerous conferences, newspaper articles, and the contributions of leading political figures at Party and Komsomol congresses were devoted to the theme of juvenile delinquency, one can infer that juvenile delinquency is widespread and represents a great social and pedagogical problem.

Nevertheless, if it should prove true that the delinquency rates in the USSR are lower than in most Western societies, this would at least partially be explained by the absence of a series of crime-inducing factors with which the West has to deal: the lack of state-controlled youth organizations, the large degree of freedom enjoyed by young people and their tenuous ties to societal goals, the proliferation of trash and pornographic literature and of inferior films, the marked materialist thinking, etc.[78] Soviet young people, in contrast, are subjected in a much greater degree to social controls in schools and youth organizations; through the creation of the system of cooperation between the family, the school and the public, they are confronted with censored information and entertainment media. On the other hand, affluence and materialist attitudes have not yet progressed so far that the affluence delinquency, which is gaining the upper hand in the West, could have developed. To be sure, in the Soviet Union too, theft accounts for the absolute majority of court-handled crimes—according to Strumilin (1960), 95%, an alarming phenomenon in a society which claims to have solved the problem of property through the abolition of capitalist exploitation and to have put an end to the ideology of property. In the case of thefts in Soviet society, it frequently seems to be a matter of the illegal acquisition of social property, and this can sometimes be explained by a hostile attitude toward the state's ownership monopoly or by an attempt to change individual material hardship.

As for other factors, despite the differences already mentioned, there are general causes for the spread of juvenile delinquency which are just as operative in Soviet society as they are in the West: the concentration of population masses in large cities (although Soviet urbanization is less advanced than in Western industrial societies); the social insecurity of people because of population movements (rural exodus, new communities, etc.) and change of job; the nonsupervision of students during their free time and the growing influence of the street and of informal youth groups and gangs which grow out of such nonsupervision; etc. In connection with poor material living conditions and with deficiencies in the moral education of youth, these factors can lead to the alienation of the individual vis-à-vis society and its values.

The problem of juvenile delinquency in the Soviet Union requires multi-dimensional treatment. The following section will give close consideration and analysis of only one aspect: the insufficient ethical value orientation of youngsters—through deficient or negative family influence or through the socioeconomically conditioned loss of the family's educational function—as a cause of antisocial behavior among minors. The isolation of this single aspect is justified by the following results of Soviet social research in recent years:

1. There is a tendency to a particularly high degree of antisocial behavior in children from incomplete families and from families in which unstable and disharmonious relations exist.

2. As long as social institutions cannot assume the educational functions of the family, the restriction of the family's educational role due to the employment of both parents, their low educational level, and their standard of living, significantly contributes to the spread of juvenile delinquency.

The Effects of Family Disorder and Broken Homes

A survey of 500 cases of juvenile delinquency in Leningrad (1959-60) showed that of the young people involved, 267 had only a mother, 25 had only a father, 8 had no parents, 2 had a father and stepmother, 13 had a mother and stepfather, and 185 had both parents. Charčev concluded that "the deviant behavior of children finds significantly more favorable conditions for its development in incomplete families than in complete [families] " (Charčev 1964, p. 276).

A number of additional research results substantiate his findings. Zjubin reports (1966, p. 8) that 40 to 50% of the delinquent juveniles grew up without a father. Titarenko (1967, p. 13) agrees with this finding, and states that the incomplete family appears "most problematic when considered from the standpoint of educational potential. . . . Thus, on an average, 40% of the delinquent youths were raised in an incomplete family. Analogous data from foreign researchers are cited."

The incomplete family's deficient or negative educational effect can be explained in various ways. One must first proceed from the fact that the specific, chiefly emotional, importance of the family as the source of education is most closely connected with the parents' marital relations; this forms the nucleus of the family and represents the foundation of trust and security for both adults and children.[79] In addition, the lack of a father, of his authority and his example, and the impossibility of identifying himself with an adult of the same sex seems to have a particularly negative effect upon male adolescents. In those cases where divorce is responsible, the children have frequently experienced the process of the internal breakdown of the parents' marriage and have suffered under it. A psychological burden must be added in those cases when incompleteness is due to illegitimate birth, for even in Soviet society single mothers and illegitimate children have a negative social status and must struggle more than others for recognition.[80] Single mothers depend upon full-time employment and often must entrust their youngsters to children's homes and boarding schools, where they generally receive less individualized care and education than family-educated children. However, if they do grow up in the mother's household, the children and adolescents experience miserable economic and living conditions because of her low earnings.

Despite these psychological and financial burdens, the structural incompleteness of the family in itself does not automatically have to lead to antisocial behavior among children. If this were the case, many millions of Soviet war widows and millions of single and divorced mothers would have produced a huge number of delinquent youngsters. On the contrary, it can be shown that family incompleteness becomes a crime-inducing factor only—or in any case mainly—when the single mothers themselves have lost their psychic balance and their social value orientation (this is not true of all cases). Charčev's survey group showed that of the 267 single mothers whose children became delinquent, 234 led an unordered life themselves, characterized by drunkenness and frequent partner change, and consequently could not convey to their children an example of moral behavior.[81] It is safe to assume that society shares a certain responsibility for these single mothers' status as social outsiders, and that it is not simply a question of individual failure.

Several studies have come to the uniform conclusion that between 40 and 50% of delinquent juveniles come from families with both parents. Closer analysis did indeed show that in many cases it was a question of parents living under a strained or broken marital relationship: 200 out of 500 delinquents in Charčev's survey group had both parents (including stepparents), but 160 out of these 200 cases showed evidence of the breakdown of the parents' marriage. Most commonly responsible for such breakdown was alcoholism: in 121 cases the father was an alcoholic, in 9 cases the mother, and in 30 cases both parents were alcoholics.[82]

The studies on juvenile delinquency cited thus far indicate that adolescents who find no psychic support in the family, and who do not witness and receive a behavior example within the family that corresponds to the moral values of society, very easily become social outsiders. Where the family fails as the authority that imparts the emotional identity of the personality and the values of society, the youngster's social integration into society generally fails altogether. In other words, at the same time that the family represents the most important socialization factor, negative family influence cannot be fully compensated by means of a strengthened societal education. Children and adolescents from incomplete families are often educated in children's homes and boarding schools, but many of them still become delinquent. In commenting on this, a Soviet researcher observed:

What really appears as the main function of the family? Indeed, the education of the younger generation. A child who is born outside the family, and is educated even by very good teachers, nevertheless does not receive all those necessities of life that a healthy family can and does give (Zjubin 1966, p. 12).

Work Overload of Mothers and Other Factors

A certain number of delinquent juveniles, about one-third according to Zjubin, come from families which are neither incomplete nor internally disorganized, but must be described as "formally well-ordered" (Zjubin 1966, p. 12). For this reason there must be a series of social and psychological factors which can restrict even the educational potential of a normal family to such an extent that it cannot give its children the necessary education.

The parents' lack of time, especially the mother's, has been repeatedly mentioned as an important factor that burdens the educational activity of the family. Although the time factor should not be isolated, its impact on the spread of juvenile delinquency remains real as long as young people do not attend full-day educational institutions. A survey by the Latvian sociologist Baerjunas indicates that 58% of the youthful lawbreakers come from families where both parents work for a living.[83] Moreover, since 30 to 50% of delinquent youths come from incomplete families, where the mother without exception has to work, it can be inferred that, in almost all families from which delinquent youngsters come, the mother is employed outside the home, while practically no juvenile delinquency occurs in complete families where the mother is solely a housewife. There is not enough representative research material available to permit generalizations on this point. However, there is no doubt that the mother's employment and her role as chief homemaker are responsible for the fact that young people spend most of their free time outside of the educational supervision of the family and are thus susceptible to the influence of the street and of informal groups. Moreover, the working mother's job overload and nervous strain can lead to a conscious renunciation of educational activity on her part or else to purely emotional or impulsive educational attitudes, which may be characterized either by complete *laissez faire* or by exaggerated strictness in the event of conflicts between parents and youngsters.

Naturally, the time element is not the only factor, for parents with genuine understanding of their growing children and with great educational authority, despite the short time available for interaction, do exert a strong and positive influence and can affect their children's behavior even without direct supervision and constant presence. It can be demonstrated that children whose parents both work generally become delinquent only when additional factors which restrict the educational potential are added, that is, mainly when the parents concerned have a low educational level and commit serious educational errors, and the particular family lives under poor economic conditions. Titarenko's study (1967) shows that 71.2% of the youngsters with deviant social behavior were raised in families where the parents had, at the most, an elementary school education; the rest were raised primarily in families where the parents had four to seven years of schooling. The inability of parents to apply considered and balanced educational methods frequently seems to correspond to their low educational level. Both Zjubin and Baerjunas have come across "typical educational mistakes" by the parents of delinquent juveniles in the course of their investigations. Zjubin (1966, pp. 12-13) cites "spoiling or neglecting or overtaxing" and, while referring at the same time to the fact that "little time [is available] for activities with the child," indicates that such wrong educational attitudes are due not only to a lack of education and pedagogical knowledge but also to the lack of time for a relaxed educational relationship. Baerjunas also names "educational neglect since early childhood or rash efforts to overly educate the children; strict authority from early childhood on and the inability, also in adolescent years, to maintain control over the children; the granting of complete freedom from early years on, with which the children cannot cope" ("Socializm i sem'ja" 1967, p. 139).

The parents' low educational level and the pedagogical errors stemming from it, burden not only the relation between parents and children but also the youngster's relation to society. Parents with a low educational level contribute relatively little to their children's adaptation to societal values in general and to school demands in particular. As the preceding chapter has shown, children of poorly educated parents lag in their general social value orientation and in school achievement and as repeaters frequently become outsiders of the school community and society. Zjubin's data show that 70 to 80% of the delinquent juveniles have only four to seven years of education, clearly indicating that delinquency and grade repetition or the premature dropping out of school are closely connected.[84] A youngster's failure in school, combined with the teacher's ignorance of his difficult situation, is frequently the first reason for his breaking away from the family and the school, for roaming about in gangs, etc.[85] Deficient school education, then, impedes the future professional and social integration of these young people.

By now it is apparent that society bears a large share of responsibility for juvenile delinquency. While the one-sided assignment of a woman's social role to her role as a worker in itself leads to an often unreasonable restriction in her role as mother and educator, the simultaneous lack of full-day societal educational institutions and of compensatory education for children of the lower educational strata inevitably has serious results. Those low-achieving students who come overwhelmingly from families with little education are not only not given special encouragement, but are frequently removed prematurely from the regular school and placed in various types of special schools as soon as they exhibit deviant social behavior. A number of these special schools—for example, special vocational-technical schools—resemble juvenile reformitories which in themselves become a favorable breeding ground for antisocial behavior patterns.

Measures against Juvenile Delinquency

In combating juvenile delinquency one must differentiate between immediate measures aimed at resocializing those who have actually become delinquent, and preventive measures aimed at the removing of the causes of the deviant behavior.

It is not possible here to describe in detail the countermeasures of an immediate nature that have already been taken, and thereby provide a complete picture of Soviet youth legislation and welfare. The following pages will briefly mention only two main programs against juvenile delinquency:

1. Social isolation in special educational institutions, for example, in boarding schools or vocational-technical special schools; attempts to remove the young person from a crime-inducing environment—family, youth gangs, etc.— and to prevent other young people from being "infected." Social isolation was the sole solution sought until 1936. Since then it has had a high priority, but is no longer used exclusively.

2. A system of social and pedagogical controls over delinquent juveniles. It seeks to keep youngsters in the family and in their regular school, but it is supposed to guarantee an effective societal educational influence, mainly during free time. In this connection, the Councils for Cooperation with the Family and School, the Commissions on the Affairs of Minors, parent patrols, and Komsomol units must be mentioned, among other groups and organizations, which, in cooperation with industry and schools, control the educational activity of parents and the free time of young people and organize extracurricular programs. In addition, they establish guardianship. Apparently this second type of measure has been developed because, among other things, complete removal of the youngster from the family has not proven fully successful.

This trend of improving the education of youth—not by replacing family education and including young people in a system of exclusively social-institutional education, but by exerting social influence on the family and intensifying free-time education—is even more evident in the preventive measures than in the direct measures against juvenile delinquency. The Soviet Union currently looks upon its preventive program against juvenile delinquency primarily as an attempt to strengthen free-time education for all youngsters and to strengthen the family or increase its educational potential.

A special study by the Laboratory for the Investigation of the Causes and Measures against Juvenile Delinquency of the Institute for the Theory and History of Pedagogy of the APN pointed out, with respect to the problem of free-time education:

> It is particularly in the out-of-school sphere that children are exposed to the most negative influence, and the overwhelming majority of socially

inimical acts and crimes are committed by students during the extracurricular hours. . . . Laboratory research has shown that one of the most important causes of delinquency is the nonsupervision of children, frequently combined with thoughtless, asocial use of their extracurricular time" (Davydov 1967).

As has been noted, youth organizations have increasingly been given tasks having to do with out-of-school education in residential areas and in cooperation with the housing organizations. Apparently only a small number of young people, and at that only sporadically, have until now been involved and influenced by the youth organizations' out-of-school activities. There are growing demands for systematizing out-of-school free-time education, and such ideas and expectations are reflected in the following thoughts of the sociologist A. G. Charčev:

> Since young people's free-time activities are basically unregulated, in order to achieve social control over their pastimes one must create complex free-time youth centers in district and urban youth clubs with a variety of entertaining activities. The structuring and supervision of free time represent an element in the campaign against alcoholism. Immoral actions and crimes are a result of the fact that young people join together in small gangs. Creation of a complex free-time center helps to overcome these phenomena (Charčev 1967, p. 155).

Of even greater importance than the comprehensive systematization of the educational work of youth organizations, however, is the lengthening of the school day and the strengthening of school-based free-time education while parents are at work. In recent years the full-day school has been advocated as the most suitable form of linking instruction, school-based free-time education, and family education. Based on early reports, the pedagogical successes of the full-day school and its advantages, on the other hand, over the necessarily fragmentary free-time education given by youth organizations and, on the other, over an exclusively extrafamilial education in boarding schools are indisputable. According to Kostjaškin, the limited out-of-school activities sponsored by youth organizations in Pioneer Houses, Technical Centers, Clubs, and Children's Corners "cannot guarantee . . . the necessary regular daily routine, the continuing and daily instruction and educational work with the children, their nourishment, their fresh-air outings. . . ." Moreover, he believes that boarding schools, despite their accomplishments in the area of free-time education, must be seen as exceptional "ersatz" institutions for children from antisocial families since they unilaterally exclude the family as the source of education and are economically unprofitable. In contrast, full-day schooling guarantees "not only the supervision [of children during extracurricular hours] and improved teaching efficiency [through the supervision of everyone's homework assignments] and education, but also directly increases the family's pedagogical, material, and intellectual potentials, strengthens them, and encourages their unity and cooperation with the school and with all of society" (Kostjaškin 1967, pp. 56-57).

There are several advantages to the further development of full-day schools, which so far provide for only about 10% of the school population. It helps not only to eliminate the causes of juvenile delinquency by expanding the program of free-time education but also helps bring about a compensatory education in full-day schools for educationally underprivileged lower-strata children who very often become social outsiders. This can be accomplished through the general supervision of homework assignments and through the differentiation and individualization of instruction.

This shift of emphasis from the boarding school in favor of the full-day school as a prototype,[86] and the interpretation of full-day school education as a supplement to family education and as a means of parental education indicate that no one in the Soviet Union today can envisage any improvement in the education of young people without the cooperation of the family.

Some of the numerous measures aimed at strengthening the family are: making divorce more difficult and requiring fathers of illegitimate children to assume more responsibility for the economic and pedagogical care of these children; increasing parental responsibility for the antisocial behavior of their children; strengthening pedagogical propaganda and various social controls over parents by means of an organized public in industry, schools, and housing organizations in the campaign against alcoholism, neglect of educational obligations, etc.; intensifying the moral and sex education of young people in order to better prepare them for marital and family life; raising the minimum wage, generally improving the standard of living, and stepping up housing construction; shortening the workday, introducing the five-day workweek, and lessening the work burden of housewives by more public service programs; and continually raising the educational level in all population strata.

The goal of these measures is to create a psychically, socioeconomically stable family unit whose members identify with Soviet society and with the values of communist ethics. In his dialectical conception of the relation between family and society, Charčev pointed out:

> every advance in the field of marital and family relations is at the same time an advance in the field of education. Insofar as socialism does not lead simply to an alteration but, rather, to a qualitative change of these ties, to the growth and development of a principally new type of family, it (socialism) also produces a series of new factors regarding the effect of the family on its children. . . . The most important factor is that organic unit of the private and the social spheres, which is unique both to the socialist social order in general as well and to every socialist family (Charčev 1964, p. 278).

How little the qualitative change in the marital and family forms that Charčev speaks of has so far progressed in Soviet society, how little that "organic unit of the private and the social spheres" is expressed in the present-day social and family structure, emerges not only from the preceding analysis of juvenile delinquency and of the marital and family structure (see below), but is also inferable from the following analysis of the role of specific societal educational goals and values in family education and in the consciousness of the people.

5

Aims and Outcomes
of Soviet Education

In differentiating between functional and intentional factors in educational practices or, as the Soviet sociologist Mansurov (1967, p. 70) does, between direct and indirect personality experiences, the living and educational conditions of the family (standard of living, educational level, harmony or disharmony of the marriage, completeness or incompleteness of the family, etc.), as well as such factors as the neighborhood and the street, belong mainly to the area of functional education or direct experience. The system of organized training and education and the means of mass communication chiefly determine the indirect experience, the "acquisition of sociohistorical experience through the personality" (Mansurov 1967, p. 71), and therefore belong to the area of intentional education. The development of the personality and its integration into society seem to depend upon both factors, particularly upon their interrelationship. If the direct experience of an adolescent, for example, in a conflict-ridden family contradicts the principles of societal education, the danger of a value conflict with society arises and can result in antisocial behavior. In this connection, juvenile delinquency must be considered symptomatic: the impact of negative social and moral experiences in the family easily results in the youngster's losing every social support and becoming delinquent. On the other hand, delinquency must be considered an exception among social phenomena. In other words, the average family generally provides the youngster with a direct social experience which can serve as the foundation of indirect social experience and of unencumbered integration into society.

The relation of functional and intentional education, or of direct and indirect personality experience, must be analyzed on another level. It is well known that communism aims toward a new social order which will be created by a new man. In an individual's awareness in a society liberated from exploitation, one's individual needs and interests should coincide with those of society. The axiom of the conflict-free compatibility of individual and societal interests, or of their identity, leads in practice to the subordination of the former to the latter:

> Socialist society, which overcomes the alienation of the individual, creates the real foundations for the attainment of individual happiness on the basis of social happiness. Since the practical realization of this social attainment depends upon the effectiveness of the socially useful activity of the people, socialist society demands from its members the *conscious* subordination of personal to societal interests, and this also appears as a determining principle of the new morality (Archangel'skij 1968, p. 68).

In light of these demands upon the individual, communist society cannot rely upon the spontaneous, functional, and unconsciously operating factors of personality formation within the framework of the family and other informal groups, even if these do not produce "antisocial" behavior in the sense of delinquency. Rather, communist society is anxious to organize a comprehensive system of societal education which produces a personality type that consciously and actively orients itself to the values of communist society. The leading position of societal educational institutions over that of the family is ideologically paralleled by the priority position of societal educational goals and values (imparted through indirect social experience) over those individual-familial goals and values which spring chiefly from direct individual experience. A personality type in which direct experience assumes priority does not correspond to the ideal of the communist personality. "Such people rely more upon their own impressions and observations; they occasionally mistrust the press, tend toward selfishness; and sometimes act against the collective" (Mansurov 1967, p. 72). In contrast, the ideal image of man in communist society is a "well-rounded personality" which is at the same time "animated . . . by the spirit of collectivism" (*The Foundations* 1964, pp. 46, 206). The ideal lies "in the identification of societal and personal interests, whereby priority is always given to societal [interests] . . . . The Soviet man is everywhere a collectivist—at work, at home, and also where he is a total stranger" (Celikova 1962, pp. 26ff.).

A system of values which should determine the education of people under communism corresponds to the picture of the collectivist personality. This value system is officially formulated in the Moral Code of the Builders of Communism, which has become part of the Program of the CPSU (1961). In addition to general ethical principles that are valid in all civilized societies, the code enumerates the following specific principles of communist morality:

> Loyalty to the cause of communism, love of the socialist homeland, love of the nations of socialism;
> conscientious work for the good of society; he who does not work shall not eat;

individual attention to the maintenance and increase of social property;

a high sense of social duty, intolerance of violations against societal interests;

a spirit of collectivism and mutual comradely assistance: one for all, all for one;

an uncompromising attitude toward the enemies of communism, of peace and international freedom ... (*The Foundations* 1964, pp. 166-167).

The Moral Code of the Builders of Communism demands of each individual active identification with the communist social order and ideology, active societal involvement, work that serves society and its interests. In this way the mobilization of the collective psyche against enemies of the communist society, both at home and abroad, encourages the formation of a uniform ideological awareness. As has already been pointed out, a collectivist value system of this kind can be transmitted only through purposeful education in social institutions and collectives. However, an exclusive organized societal influence over the life and education of children and adolescents does not exist in the USSR, for young people are also greatly affected by their direct experience in the family, in the neighborhood, and on the street. The uniform social value orientation of adolescents can be achieved under these circumstances only if the youngsters' direct experience in the social environment outside public educational institutions also bears the stamp of specific societal values. For this reason it is important to examine the role that collective values assume in family education as the most important area of out-of-school education. This will be illustrated in a discussion on the participation of Soviet parents in their children's education for work and for communist ideology.

Since little research material is available concerning actual educational practices in the family, the attitude of young people toward work, their ideological awareness, or their sociopolitical activity must be made the gauge of familial educational influence. In so doing, the reflections of individualistic value orientations in the adolescents' attitude and actions will be interpreted as the result of direct experiences and educational influences. Of course, one could just as easily support the view that individualistic value orientations are not based upon definite educational influences—for example, those imparted by their parents—but simply express the spontaneous tendency of people in every society to allow themselves to be led in their everyday life "chiefly by the immediate needs of life and interests whose satisfaction results in the attainment of personal happiness" (Archangel'skij 1968, p. 67). Communist education, however, is especially directed against this spontaneous trend toward individualism and selfishness. The problem is that a collective-oriented society fights against individualistic work attitudes, social passivity, ideological indifference, and diversity, all of which it considers to be socially inimical phenomena. As long as the Communist Party's claim to leadership is maintained in all areas of life, the transmitting of individualistic value orientations from generation to generation presents an obstacle in the path toward establishing the communist social order and is compensated for by society's strengthened ideological-political influence over the younger generation and their parents.

WORK EDUCATION AND YOUNG PEOPLE'S ATTITUDES TOWARD WORK

The idea of work education has always occupied a prominent position in Soviet pedagogical theory and practice. According to their understanding, education for work and through work has the purpose of transmitting not only skills but the essential values of communist ethics and the formation of an altruistic attitude toward the collective. The attitude of students toward work particularly reflects their "understanding of their social duty" (*The Foundations* 1964, p. 171). Work becomes the symbol of the individual's service for society and, like the latter, it should not be elicited by necessity or coercion, but become a need. According to one of Lenin's definitions, communist work is understood as "work which is performed without thought of remuneration . . . based on the habit of working for the common good, . . . as the need of a healthy organism" (ibid., p. 192). The training of the younger generation for such an attitude toward work is "the most important task of moral education" (ibid., p. 170). Accordingly, the 1961 Program of the CPSU states: "The Party sees as the main task of education the development of a communist attitude toward work among all members of society" (ibid., p. 189).

Education for a communist attitude toward work can best be realized by organizing systematic work activities within the framework of a collective—"communist ethics originate, above all, in work, in actions and deeds" (ibid., p. 171)—as well as by imitating models. In both forms of work education, the family is assigned an important function, one that supplements societal education: as a small collective, the family should transmit work habits and provide youngsters with exemplary behavior patterns through the parents' work activities and work attitudes. Here too, as in the case of preschool education, one finds many contradictions between these pedagogical demands for familial work education and the everyday reality of family education.

As far as practical work education goes, the general shifting of the work process into the extrafamilial sphere and the time strain on both parents because of full-day employment lead to an extreme restriction of practical work education possibilities in the family. According to Titarenko's (1967) already cited research results, regular duties and a fixed daily routine for children and adolescents could be demonstrated in only half of the 647 families surveyed.[1] On the other hand, the time budget research by Davydov and Pelipenko (1968) with 537 students in grades five through ten has shown that 95% of all students do household work every day: an average of 50 minutes on weekdays and more than an hour on weekends. Supplementary data from the same investigation indicate that only 10.5% of the students had a regular daily routine and followed it systematically, and that only a few upper-grade students spent their out-of-school time together with their parents. This leads one to assume that the household work of students is mainly limited to taking care of themselves during their parents' absence, to minor shopping, etc. The demonstrable household work of students can be considered in most cases as an expression of growing independence; it does not, however, resemble collective work and mutual assistance, and lacks adult pedagogical supervision. In general, then, one cannot speak of actual work education through the allocation of household responsibilities. Moreover, the lack of systematic practical work education in the family apparently stems not only from the limited time available, but also from the educational attitude of many parents toward their children's work activity. Based upon her own studies, observations, and conversations, the pedagogue E. I. Volkova had to point out that, even in those cases where parents do urge their children to help with household duties:

> The housework of boys and girls was not infrequently limited to the performance of sporadic chores assigned by adults, and they have no responsible duties as members of the family collective. The housework of upper-grade students is often purely utilitarian; its educational importance is underestimated. . . . Many parents do not obtain their children's systematic participation in housework; they do not make the appropriate demands. As a result the upper-grade students lack a feeling of responsibility (Volkova 1959, pp. 86-87).

In the short time the family spends together, many parents fail to make pedagogical demands upon their children; many justify this by saying that students are too tense to be able to perform household duties too.[2] This is an understandable attitude on the part of parents if one considers that, as time budget studies show, upper-grade students have to work an average of more than eight hours a day.[3]

It appears that the Soviet family generally imparts to children no systematic practical work education that could be considered preparation for subsequent work in adult society. The schools, however, are making efforts to encourage students to be more cooperative at home. They do this not only through pedagogical propaganda among parents, but also by influencing the students themselves in the youth organizations. The Pioneer and Komsomol groups of a Leningrad school, for example, made posters illustrating the types of household work appropriate to students in grades one through ten. In addition, they offered suggestions for certain other tasks, according to the conditions of family life.[4]

The question of whether, through their own example, Soviet parents instill a communist attitude toward work in the household and in social production is even more difficult to answer than the question concerning practical work education in the family, for here, too, little empirical research material is available. The negative traditional allocation of masculine and feminine roles and functions in the Soviet family has already been noted in connection with preschool education. The contention has often been made in Soviet pedagogy that one must "put an end to the remnants of an order wherein the total burden of housework lies solely upon the female part of the family" (Volkova 1959, p. 86). In most families the husband still takes little or no part in sharing the household chores, and parents therefore are not a living example of mutual help in the eyes of their children. As an indirect result of the one-sided approach to housework, most mothers call upon daughters for help. Volkova made the same observation (1959, p. 87).

The parents' job activity does not seem to occupy an important place in many family conversations. A survey of 139 elementary school pupils showed that, even as late as the fourth grade, more than one-third of the pupils did not know what their parents did at work, and almost half of them had no idea of the "value" of their parents' work "for other people" (Burštejn 1961, p. 65). Although this survey contains no representative data and refers to younger schoolchildren, it does indicate that many parents do not include discussion of their work in family conversations, expecially the societal aspects of their jobs. A clear gap seems to exist in many cases between the working world and family life, between the social and the private spheres. This gap is expressed not only in the children's scant knowledge about their parents' jobs, but in the failure of many parents to support students' societal work activities—a factor in the ideological education of young people—and in the growth of negative attitudes toward physical labor on the part of both generations. Although physical labor determines by far the predominant aspect of work and represents the most important form of human employment "for the good of society," and will continue to do so in the near future, many parents want a better career for their children than what they themselves have. They therefore impart a perspective on work which mainly takes the need for individual satisfaction and social prestige into account and neglects societal needs. The significance of this problem of a divergent development of individual and societal interests can be judged from the fact that Khrushchev himself repeatedly criticized it publicly. His most detailed statement was made at the All-Union Teachers Congress in 1960:

> We should not forget that the struggle for the new way of life, for the new ethics, still continues in battle against the remnants of the old which stubbornly persist. . . . Among a small number of youth who did not go through a good school of life, one still observes a frivolous or even contemptuous attitude toward physical labor, an idle disposition, and one finds cases of a lack of idealism and a type of nihilism. . . . Unfortunately all parents and teachers still do not understand the significance of training for the choice of an occupation, for work activity which also embodies the meaning of life. Many are still unable to abandon the old views about secondary education and believe that the inevitable result of such an

education must be this or that managerial position, a small one, maybe, but a managerial position nevertheless, or else a "clean," "light" job. . . . A few words must be said about the role of the family in education. The parents' example and that of the older members of the family is very important in the formation of views and ideals, intentions and habits. The old proverb still holds true: "The apple doesn't fall far from the tree" (Khrushchev 1961, pp. 24-25).

Within this context of an inadequate education for work, Khrushchev demanded that the education of children in the family not be considered the purely "personal affair of the parents," but rather "one of the very important areas of Party work" (ibid., p. 27). This means simply that in the area of socially oriented work education the family has proven to be an unreliable partner of social educational institutions, and that a strengthened ideological-pedagogical influence over parents and children is needed to prevent the further spread of an individualistic attitude toward work.

In addition, in practice the problems of work cannot be solved by appeals to the collectivism of workers. Among other things, the problem of turnover demonstrates this. The USSR is paying more and more attention to increasing labor turnover based on employees' notices. An evaluation of 11,000 questionnaires from Leningrad industrial enterprises indicated that there were three main reasons given for job change: 37.4% were dissatisfied with the type of employment (heavy and dirty work, work not commensurate with their training); 29.9% wanted to improve their living conditions or find a job closer to home; and 23.5% sought to improve their wages.[5] In the interest of effective economic development, a workers' organization which takes the individual needs of the working people into consideration will be needed to solve the problem of turnover. The rising level of people's demands and the growing individualization of work attitudes are forcing ideology to adapt to realities: one can today no longer emphasize only the collective aspects of work, but encourage employment through moral and material incentives.[6]

While Khrushchev's statements could still give the impression that inadequate social value orientation in the area of work education represents an exception and is based upon educational errors in several families, an analysis of research material about studying and working Soviet youth shows that an individualistic value orientation among the younger generation in their attitude toward an occupation and work has gained in strength and is already widespread.

An important index of young people's individualistic value orientation is the contradiction between the occupational desires of young people and the vocational orientation in schools, where the needs of the Soviet planned economy are taken into consideration. This discrepancy is expressed, among other places, in a definite preference for intellectual work and in a low estimation of the mass occupations characterized by physical labor, which now, as before, predominate in industrial and agricultural production as well as in the service sector. Despite the polytechnical education and practical work phases in vocational training, etc., introduced in the Soviet School in 1958, most upper-grade secondary school students tend toward careers with intellectual work, although under the current conditions only a small number of graduates can be accepted in universities and be trained for such careers. A 1964 survey of a representative number of 4,500 upper-graders in Kazan and Ufa indicated that "about 80% strive for intellectual employment. . . . In view of the fact that the majority of secondary school graduates will try in vain to enter a university, the lack of psychological preparation for physical labor will in the future lead to a serious life disappointment and produce a negative attitude toward the career which the young person, forced by necessity, takes up despite his plans" (Aitov 1966, p. 24).

A survey by Šubkin (1968, p. 60), covering 10% of the 1963-64 school graduates in Novosibirsk, showed that the career desires of 89% of the young people had no connection with the schools' polytechnical work instruction. The career desires of most of them concentrated on less attractive occupations involving intellectual work. The growing rural exodus of young people who dislike agricultural labor, as well as the low appeal of the service jobs which are becoming more numerous, has had disastrous effects on the national economy.[7]

It would be one-sided to interpret the overwhelming trend among students toward university and intellectual careers solely as an escape from physical labor, for this trend also expresses a strong educational desire and the high social prestige which very skilled work brings with it in modern society. On the other hand, the research data prove that the career desires of young people very much contradict the economic needs of society and the school's socially oriented career guidance, and therefore reflect chiefly individual inclinations and interests.

The individualistic motivation of career choice among adolescents must be seen as a further index of the individualistic value orientation of the younger generation. Indeed, while in surveys youngsters frequently name ideologically conforming collectivist motives for their career choice, personal motives are taking on increasing importance. For example, 25% of Šubkin's survey group answered the question, "What do you like about the career you want to pursue?" with a reference to its "importance for the national economy"; 45%, however, referred to the "creative nature of the work"; and 2% spoke of "high earnings" (Šubkin 1964, p. 20).

Individualistic motives of career choice predominated even more clearly in the statements of 250 female and 250 male secondary school graduates in Nižnij Tagil. In reply to the question of which factor has most influenced the formation of their life plans, only 17.5% of the girls and 22.4% of the boys named a clearly collectivist motive, the "awareness of social duty"; 46.5% of the girls and 33.6% of the boys named a "serious interest in a certain activity"; 15.2% of the girls and 24.7% of the boys named the "endeavor to find a secure position in life as quickly as possible"; 12% of the girls and 6.8% of the boys wrote "material considerations"; and 8.8% of the girls and 12.5% of the boys referred to the influence of parents and friends. In contrast, school and youth organizations did not appear as influence factors, but could be assumed in the statements about "awareness of social duty."[8]

Of course, the motivation of career choice with references such as those to individual interests, in the sense of a "serious interest in a certain activity," do not fundamentally contradict societal interests and a social value orientation. Such a motivation can be described as individualistic in the sense of a lack of consideration for society only because the planned Soviet economy and communist ideology and education proceed from a definite priority of societal over personal interests, but, as has been shown, the personal interests of many young persons do not correspond to the needs of society. Archangel'skij and Petrov argue exactly from this perspective. On the one hand, they emphasize, there is a positive connection between societal interest and the "creative interest" which "reflects the individual differences in inclinations and endeavors" (Archangel'skij and Petrov 1967, p. 72). They also point out that there are "always still many cases of opportunism where graduates, following completion of school, do not want to consider the demands of social need in determining their life plans. With sufficient development of intellectual interests, a superficial adoption of the ideals of service to society leads to intellectual snobbism, to enthusiasm for knowledge for its own sake. . . ." This type of mental attitude, however, is "in contradiction to the ideal of well-rounded personality development" in communist society (ibid., p. 74).

The sociologist Mansurov discovered an interesting aspect of adolescents' motivation for career choice: the receptivity of young people to the needs of society depends upon their age and upon the intensity of their newspaper reading. He showed that the younger the age, the greater was the consideration of societal interests or the repetition of ideological standpoints in the statements of young people—that is, the most abstract the question of career choice appeared to them, and the more they were impressed by regular newspaper reading. A comparison of students of different age groups who read a newspaper daily with students who only occasionally read it, and study of their career choice motives, led Mansurov to the following conclusions: all students, regardless of age and of the intensity with which they read a paper, assign first place to "love for the career" and "skills for the career." Next, the collectivist motive of the "necessity of the career for the country" was named significantly more often by students of the 7th and 8th grades than by those in the 10th and 11th grades, and in both age groups significantly more often by those who read the paper daily: 42% of the younger and 25% of the older students who read it daily as compared to 37% of the younger and 12% of the older students who read it only occasionally. In contrast, the individualistic motive of "material reasons" for a career choice were named by 9% of the younger and 20% of the older students who read a paper daily, in contrast to 43% of the younger and 37% of the older students who only occasionlly read it. Mansurov concluded that newspaper reading can "contribute much to the formation of those motives of career choice which correspond to socialist norms" (Mansurov 1967, p. 82).

Meanwhile, it remains true that career choice motives which conform to ideology recede into the background with increasing age, and that in the awareness of even intense newspaper readers among the older students the individualistic motive of "material reasons" is almost equally as important as the collectivist motive, the "necessity of the career for the country."

The attitude toward work activity actually performed in production after school graduation must be discussed as the final and most important index of young people's value orientation. This index is especially important insofar as it does not include (as the first indices do) expressions about anticipated work activity, but, rather, statements about the actual attitude toward work and objective data concerning the employment and the social initiative of young people in the factory. Such a discussion presupposes the fact that, in practice, integration into career life is a matter of interest for society and the planned economy. In other words, school graduates, sometimes against their wishes, interests, or skills, are employed in branches of work which are important for the national economy. The trend toward individualistic attitudes to work can be significantly strengthened by the frequent discrepancy between personal career desires and actual employment. An active identification with societal work and with the factory collective, which demands the communist ethic from the worker, can be developed only with difficulty in an activity which does not correspond to his inclinations and skills. This fact must be considered in evaluating the survey results concerning the young person's attitude toward work.

The most thorough investigation in this area was carried out by the sociologists A. G. Zdravomyslov and V. A. Jadov. They explored the "attitude toward work and the value orientations of the personality" among 2,665 young workers in 25 Leningrad factories. The study, which rested partly upon data from factory managements and partly upon an evaluation of questionnaires, showed that most young workers (about 95%) fulfilled and exceeded the production norms, that the majority demonstrated a good (60%) and average (40%) quality of work; however, only a minority developed initiative on the job and in the factory by contributing suggestions for greater efficiency, etc. Specifically, the following groups could be differentiated: workers "with overfulfillment of the production norms, with average work quality, and without initiative"—36.6%; workers "with fulfillment and overfulfillment of production norms with good work quality, but without initiative or with average initiative and average work quality in the fulfillment and overfulfillment of production norms"—31.9%; workers "with overproduction, high reliability in the assignment of responsible tasks, good work quality, but average initiative"—15.9%; "the best workers," with high indices in all three categories—11.2%; and workers with low indices in all three categories—4.1% (Zdravomyslov and Jadov 1966, pp. 193-194).

It can be inferred from these data that for most young people, that is, for about two-thirds of the 2,665 young workers surveyed, factory work is a "job" which they perform without personal commitment in the sense of initiative. Only for a few has the development and efficiency of production become a matter of personal responsibility toward the factory and society. In many cases the lack of personal on-the-job initiative corresponds to the young people's view of their work, not for its societal significance but for its wages. Indeed, 617 of the 2,665 survey subjects considered that work was good "where one is more needed," and 830 admitted that one should "not forget the earnings, but the main sense of the work is its social value"; 819 young workers, however, stated that for them the earnings "were the important thing, but one must also think about the sense of the work"; and 399 even stated that "any kind of work is good if it is well paid" (ibid., p. 195).

The division of the survey subjects into "groups of value orientation" that reflect the predominant interest area of young workers, an area with which they identify and to which they want to devote more time in the event of an eventual shortening of the workday, is also informative. Investigation of the main value orientation of the personality and of the effect of this value orientation on the attitude toward work shows that the family is most frequently (38% of those surveyed) named as the orientation point. If one adds to the chiefly family-oriented young workers those who have absolutely no fixed orientation (36%) and those who are predominantly oriented toward earnings (6%), this embraces that majority of workers who develop no or little initiative. According to Zdravomyslov and Jadov, this group is guided by direct interests or possesses absolutely no fixed interests, and their attitude toward work is characterized by a deficient or weak understanding of the societal importance of work, a fact which is particularly emphasized by the large group of workers without a fixed value orientation.[9] In contrast, a large minority, encompassing about one-third of the survey subjects and corresponding to the group of workers with initiative, are oriented toward "societal work" (12%), "work in a factory" (10%), and "education" (23%). A higher degree of understanding for the societal importance of work prevails among these workers.[10]

Zdravomyslov's and Jadov's survey results permit the conclusion that a large number of the young worker generation do not demonstrate a true communist attitude toward work. The question arises of whether the growth of passive and individualistic attitudes toward work is based on the already mentioned fact that many young people have a job which does not correspond to their career wishes, interests, and abilities, and that this work for the most part involves physical labor. However, not only the relatively high index of satisfaction with their work in all survey groups, but especially in the socially passive groups of the cited study,[11] speaks against an overestimation of these factors. Data showing that passive work attitudes are also widespread among students who are preparing for careers in intellectual work also speak against this. The teachers' newspaper, under the headline "Against Intellectual Apathy " recently reported a study in a teacher training institute which showed that 47% of the students "study without particular exertion of their abilities" (Slastenin 1969). The main problem, therefore, seems to lie not in the young person's disagreement with the actual content and conditions of his work life, but in his fundamental attitude toward work as an area of societal activity. Most young workers have an attitude which amounts to a "retreat into the world of personal interests," an attitude which the Soviet Union likes to represent as indicative of youth in "bourgeois society" (Archangel'skij and Petrov 1967, p. 68). On the one hand, such an attitude measures work by subjective satisfaction, by its pay, etc., that is, by individualistic standards; on the other hand, one's work appears as an area of life severed from private life and of secondary importance to it, an area of life with which the individual only slightly identifies.

In summary, the following factors can be named for the preponderance of the "individualistic" or "individualistic-familial" value orientation of the younger generation in their attitude toward work:

1. A general increase in the material and intellectual needs and demands of people with respect to the growing consolidation and growing prosperity of the entire society. An increase in material demands leads particularly to "consumer egoism" and social passivity in that large group of young people who have not found a fixed value orientation in their families or in extrafamilial society.

2. The neglect of a collectivist work education in the young person's families: in Soviet society, just as in the West, the modern small family betrays a trend toward self-limitation upon its own intimate world. This trend seems to be gaining strength in the younger generation; characteristically, their personally founded family is the most important orientation point for the largest group of young workers.

3. The neglect of the values of the personality, of individual inclinations, interests, and abilities in the school-based work education and vocational preparation, as well as in the employment allocation in the centrally planned economy. Rigid implementation of societal interests leads to a weakening of personal commitment and of the identification with the factory collective and society as a whole.

The attitude toward work poses a problem of both the individual's general awareness and ideological awareness, as well as of the actual professional guidance and work organization. Both aspects are mutually dependent. Accordingly, the Soviet Union today is seeking a solution by strengthening ideological education and reforming career guidance and work organization. The question of ideological education has been repeatedly touched upon and will be disucssed in detail in the following section. With respect to practical reforms, however, the economist A. Zvorykin pointed out: "The problem of choice of life paths," which is currently determined by the fact that "there is a large gap between the young person's dreams and real life," can be solved only "if one takes the characteristic of each individual as a basis, that is, if one proceeds from the person to the career" (Zvorykin 1968). And the sociologist M. T. Iovčuk characterized the economic reforms in the USSR, which, among other things, should amount to the "strengthening of the collective and individual commitment," as a means to "overcome the insufficient interest among a number of workers which is apparent in the development of socialist production" (Iovčuk 1968, p. 29). For the time being, of course, just how far this type of reform suggestions will be realized remains questionable, especially the extent to which these types of reforms will lead to a change of ideology itself in the direction of a stronger emphasis upon the values of the personality. At the moment one should no longer speak of an individualistic value orientation in the attitude toward work where it is frequently a matter of only the individual's drive toward self-realization and of his striving toward personal work satisfaction and material prosperity.

POLITICAL EDUCATION AND YOUNG PEOPLE'S POLITICAL ATTITUDES

The greater time lapse since the October Revolution, the further the economic consolidation of Soviet society, and the wider the information radius for the population the more difficult the realization of the Communist Party's goal of a uniform ideological education for all seems to become. Although the Communist Party exercises constant and strict control over schools and universities, youth organizations and factories, the press, radio, and television, the past few years have witnessed more and more discussion about deficiencies in the ideological education of the younger generation. The Party has to admit that many youngsters leave school without fixed political convictions and with inadequate identification with the fundamentals of communist ethics (as is apparent, among other things, in their attitudes toward employment and work), and that many university students and instructors neglect the social science courses which are especially geared to ideological education.[12] Critics emphasize that young people

who are just entering life do not yet possess that ideological tempering which their fathers and mothers have acquired. They are sometimes incapable of correctly and thoroughly judging domestic and international events; they represent a consumers' point of view, demonstrate political immaturity, and succumb to the influence of alien morality. The work discipline in industry bothers such people, and studying does not interest them. Naturally all this involves only a small number of youth, but that too gives reason for concern. It is therefore necessary to talk about the unsolved questions of adolescent education and perhaps even about exceptions to the general rule. Why does a boy or girl born three decades after the revolution suddenly appear as the bearer of infamous relics of the past? (Eštokin 1965).

In the past few years, even in the official Komsomol youth organization, trends toward ideological diversion and toward the establishment of a youth culture independent of the Party have become noticeable. Even though these trends are necessarily doomed because of the authoritarian structure of the government, they are characteristic of the younger generation which does not unquestioningly accept the revolutionary heritage of their fathers but emphasizes their own personal interests. On the occasion of the fiftieth anniversary of the founding of the Komsomol, it was expressly emphasized that the Party and the Komsomol "have unmasked the falsity and damaging effects of the idea of the 'equal rights' of the youth organization with the Party, of its 'neutrality' and political independence." Absolute independence could lead to the separation of the youth organization from the Party, to uncontrollable developments in the communist youth movement; at a time "of violent class struggle, the struggle for youth included," there could be "no 'neutral' positions and no 'no-man's land.'" At this point the developments in Czechoslovakia in 1967-1968 were deliberately referred to: "Several youth associations began to 'split off and to declare themselves independent' of the national youth organization and to establish themselves according to age, occupational, and ethnic features. . . . Moreover, it is clear that a mosaic-type structure, so-called pluralism, led to the undermining of the unity between the working and studying young people in the youth movement in Czechoslovakia" (Apresjan 1968).

These few references make it clear that the CPSU sees a threat to the uniformity and effectiveness of ideological schooling. The Party considers every weakening of uniform ideological awareness, every trend toward sociopolitical passivity and ideological pluralism, as a danger to its power position in the state and in society, and reacts by sharpening the ideological struggle and societal controls. Here are some examples. After the Twenty-third Congress of the CPSU (1966), following the introduction of the subject "Foundations of Political Knowledge" in the upper school grades (1960) and of the subject "Foundations of Scientific Communism" in the universities, ideological instruction in schools and universities was strengthened by the introduction of military basic training (140 class hours in the upper grades) and by the expansion of obligatory social science subjects in universities. In addition, the Komsomol was subjected to stronger Party control.

If even the school, the university, and the Komsomol—educational institutions under the direct control of the Party—perform inadequate work in the field of ideological education, this must be even more true of the family, which, as our discussion of work education shows, inclines more than any other social institution toward the passing on of individualistic value orientations. As a result, the ideological struggle necessarily includes measures for control over parental educational activity. The campaign against "remnants of the past in the consciousness of the people," which the Party feels are primarily preserved in the family, has been sharpened in recent years. Next to the organs of the state and industrial jurisdiction, it is chiefly the school which is charged with the task of societal control over the family. The *Foundations of Communist Education* points out:

> Formation of the communist world view means at the same time the overcoming of every remnant of capitalism in the minds of the people. These remnants, however, are very difficult to eliminate. They find expression in individual Soviet people in a lack of ideals about, and indifference to, political life, in the discrepancy between their words and deeds, in sloppiness and idleness, selfishness and greed, in bureaucratic behavior, in the violation of the rules of socialist collective life, in alcoholism and rowdyness, in relapses into ethnic factionalism, in religious and other superstitions, etc. . . . .
>
> The school collective plays a decisive role in the struggle against individualism and selfishness as well as against other such remnants of the past, all the more so when the principle of collectivism is often ignored in the parental home. In this sense the school exerts its influence not only upon the student, but also upon the family in that it contributes to the destruction and elimination of remaining petty-bourgeois views (*The Foundations* 1964, pp. 125, 212).

The *Foundations of Communist Education* also emphasizes the great influence of parental example on the ideological education of children: "The education of the younger generation in the spirit of communist ideology" begins "in the family and in preschool establishments" and "in many instances the attitude of the Pioneer toward his organization and toward societal tasks" depends upon his parents (*The Foundations* 1964, pp. 128, 319).

The following pages will examine whether and to what degree Soviet parents have a great influence on the education of their children in the sense of societal demands, whether and to what degree they give them a living example of collectivism through their own general social value orientation, political interest, and sociopolitical activity, and whether and to what degree they participate in the conscious transmittal of the communist world view and encourage sociopolitical activity by their children. If the research material available about these questions confirms the thesis that the family is strongly concentrated on personal interests and on its own intimate world, then, based on the data about ideological awareness, the sociopolitical activity and the life plans of young people themselves must be examined with respect to just how far the orientation on individualistic-familial values influences the younger generation and how it weakens their collectivism.

One can well assume that the majority of the adult population favors a fundamental identification with the socialist order, with the Soviet state and its political leadership. Adults have consciously experienced the gradual consolidation of Soviet society, the increase in the standard of living and the shortening of the workweek, the development of the Soviet Union into a world power, the successes of Soviet science and space exploration, and the loosening of social restraints following the Stalin era. Add to this the fact that the people have no possibilities of making comparisons with other societies and therefore believe the mass media information which asserts that no state does more for the working man than their own. A democratic tradition, one that could be alive in the consciousness of the people, does not exist in the USSR. Hence, to the masses, the overall development of Soviet society appears all the more as continuous progress. Even the critical intelligentsia, which has more information than the masses at its disposal, would like to see reforms realized only within the existing socialist political system. If this is true, one could assume that parents will not educate their children against the state and its social order, but toward fundamental identification with it and adaptation to it.

More difficult to answer is the question of whether fundamental identification with the state and social order includes that active interest and participation in sociopolitical life which the collectivistically oriented socialist society expects of every one of its members. Numerous recent research data indicate that the majority of people incline toward more or less passive identification with the life and value system of society, or at best to a priority emphasis of individual and familial interests. Examination of the interests among workers' families in a large industrial enterprise has shown that 52% of the workers emphasized "mutual help in the education of the children;" 50%, "mutual help in the household"; 47%, "common administration of the household budget"; and 39%, "common relaxation and diversion in the family." Only 33% emphasized an "interest in the production work of the family members" and 25% an "interest in societal work." The division of the entire survey group into groups of prevailing interest orientation showed that 47% of the families were characterized by "a focus upon domestic interests," while in 39% of the families "the interests [were] divided between domestic life and the social sphere." In 7% of the families—for the most part married couples without children—"the focus toward societal interests" predominated (Balaguškin 1968, pp. 197-198).

In addition to general interest orientation, the reading of political literature and participation in societal work and in the political-educational work of the Party in factories and organizations can be cited as further indices of the sociopolitical receptivity of adults. Grušin's representative time budget research shows that 81.6% of the population read newspapers on a daily basis and 7.7% do so several times a week; 16.6% take part in daily societal work, 21.5% participate several times a week, and 34.2% a few times a month; 19% participate in political instruction several times a week and 19.6% several times a month.[13] These data require careful interpretation.

First of all, with respect to the reading of daily newspapers, studies on the reading habits of young people have shown that in many cases these readings concentrate less on the political part of the press than upon local news and sports. Other research studies have also demonstrated the fact that, especially among adults, politically oriented literature is not widespread. In a survey of 840 workers, those over the age of 36 hardly mentioned the reading of sociopolitical magazines and social science literature; on the other hand, Soviet and foreign entertainment and technical literature clearly held their interest.[14] Moreover, Grušin's point that one-tenth of the population "reads practically no newspapers, one-quarter no magazines, and one-fifth no books" (Grušin 1967, p. 90) must also be taken into account.

As far as societal work goes, chiefly participation in political instruction, Grušin's data already show that these activities apply to less than 50% of the adults' weekly time budget, and are significant for that very reason. The earlier mentioned survey of 2,306 parents in Armenia which Asratjan (1968, p. 41) reports about yielded similar data: about 50% of the parents surveyed performed societal work in their collectives. According to Zemcov (1965, p. 68), societal work took up, on the average, about one hour of the weekly time budget of all male workers; "rest and recreation," on the other hand, amounted to about 20 hours. In evaluating the workers' sociopolitical activity, one must also consider the fact that in many cases it has a more or less obligatory nature—for example, when a worker assumes a responsible position in the factory or wants to attain such a position. Those 40 to 50% "active" workers, therefore, include many whose activity is not motivated by voluntary commitment. Gurjanov's cited study about the intellectual interests of 804 workers shows how little sociopolitical activity correlates with sociopolitical interest: with an eventual shortening of the workday and a corresponding lengthening of free time, only 18% of those questioned would want to spend more time for the factory collective, while the rest would prefer individual family-oriented free-time activities.[15]

A further indication that political activity is largely motivated by societal obligations is the fact that workers are much less active if local Party organizations and factory Party groups engage in little political orientation. The political awareness of the adult working population outside of the large cities seems to be particularly weakly developed; in such areas, among other things, the mutual familiarity of the people can undermine the Party's social control mechanisms. Zemcov reports about the Leninskij workers' settlement in the district of Tula:

> Political instruction is neglected, extemely little free time remains for self-education, attendance at lectures, the reading of newspapers, etc. Of 136 individuals who filled out the questionnaires, 39 read no newspapers, 88 no magazines, and 54 no books. . . . A total of 24 people took part in political instruction. It is understandable that all this was in no way conducive to overcoming the remnants of the past in the consciousness and actions of the people (Zemcov 1965, p. 66).

As an example of widespread "remnants of the past," Zemcov cited the fact that many men drink heavily and that "of the 136 individuals (including 109 workers) who filled out the questionnaires, 73 enjoy playing cards, dominoes, lotto, etc., and most of them play daily or several times a week" (ibid.).

Avoiding the risk of hasty generalizations, one can determine, on the basis of available research results, that at least half of the adult Soviet population engages in no sociopolitical activity in everyday life, while the determinable activity of the other half frequently does not rest upon sociopolitical interest and voluntary commitment, but upon societal obligations, and is performed as an exercise of duty. Most people's interests are concentrated on domestic life, on individual activities, and on relaxation within the family circle or informal groups. Only in a few families do parents appear to their children as social activists, as collectivists, and those few families are opposed by others in which parents ignore every social value orientation and devote their nonworking hours to drinking, card playing, etc.

One can therefore assume that families engage in conversations about ideological questions as seldom or even more seldom than conversations about the socially relevant aspects of the parents' actual factory work.[16] References are often found in the pedagogical press about parents not giving sufficient support to the political-educational work of teachers. A district Party secretary, for example, finds fault with the fact that the educational efforts of teachers in shaping their students' world view occasionally "strike against the mute wall of political 'neutralism' in the family and sometimes also come into a conflict with the apolitical conversations and the wrong conduct of parents" (Antipin 1969).

One can hardly expect that parents who themselves engage in no sociopolitical activity will consciously encourage such activity among their children. Just as in the case of their children's career choice, they emphasize personal inclinations and abilities; assigning greater importance to the interests of their children than to those of society,[17] they will want to see to it that their children have as much free time as possible and spend it with the family. Although there are little exact research data available about this point, one finds significant references in the pedagogical literature about the fact that many parents demonstrate an indifferent or even negative attitude toward their children's activities in socially useful work. These activities, which are organized by the school's youth groups and include the care of school establishments, employment in different branches of production, etc., are often scheduled for weekends and vacations—in other words, when there could be a more intensive family gathering than is possible during the normal workdays. I. Svadkovskij, a member of the Academy of Pedagogical Sciences, reports about parents "who not only do not train their children to work, but also even encourage them to avoid appropriate work in school" (Svadkovskij 1961, p. 2). *The Foundations of Communist Education* states in this same connection:

> Many parents are dissatisfied with the growing societal activity of their children because they believe it is detrimental to their school work. They try to induce the Pioneer to turn down societal assignments with every conceivable excuse. In this way they raise conflicts in the children's minds, in their attitude toward societal duties, and damage their education (*The Foundations* 1964, p. 319).

Of course, many parents are interested in organized free-time activity for their children outside the family, since they themselves can supervise only a small portion of their children's free time and are often unable to offer their youngsters [suitable] ideas. In addition, a substantial minority of parents actively participate in the youth organizations' group work. The already mentioned survey of 2,306 Armenian parents showed that 30% of them participated regularly in group evenings, and that 13% served as leaders of hobby circles, sport groups, etc.[18] However, one characteristic of this type of group work is that it is more a matter of stimulating free-time activities according to the youngster's free choice and interest than of setting up ideological-political schooling, of assignments for social control over others (such as Pioneer and Komsomol groups, which form "patrols" in the campaign against juvenile delinquency, etc.), or of unpaid and vocationally and educationally neutral work for the good of society.

The neglect of conscious ideological education in the family is perhaps most clearly expressed in the parents' failure to give their children an atheistic education, a significant element of Soviet ideological education. It has already been mentioned, in connection with preschool education, that, according to the results of surveys in various areas of the USSR, up to 50% of the parents have their children baptised. Chiefly under the influence of grandparents and mainly in rural areas, religious ideas have also been maintained in addition to external rites. In the Leninskij workers' settlement, Zemcov observed:

> Ikons hung in 64 of the 152 families surveyed. Older women explained the presence of the ikons in the following manner: "I believe and I teach the children to believe, we won't let you bother us in this. . . ." They [the ikons] also do not disturb the intelligentsia of the settlement who do not perform any kind of orientation work among the population (Zemcov 1965, p. 66).

Because of the parents' neutral and indifferent—sometimes even positive— attitude toward religion, many youngsters can be converted to conscious atheism only under the systematic influence of societal education and by the mass communication media. A study by the sociologist Mansurov indicates that convinced atheists are clearly in the majority only among those young people who are strongly influenced by the press: 87% of the upper-grade students questioned and 77% of the vocational students who read a newspaper daily—but only 62% of the upper-graders and 44% of the vocational students who seldom read the paper—described themselves as "convinced atheists." Even 10 to 20% of the regular newspaper readers, and as high as 32 to 33% of the occasional readers, had "still formed no fixed opinion in this respect" and 3 to 4% of the occasional newspaper readers called themselves "believers" (Mansurov 1967, p. 80).

These data complete the transition from the description of the ideological-political value orientation and educational activity of the parents (and

grandparents) to that of the younger generation and their ideological-political
value orientation. . . . Since the family is the only institution in Soviet society
that continually embraces children and adolescents, the fact that many young
people are not convinced atheists—and that some even describe themselves as
believers—can only be traced back to the influence of the family.

The following pages will discuss the general ideological-political orientation
of young people, their sociopolitical activity, and their life plans. Although
attitudes which deviate from social norms will be pointed out, one should not
assume that the connection with family education is as exclusive as in the area of
religious traditions or deficient atheistic convictions among the younger
generation. Instead, one will have to consider that young people encounter
ideological indifference, ideological pluralism, and sociopolitical passivity not
only in the family but also in the school, in the university, and in youth
organizations, and, above all, in informal friendship groups. One should also take
into account the young person's spontaneous tendency toward priority emphasis
on individual interests and his spontaneous reactions against every type of
dogmatism and formalism which confronts him in the ideological-political work
of social institutions and organizations.

In describing the young person's ideological-political orientation, one should
differentiate, on the one hand, between a basic and general identification with
the Soviet state and the socialist social order and, on the other, with ideological
conviction, political interest, and sociopolitical activity. All Soviet studies show
that, upon questioning, almost all young people endorse the Soviet state and the
socialist social order. For example, 95% of the secondary school and vocational
students surveyed by Mansurov and Lunkov (1967) gave a clearly positive
answer to the question, "Are you proud to be citizens of a socialist state?" In
the same survey group, however, as has been mentioned, there were several who
did not describe themselves as convinced atheists. Mansurov emphasizes that
"there is no direct correlation between political conviction and the pride of
being able to live under socialism," that "the pride of socialist citizenship does
not extend to the political orientation and education of the students" (Mansurov
and Lunkov 1967, p. 89). It can be assumed that the fundamental and
predominantly emotional identification with one's own state and with the
socialist social order, as Mansurov emphasizes, is "a general feeling among the
overwhelming majority" of young people (as well as of their parents), but that
this general identification does not preclude ideological diversity, political
indifference, and sociopolitical passivity. To comprehend such contradictions,
one should not rely solely upon the general statements of adolescents, "often
replete with jargon and phrases" (Archangel'skij and Petrov 1967, p. 71);
instead, the actual forms of expression of political interest and sociopolitical
commitment must be analyzed.

Mansurov's findings on the extent of newspaper reading among secondary
and vocational school students are informative in this connection. He discovered
that the intensity of such reading increased with age: 45% of the secondary

school students in the tenth grade read the newspaper daily and 31% do so frequently; the corresponding figures for the tenth grade vocational students of the same age are 35 and 33% respectively. A considerable minority of 17-year-olds—one-fourth to one-third of the survey groups—read the paper "only occasionally" or "almost never." A closer analysis of newspaper reading showed that in their reading the students were chiefly "interested in what they knew", namely, local news and sports reports; for most secondary school students, political articles took second place behind local news or sports reports, and for most of the vocational students they took only third place behind local news and sports reports. Accordingly, even among regular newspaper readers, only 34 to 35% admitted that they followed political events with interest; the majority refrained from answering this question.[19]

Mansurov's research results indicate that a certain detachment with respect to the political sections and a certain indifference to ideological-political questions—for example, in relation to religion—are widespread among Soviet youth. These findings are confirmed by numerous observations indicating that many upper-grade school essays are distinguished by "poverty and dryness from an ideological-political point of view" (Antipin 1969), and that a large number of students neglect to study social science subjects. A large number of students, chiefly those studying the natural sciences, seem to "possess great knowledge in their special field . . . but on questions of world view or, more precisely, on their awareness as citizens, they are completely helpless" (Rumjancev 1967).

At the 1967 symposium on "Youth and Socialism" in Moscow, the sociologist V. G. Mordkovič reported on a representative survey of 10,228 young people in the areas of Sverdlovsk, Čeljabinsk and Kurgan. The survey was devoted to an analysis of the sociopolitical activity of the younger generation. According to Mordkovič, the survey data on the fulfillment of societal assignments indicate that, on an average, 47% of the young people take part in "societal work"; among them, members of the Komsomol predominate (to which about half of the upper-grade students belong). Komsomol members are two and a half times more active than nonmembers.[20] This means that the active young people are largely recruited from the organized youth, while those who are not under the influence of Komsomol, but mainly under the influence of the family and of informal groups, engage in only minimal sociopolitical activity. Since the average value of the activity of all age groups, according to Mordkovič, amounts to 52.3%, it follows that on the whole young people are less sociopolitically involved than adults. The activity of working youth between the ages of 15 and 18 seems to be especially weak: "The participation of adolescents of this age in societal activity hardly exceeds a third [of the participation] in the best collectives" (Mordkovič 1968, p. 28).

Other survey results give the impression that students of the same age group demonstrate higher indices of sociopolitical activity than young workers: the study, by a Leningrad sociologist, of 1500 upper-grade students showed that 63% engaged in societal work.[21] Meanwhile, the fact that "every third person is not satisfied with his participation" makes it clear that the high indices are explained chiefly by the fact that the school organizes a system of sociopolitical activities that are very difficult to avoid, especially since they are more or less obligatory. Just as with adults, one cannot come to any conclusion about a young person's interest in sociopolitical activity based on his or her actual activity in this field. The data cited about secondary students are confirmed by data on the young scientific generation, chiefly in the natural sciences, in Soviet universities. According to an inquiry at the Obninsk Institute for Physical Sciences, only 14% of the young scientists working there fulfill the societal and political directives of the Party organization with a certain degree of enthusiasm. In contrast, according to their own admission, 76.3% do this only because they are obliged to do so; they find no moral satisfaction or use for themselves in it.[22]

The research results cited underscore the point that could be made in connection with the analysis of young workers' attitudes toward work and their initiative: only a considerable minority of young people take an active and voluntary part in the life of the collective—the factory, the school, the university, etc.—and of society. In comparison with their parents' generation, the distance they maintain with respect to societal life and their sociopolitical passivity seem on the whole to be increasing among younger people. The influence of the Komsomol which, next to the Party, is responsible for organizing sociopolitical activities, seems to be weakening. The crisis of ideological-political education work among youth is at the same time a crisis of the Komsomol, and evidently rests, above all, upon the fact that, for young people, one's private life and individual interests are increasingly becoming the center of their thoughts. However, social institutions and organizations persist in their collectivist claims upon the individual, often persisting in dogmatic and formalistic bureaucratic methods in assigning societal tasks and duties, methods which turn the youth off. Mordkovič feels that the main deficiency in the winning over of young people for societal work lies "in the failure to consider their interests, which are determined, above all, by their specific age" (Mordkovič 1968, p. 28).

In fact, young people are increasingly making their societal commitment dependent upon whether or not it furthers their individual interests and considers their needs. Sociopolitical activities are undertaken not so much "for the sake of society," but only if they are interesting, if they afford relaxation or the development of individual abilities, if they are connected with earning money, etc. A characteristic example of one such individualistic motivation of societal activity is found in the students' answers to Mansurov's survey question, which asked how the young people would feel about going to an economically important frontier construction site for three years. Almost half of the secondary school students and a third of the vocational students questioned made their participation dependent upon whether it is "interesting to work there"; about 15% of the secondary school students and about 8% of the vocational students related their answer to whether one "could work there in a chosen field"; about 6% of the secondary school students and about 20% of the vocational students said it depended on whether "one could earn well" there; and about 10% of the secondary school students and 1 to 2% of the vocational students rejected participation altogether. Only about 19% of the secondary school students and about 15% of the vocational students wanted to go to the youth construction site because of a collectivist motive: "it is necessary for society."[23]

Mordkovič undoubtedly strikes at the core of the attitude that is characteristic of most young people toward sociopolitical activity when, in answer to the same question of motivation, he points out that "a particularly strong personal incentive toward increasing the societal activity of young people" is "the aid which the Komsomol organization extends to them in the realization of their life plans" (Mordkovič 1968, p. 34). Their life plans, however, are so strongly individualistically oriented that a youth organization which is not conceived of as a youth-interest group but as an interest group of the Party and of the state can hardly support them.

In the survey of 1,698 young people concerning their most important life plans for the near future, the Leningrad sociologist V. T. Lisovskij received the following answers most frequently: "to receive a higher education"—1,019; "to have an interesting job"—999; "to spend time in other countries"—952; "to achieve material prosperity"—940; "to find good housing and living conditions" —928; "to improve one's career qualifications"—750; "to find one's love"—743; "to raise children to be good human beings"—727; "to find true friends"—709; "to marry"—558; "to get an automobile"—545; "to finish secondary school"— 427; "to go to one of the new construction sites"—344; "other plans"—96.[24] Many things speak for the fact that young people make their Komsomol membership and activity dependent upon whether they find support for the realization of at least a few of the above-mentioned life plans. Such plans, except for the plan "to go to one of the new construction sites," express solely individual interests. To the question, "If you need the help of the Komsomol organization, exactly why do you need it?" 21.8% of the young people in Lisovskij's survey group said they wanted help in getting an apartment; 15.7%, help in enhancing their career qualifications or a promotion; 14.4%, help in the "struggle against bureaucracy"; 14.4%, help in their free-time activities; 12.9%, help in improving their sports work; 12%, help in "admission to the university"; and 6.3%, help "in other respects."[25] It is certainly not surprising that the question, "Has your Komsomol organization helped you in the realization of your life plans?" was clearly denied by 70.6% of the young people; 7.9% replied "yes", 11.9% said "very seldom," and 9.6% refrained from answering. The fact that most adolescents find no support for their individual interests and life plans in the Komsomol leads to weakening the sociopolitical activity in the younger generation. A solution to this crisis seems to be possible only if the work of the Komsomol is more directly aimed at the interests and values of the personality, for this will create personal incentives toward cooperation among young people. Only a restoration could probably be an alternative to this reform, which would have to lead to the strengthening of indoctrination, to the restriction of the family's educational functions, and to the establishment of mechanisms to force the activation of people for purely obligatory service to society.

One can further state that "the development of the sciences has made the thinking of youth more pragmatic and strengthened the endeavor toward independent acquisition of information" (Simposium 1967, p. 155). This fact leads to a diminishing of "ideological collectivism" and to the spreading of a certain detachment, or even skepticism, with respect to ideological propaganda among the younger generation. With growing age and a rising educational level, young people increasingly tend toward the independent formation of opinions, and the exclusive sanction of the Party's and the Komsomol's interpretation of ideological-political questions is diminished.

STATE GOALS AND FAMILY PRACTICES— CONCLUDING PERSPECTIVES

Work education and ideological-political instruction have shown that Soviet parents transmit few specific values of communist ethics and ideology to the younger generation. The question arises as to whether there are any characteristic features of actual education in the Soviet family which are connected with the social structure and the social value system and which distinguish Soviet family education from that of other societies. Do the conceptions of Soviet parents regarding the desirable personality traits and capabilities of their children differ from those of German or American parents? Do the educational practices of Soviet parents indicate a specific pedagogical awareness or a specific internal family structure, a particular relation between parents and children?

These questions are difficult to answer mainly because there is a lack of representative research material in the USSR about parental educational goals and practices. In addition to Titarenko's frequently cited dissertation (1967), which is limited to an analysis of the goals and forms of moral education in the Soviet family, there is evidently only one single empirical study concerning this topic. This study, undertaken in 1965, covered 250 families in the city of Voronež, but its information value is meager because the author did not take into consideration the educational level, the occupational and social strata membership of the parents involved, the age and sex of the children, and other factors which can influence parental attitudes toward goals and their educational practices. It is also deficient in other respects: only the primary eduational goal and the single preferred means toward its attainment mentioned by parents were given in each case. Nevertheless, despite serious methodological weaknesses, the study must be utilized because it can provide certain information about the actual shape of present-day Soviet family education.

Kaliničenko (1966, pp. 198-199) presented a summary of the results of the parental survey on the goals and means of family education. (See Table 1.)

Table 1

How Parents Imagine Their Children as Adults	No. of Answers	The Most Effective Means of Education in the Parents' Opinion	No. of Answers
1. Ethical Honest Industrious	78	Persuasion	27
		Personal example	24
		Praise	11
		Strict demands	8
		Deprivation of entertainment	5
		Physical punishment	3
2. Well-rounded development Cultured	12	Persuasion and personal example	8
		Recognition for good behavior	2
		Don't know	2
3. Socially useful	29	Trust	3
		Reward	6
		Stand in the corner	2
		Deprivation of entertainment	5
		Suggestion	10
		Strict demands	3
4. Acquire a higher education	44	Reproof and explanation	8
		Persuasion	5
		Physical punishment	5
		Punishment through work	2
		Stand in the corner	14
		Coercion	7
		Don't know	3
5. Naming a definite occupation (physician, engineer, teacher, construction worker, musician, journalist, etc.)	39	Persuasion	4
		Suggestion	12
		Personal example	2
		Reward	6
		Physical punishment	3
		No supper	1
		Not allowed to go out	11

Table 1 (continued)

How Parents Imagine Their Children as Adults	No. of Answers	The Most Effective Means of Education in the Parents' Opinion	No. of Answers
6. Skilled worker with musical education	1	Recognition and personal example	1
7. Good	47	Persuasion	4
		Personal example	1
		Stand in the corner	13
		Deprivation of entertainment	8
		Strict demands	2
		Praise and punishment	3
		Physical punishment	8
		Don't know/no answer	5
Total	250		250

The answers to the question concerning educational goals are striking, for only a small minority of parents named goals which can be considered to be typical components of the communist educational ideal: 17% of the parents questioned want their children to be, above all, "well-rounded, cultured" people (12 answers) or people who are "useful to society" (29 answers). Marx and Lenin considered "well-rounded personality development" as one of the important goals of communism, a prerequisite for easing both the capitalist rigid division of labor through adaptability to other functions and the "individual" freedom found in capitalism by means of society-oriented freedom under communism. According to a more recent official definition, it is now looked upon as the "development of all one's creative abilities and talents, the development of the person as a worker, as a producer of material and intellectual goods, as a socially active person, as a moral and cultured personality, as the bearer of lofty, ethical and esthetic values" (*The Foundations* 1964, p. 47). The ideal of the individual's "usefulness" for society is not far removed from the ideal of "well-rounded personality development" and is dealt with in different forms in the Ethical Code of the Builder of Communism.[26] The reference to these two ideals of the communist personality infers a strong ideological, society-oriented awareness, at least a strong verbal identification of the parents concerned with the essential and specific goals of communist education.

Most of the parents' answers, however, have to do with general moral virtues which regulate human coexistence in all civilized societies. Exactly 50% of those questioned see the goal of their educational activity in rearing their children to be "ethical, honest, industrious" (78 answers) or "good" (47 answers) people. Apart from "love of work," a virtue whose relative priority within this group of answers is impossible to determine, the moral qualities mentioned lack all reference to specific values of the "communist ethic." "Social" virtues, such as "cooperation," "responsibility," and "collectivism," as well as the ideological values prominent in the Moral Code of the Builder of Communism are missing in the parents' conception of goals. In the main, the group of parents who want to raise their children to be "good" people remains distant from the specific values of "communist ethics"; this vaguely defined category can denote obedience, sociability, good behavior, and many other things. According to Kalinichenko, parents who follow this educational goal can be counted among the group of "pedagogically passive" parents; they "themselves cannot say what actual meaning they attribute to this abstract idea [of "goodness"]. Such parents are most frequently socially neutral: their philosophy of life consists in escaping from difficult life situations and avoiding responsibility for what happens around them" (Kalinichenko 1966, p. 202).

Titarenko's 1967 study involving 647 families confirmed the fact that the value conceptions of most Soviet parents lack a direct reference to the specific social value system. In polling parents about their goals in the moral education of their children, he learned that in most cases family education was "directed to simple norms of morality." Titarenko states that in this respect family education "does not cover the whole area of societal demands," but he feels that it does strike at the essence of these demands and therefore fulfills the tasks of communist education (Titarenko 1967, p. 17). This view is valid only if parents do not raise their children in a manner which contradicts the social value system; in every case, an emphasis on several individual virtues and the neglect of social virtues and ideological values in family education can only contribute to the individual's more or less passive adjustment to society, which does not correspond to the communist ideal of an "organic unity of the individual and the social" (Charchev).

The second largest group of parental responses about the goals of family education applies to their children's education and careers: 33% of those parents questioned felt the most important goal of education was that their children "acquire a higher education" (44 answers) or a definite occupation (40 answers). With a single exception every answer referred to occupations involving intellectual work which, in general, presupposes a higher education. Since formal education, vocational training, and vocational guidance belong more to the area of public education than to that of family education, it must seem strange that many parents consider their children's future occupation and educational standard to be a high-priority educational goal. This could also indicate a social orientation on the part of the parents, insofar as the school supports this goal by controlling the learning activity of children and society supports it by training urgently needed specialists. Meanwhile, the parents' individual accomplishments and their personal ambitions to assure their children a respectable and well-paid position in society play a substantial role. The overwhelming individualistic attitude of both parents and adolescents toward work and a career has already been discussed in detail and is especially confirmed by the almost exclusive emphasis by those parents polled upon academic education and academic careers. Such an individualistic attitude contradicts the communist ideal of well-rounded personality development and expresses an aloofness toward physical labor on the part of the parents concerned. These parents hardly bring their children up with a need to work, as is demanded by communist ethics. This is shown by the strongly repressive educational practices they apply—in some cases, even "punishment through work."

Thus it is evident that most parents who are oriented toward individual virtues, as well as those who emphasize their children's education and career, pursue individual interests and socially neutral values. This predominant pattern of parental attitudes instills primarily a passive social adjustment by young people, an adaptation that focuses on personal success and prosperity but not on the needs of communist society.[27] A large number of the Soviet families studied until now seem to be distinguished, therefore, by marked small-group selfishness. It remains to be shown, primarily through the educational practices of Soviet parents, that cooperative and altruistic behavior seems to be less rewarded and encouraged within the small family group than subordination and adjustment to parental authority, and that individual endeavors for happiness are encouraged as being opposed to the demands of society.

In drawing conclusions about cultural traditions and social structures from the spread of certain value standards among the people, one could assume that the overwhelming preference of Soviet parents for individual virtues and interests is characteristic of a modern achieving society with authoritarian traditions and structures, in which conformity, adjustment, sense of duty, and obedience count more than initiative, self-reliance, creative thinking, and self-confidence. In this connection it is interesting to point out that the educational goals of Soviet parents differ little from those of German parents, but substantially from those of Americans. As the comparative data by F. Wesley, Charles Karr, and other authors about German and American family education show, German parents primarily emphasize "obedience," "honesty," and "order." In this they resemble that large group of Soviet parents who want "honest," "ethical," and "industrious" children. German parents also place great value on their children's "good learning," and in this respect resemble that large group of Soviet parents who desire, above all, an academic education and academic occupations for their children.

In contrast, according to the survey data available, in the area of moral education American parents emphasize not so much the private but the social virtues: "sociability," "respect for others," and "considerate behavior." In the area of intellectual education, however, American parents place more stress on the formal attainment of education and less on the development of creative abilities, "individuality and self-reliance" and "curiosity and a thirst for knowledge."[28]

It is beyond the scope of this study to set up a fundamental and far-reaching comparison between Soviet, German, and American family education. However, there is no doubt that the traditions of a paternalistic system with a strong, centralized state authority, which exist in the Soviet Union and which since 1945 are gradually being removed in Germany, stamp the image of the personality and of the "citizen of the state" and define the goal conceptions in family education differently than do the traditions of a "pioneer" society like the USA, with its democratic structures and relatively weak central state government. Our analysis of the educational practices of Soviet parents reveals these problems even more clearly.

When asked about the educational means they preferred, it is striking how few of the parents surveyed by Kaliničenko referred to verbal and nonverbal methods of approval: only 10% of the parents questioned consider "trust" (3 answers), "reward" (6 answers), "recognition" (3 answers), or "praise" (13 answers) as the most effective means of education. These educational practices, which point to loving parental concern about the child's or adolescent's personality, carry a certain weight only among those parents who want to raise their children to be "honest," "ethical," "industrious," or "socially useful."

The number of those parents who rely upon the functional effect of their own behavior on their child is also small: 12% (31 answers) of those interviewed named "personal example" in this sense as the most important means of education. These parents pursue educational goals that are similar to those of the parents in the above-named group; they place more value on self-control than on regulating their children's behavior. Parents who consider the imitation of parental behavior and the child's internalizing of such behavior norms as one of the most important mechanisms of family education demonstrate a mature pedagogical awareness.

Soviet parents frequently apply verbal means of education. Aside from the already-listed forms of supporting the child through praise and recognition, the most popular verbal means of education serve to implement the parents' will or idea with respect to the child. In this sense about 29% (44 answers) of those questioned consider "persuasion," "suggestion" (22 answers), or "reproof and explanation" (8 answers) as the most effective educational means. "Persuasion" is the most frequently named single means of education in Kaliničenko's survey group, and it is especially popular among those families who want their children to be "honest, ethical, industrious" and "well-rounded, cultured" people. The "persuasion" approach in education presupposes a certain trust in the child's or adolescent's understanding, and speaks for a nonauthoritarian relationship between the two generations or for an emphasis of ethical above personal authority. In contrast, the verbal means of "suggestion" easily bears an authoritarian character, and it is probably no coincidence that this procedure has great weight mainly among those ambitious parents who see the most important goal of education as the guaranteeing of an academic occupation for their children.

By far the largest group apply strictly demanding, repressive, and punitive means of education: on the whole, 39% of the parents questioned consider "strict demands" (13 answers), "coercion" (7 answers), making the child stand in the corner (29 answers), various prohibitions as punishment for bad behavior (30 answers), or physical punishments (19 answers) as the most eft:ctive means. Such educational practices are especially prevalent among parents who want to have "good" children. One can conclude that, for the parents concerned, this "virtue" means primarily subordination, obedience, good behavior, etc. Achievement-oriented families also place great weight upon repressive and punitive educational practices.

Kalinicenko's data on the educational practices of Soviet parents show that the choice of educational means depends greatly, although not without exception, upon the choice of educational goals. While parents, who are oriented toward definite moral personality qualities—"honesty," "decency," "love of work," and "well-rounded development"—often apply nonauthoritarian educational means, repressive authoritarian practices are most common among those who are oriented toward the vague conformist virtue of "goodness" or individual achievement and occupational status. Kalinicenko's survey results unfortunately do not allow a correlation of the different educational goals and educational practices with the strata membership of the parents' groups concerned; such a correlation would undoubtedly facilitate an analysis of the data. As a generalization one can say that, on the whole, the families surveyed place greater weight on repressive authoritarian educational practices. If one counts persuasion among the authoritarian forms of influence, 122 of the 250 parents questioned incline toward repressive authoritarian educational practices, while 108 prefer nonauthoritarian practices and 10 were undecided.

The work overload and nervous strain of parents (especially of working mothers), the limited time available for parent-child interaction, cramped living conditions, and low educational levels have already been mentioned as possible causes of the growing popularity of authoritarian educational practices among Soviet families. An authoritarian relationship between husband and wife in many families can also be cited as an explanation for such practices in family education. However, as other studies have shown, educational authority over children actually lies primarily with the mother. A further sociological component of authoritarian education must be taken into account here. If one proceeds from the fact that family educational practices are always socio-culturally determined, one must then assume that authoritarian educational practices in a great number of Soviet families have some connection with the authoritarian structures of Soviet society. The pressure toward subordination and adjustment, which exists in Soviet society and in state educational institutions, seems to enter also into family education as an important mechanism.[29] The problem is that authoritarian educational means in a strong family group evidently encourage only a certain group selfishness; such families raise their members as conforming personalities, but not as active citizens of the state. The Soviet psychologist A. G. Kovalëv's statement that authoritarian education produces "a passive, apathetic character type" bears repeating. Such a character type may indeed be characteristic of an authoritarian society, but it in no way corresponds to the ideas of communist ideology regarding the ideal communist personality and builder of communism. Here the discrepancy between ideology and reality raised by many Western critics of the Soviet system is particularly clear. Soviet ideology anticipates a society liberated from exploitation, a "well-rounded" personality, the unity of individual and societal interests; but in social practice one observes a neglect of the values of the personality on the part of society and the spread of authoritarian governmental forms which determine the social climate and contribute to the formation of a passive and apathetic character type.

Authoritarian education can lead not only to suppression of the individual's intellectual and social initiative, but also potentially to conflicts between the young people and their parents and society, which in turn makes their integration into social life more difficult. Kon (1967) and Dunaeva (1968) agree that authoritarian parental educational attitudes are the most important factors burdening the relations between parents and adolescents. Moreover, excessive strictness is one of the most frequent educational mistakes made by the parents of delinquent youngsters, and the disregard of parents (or of the teachers and youth group leaders) for their adolescents' personality can easily lead to the social isolation of the latter. It is chiefly emotional security and confirmation that young people evidently seek in the family and, vice versa, the family seems to lose its particular potential for influencing the growing children exactly when the parents do not deal with every aspect of their children's individual personalities. Kalinicenko characteristically emphasizes the "antipedagogical character" of authoritarian educational practices, and criticizes the fact that a number of parents "consider fundamentally wrong or even obviously detrimental educational means as effective." These means include primarily "severity," "force," "physical punishment," "punishment through work," and "deprivation of supper" (Kalinicenko 1966, p. 200). Kalinicenko and other authors, however, do not derive such educational attitudes from the authoritarian structures of Soviet society; rather, they interpret them as "remnants of the past in the minds of the people" which can be overcome through pedagogical propaganda among the population. On the other hand, if one traces the growth of authoritarian educational practices in the family back to authoritarian societal structures, a change in family education can only be conceived of as a result of a change in the societal structure.

If Soviet society wants to make further economic, social, and scientific progress—above all, if it wants to realize the original ideological postulates of socialism, namely, communism—it needs a type of person who possesses self-reliance, initiative, cooperation, and other social virtues, and this type of person cannot be formed in an atmosphere of coercion. As our discussion on the attitude toward work and sociopolitical activity has shown, the initiative of the younger generation can be encouraged only by eliminating authoritarian structures and giving greater consideration to individual interests and needs and to the values of the personality. This realization is already widespread among Soviet sociologists, pedagogues, economists, and other scientists. However, probably as a result of the Czechoslovakian experiment in "democratic socialism," there are many signs indicating that the current Soviet leadership is more inclined toward restoration than toward reform, since decentralization in the economic field, democratization and liberalization in the political and social area, and the condoning of intellectual pluralism could undermine the Communist Party's power position in the state and in society.

Even with continuing restoration policies, however, one can assume that the self-awareness of the family as a social group will grow stronger and that, with the continued increase in living and educational standards in all population strata, the drive toward personal happiness, prosperity, and cultural diversity will play an ever greater role in the thinking of the Soviet people.

Summary

The description of Soviet family legislation, family policy, and pedagogy, on the one hand, and the analysis of actual family education and the value orientation of the personality on the other, have shown that the relation between the family and communist society is ambivalent. The state has increasingly devoted itself to strengthening the family, which has, in turn, retained decisive functions in the area of education in Soviet society. In fulfilling these functions, however, the family meets the state's demands only to a small degree, while the state strives to place the family (as a "cell" of society) and family education (as a subdivision of the communist educational system) under societal control. In summary, several fundamental problems concerning the relation between the family and society, or between family education and communist societal education, shall be discussed. The success of the Soviet system of social planning and education will be measured for the most part against the attainment of its goals.

The well-rounded, ideologically aware, and collectivistically oriented personality is the ideal communist person. Soviet pedagogy has always supported the view that this personality type develops best under the conditions of the socially controlled education of children and adolescents in collectives arranged according to age groups. Unlike this utopian Marxist-Leninist program, which sought to organize a comprehensive societal education for all children, the Soviet family has remained the first and most important source of education.

In the USSR, as in Western societies, the child's early and crucial socialization phase is determined almost exclusively by the family. Since the child's earliest emotional tie is directed toward one person, the mother, and then to other adult members of the family, and since in most cases he remains an only child, the formation of a "collective ego" cannot take place during the early socialization process. Both the age group and collective education undoubtedly become more significant in Soviet than in Western societies when the child enters school and state-controlled children's and youth organizations, but the children and young people are not incorporated into a comprehensive youth culture. Also, the family and the unorganized and uncontrollable friendship ties among children of the same age group remain temporarily dominant when compared to the school class and the age group in youth organizations.

In the USSR, more than in other societies, the parents themselves appear as representatives or as an extended arm of society, since both teachers and an organized "public" check their educational activity. Nevertheless, family life—partly due to the spreading of the small family pattern—is characterized by great intimacy and a certain isolation vis-à-vis society.

On the whole, the child's personality development is determined more by individual identification with his parents—in certain cases also by conflicts with them—than by his identification with the organized age group or the youth collective. In cases where parents neglect their children or, through alcoholism, marriage discord, or some other factor deprive them of the feeling of security, of being "at home" and being loved, children lack the prerequisites for normal personality development and may become neurotic or delinquent. This should not be the case with a primarily collective education. Identity and self-confidence of the personality depend less upon the collective than upon individual, emotionally meaningful family relations, and, as their life plans indicate, young Soviet citizens seek fulfillment and happiness less in the collective than in their own families, where they feel most comfortable.

Measured against its own claim, Soviet pedagogy has not yet managed to develop a new collectivistically oriented personality type, probably because it still depends on the socialization of the next generation within the primary family.

The conclusion that the communist educational system could reach its goals only through complete elimination of the family as a medium of socialization is rather radical, but the fact remains that a type of family different from the present one would have been—or still would be—needed to make the family a subdivision of societal collective education. Communism has in fact set out with the goal of creating a new type of family. This new family should be characterized, among other things, by the elimination of economic dependency between family members, the abolition of private property together with the selfish drives of the individual and the family, the liberation of the woman from household and educational duties, and the individual's strong tie to society brought about by the identity of his individual interests with those of society. Whether these expectations have been fulfilled or not simultaneously touches upon the problem of social change.

Compared to that of the Russian family, the structure of the Soviet family has undergone decided changes in the course of industrialization and agricultural collectivization. The family has lost its significance as a production unit, has abandoned its patriarchal structure to a great degree, and, partly due to the integration of women into the societal work process, has increasingly become based on love marriages and has increasingly taken on the character of an urban small family made up of two generations.

All these changes in the family, which are characteristic not only of Soviet society but of all modern industrial societies, have led to a strengthening of the small-group mentality of the family and only superficially detracted from its economic and educational functions. There still exists a strong dependency, emotional and economic, between husband and wife, between parents and children. With most women in full-time employment, the economic dependency between husband and wife is now no longer one-sided, but mutual. This has hardly diminished such dependency, since in general only the joint family earnings can guarantee minimum subsistence needs. With respect to children, the family has retained its eductional and economic functions. The child is not only indebted to his parents for life and emotional security, but also for material livelihood, and he generally remains financially dependent upon his parents until he begins a job of his own. Children inherit from their parents not only possessions—although never in such large measure as children of property owners or private businessmen—but they also inherit their parents' social status in a strongly differentiated society. For these reasons, parents see the goal of their employment not perhaps in the increase of social prosperity or in their contribution to the construction of communism, but in securing the highest possible standard of living for themselves and their children and in guaranteeing a good position for their children in society. The overwhelming individualistic attitudes held by many adults and young people in the Soviet Union with respect to occupation, work, and sociopolitical involvement seem to have their emotional and economic foundations in the continued existence of the old family group. Nationalization of the means of production and ideological education in societal institutions have managed to change little in the passing on of these attitudes.

Through fulfillment of its educational and economic functions, the family seems to lay the foundation for the individual's close tie to his parents and family, as well as to individualistic-familial values which tend to weaken the tie to the collective and to collectivist values. Moreover, it is noteworthy that today's Soviet parents—adults born after the October Revolution and reared by Soviet families and communist educational institutions—pursue educational goals that seem more suited for a capitalist, individual-oriented society than for future "builders of communism."[1]

The obvious inference that the planned social change of Soviet society has had only slight effect upon the family can also be turned around: the planned change itself, primarily the planned change in human mentality, has been held up by the tendency of a strong family unit, protected by the state and confirmed in its economic and educational functions, to go its own way. One can argue that, in order to change the mentality of people, their emotional, social, and economic needs, as provided for in Marxist-Leninist ideology, a greater restriction of the family's economic and educational role in the lives of adults and children and a stronger incorporation of the younger generation into collective educational institutions from early childhood on would be needed in order to transmit a communist social order supported by ideologically aware and politically active people.

Until now, however, such a concept has been realized only in relatively small communes, such as the Israeli kibbutz. The success of the collectivist, social, and educational system in the kibbutz is based, among other things, on the fact that, in it, all economic functions are relegated to the collective (there is no private household, no paid work, etc.), that children are educated from early childhood in separate age groups, and that adults are voluntary members of this microsociety and identify with its value system.[2]

On the other hand, no large and complex society has yet succeeded in substantially taking over the economic and educational functions of the family, and it remains questionable whether this will ever be possible. The Soviet Union, too, can establish a predominantly extrafamilial collective education for children which does no harm to the normal psychosocial development of their personalities only if small and well-led groups assume the role of the family. A large state can hardly provide for the organization of such groups, and in any case it would not prove feasible. Finally, the voluntary nature of its members and the general identification of people with its value system are lacking in Soviet society, so that a consequentially collectivist social and educational system could be realized only under force.

The Soviet state has ideologically held fast to the Marxist program of socialization of the private household and of education, but in practice it has largely written this program off. Meanwhile, from the standpoint of the anticipated communist social order, the family fits (in a certain sense) Bucharin's characterization of it: a "dreadful bulwark of all the stupidities of the old regime" (quoted in Blitsten 1963, p. 223), an institution which stubbornly passes on individual emotions, needs, and values, and enables the individual to adjust to society while at the same time remaining relatively detached from it.

The family's basic "dysfunctionality" with respect to society, particularly a collectivist society, illustrates the fact that the relation between the Soviet state and the family has always been ambivalent. Of course, no one today still believes that the family can be dispensed with in the foreseeable future, along with fulfillment of its economic and educational functions. On the contrary, the educational importance of the family is being more and more strongly emphasized. In many respects ideology has to adapt to realities and to a certain degree must make allowances for the individual value orientation of the people—for example, for material interest in employment. Party leaders, and primarily Khrushchev, have repeatedly asserted that communism works toward strengthening the family, not its weakening. At the same time, however, it must be remembered that the family has proven to be an unreliable partner of state institutions in educating children toward the specific values of communist society, and measures are being strengthened to improve primarily the ideological-political education which is neglected in the family. The Khrushchev plan of making boarding schools the models of communist education must now be seen as outdated, and the propagation of communal living for adults, with full-time state institutions for the education of the young—as suggested by the "old-guard" Academician S. G. Strumilin—must be considered utopian. Other forms of an ambivalent relation between state and family must now be expected, that is, social controls over the family, primarily over the educational activity of the parents, and the sharpening of sanctions against deviant behavior by individuals. As long as its educational function cannot be taken away from the family to a greater degree than it has until now, and be transferred to state institutions, societal control over family education will represent an important lever for the success of the collectivist goals of Soviet pedagogy. As the available data about adolescent value orientation attest, this type of control leads to a growing tendency to retreat into one's private life, to increased alienation by the individual and the family vis-à-vis society. And it is this very passive resistance against the state's repressive-authoritarian influences which tends today to become the most dangerous opponent of the authoritarian communist regime. Obviously, only in the case of a sociopolitical change in the direction of a decentralized, self-governmental, democratic, and humanistic model of socialism could one imagine a lasting solution to this fundamental conflict between the family and the state in Soviet society. Whether such a change will occur remains to be seen.

Notes

CHAPTER 1

1. In addition, Marx and Engels themselves did not completely agree in their critical examination of marriage. Thilo Ramm (1957, pp. 97ff.) correctly pointed out that, unlike Engels, Marx favored a program which would make divorce more difficult.
2. See note 1.
3. All of the data cited here are based upon the 1926 or 1939 census; see Dodge 1966, pp. 44ff., 141.
4. See note 3.
5. Fisher 1959, p. 68.
6. See the letters from Lenin to I. Armand and the memoirs of C. Zetkin. Quoted in Schlesinger 1949, pp. 25ff., 75ff.
7. See p. 119.
8. Schlesinger 1949, pp. 37ff.
9. Partially reprinted in Schlesinger 1949, pp. 154ff.
10. Anweiler 1964, p. 228.
11. Reprinted in Schlesinger 1949, p. 44.
12. *Narodnoe chozjajstvo SSSR v 1968 godu,* p. 36.
13. Reprinted in Schlesinger 1949, pp. 269ff.
14. Hazard 1953, pp. 265-266.
15. Hazard 1953, pp. 258-259.
16. "Otvetstvennost' " 1967, p. 7; also below, pp. 66-72.
17. Reprinted in Schlesinger 1949, pp. 367ff.
18. For the judicial aspect, see Bahro 1966.
19. *Isvestija,* June 20, 1968.
20. During the Khrushchev era, the press reported from time to time about cases where parents were deprived of their parental rights on the grounds, among others, of having influenced their children in religious matters. For example, I. Lukin reported in the July 25th, 1962, issue of *Pravda* about a mother who joined a Baptist sect, taught her children prayers, and kept them back from activities of the Pioneer organization. The motivation for the withdrawal of parental rights in this case was explained by saying that the mother neglected her children. In this connection, H. K. Geiger was probably correct in stating that the Soviet state's interference in the private life or in family education "is probably invoked more frequently for abuse and lack of support than for giving religious instruction" (Geiger 1968, p. 266).
21. See (among others) Ruettenauer 1965, pp. 127ff.

22. *Works IV,* pp. 367ff.
23. Referred to in Medynskij and Petruchin 1955, p. 7.
24. "Obščestvo po rasprostraneniju političeskich i naučnych znanij"; renamed "Obščestvo Znanie" in the 1960s.
25. Referred to in *Istorija pedagogiki* 1961, p. 259.
26. See pp. 27 and 142.
27. See pp. 55-56.
28. See pp. 82-83.
29. See p. 120.
30. *Ličnost' pri socializme* 1968.
31. Suchomlinskij 1967.
32. See (among others) Lichačev 1967.
33. See Levšin's contribution to the discussion in *Literaturnaja gazeta,* Nr. 25, May 25, 1967.
34. Kostjaškin 1968.

CHAPTER 2

1. Ahlberg gives a detailed overview of this (1964).
2. Reprinted in Anweiler and Meyer 1961, pp. 227ff.
3. See pp. 22-23
4. Lembert 1963, especially the section "Experimentelle Forschung im Dienste der Schulreform," pp. 274-282.
5. See the detailed report "Socializm i sem'ja" 1967.
6. Fischer's *World Almanac 1967,* p. 194.
7. In 1967, the rural population still formed 45% of the total population of the Soviet Union, and 22.63% of the working population was employed in agriculture; cf. *Narodnoe chozjajstvo SSSR v 1968 godu,* pp. 10-11, 35. In contrast, as early as the beginning of the 1960s still only 16% of the working population in West Germany and only 9% of the working population in the United States were employed in agriculture; see Wagenlehner 1965, p. 17.
8. *SSSR v cifrach* 1968, p. 12.
9. Charčev 1964, p. 215.
10. *Women in the USSR 1965-1966.*
11. Kuznecova 1968.
12. Lagutin 1967, p. 58.
13. See p. 53.
14. Kuznecova 1968.
15. See pp. 96-97.
16. Based upon the author's personal information during a research trip to the Soviet Union in the early part of 1968.
17. Charčev 1964, pp. 247-248.
18. Lagutin 1967, p. 56.

19. Kuznecova 1968.
20. Sagimbaeva 1969.
21. Charčev 1964, pp. 252-253 and Geiger 1968, pp. 177ff.
22. See also the lengthy debate on this subject in *Literaturnaja gazeta*, especially the article by the economist V. Perevedentsev in the November 20, 1968 issue, in which he supports a general freeing of women with small children from employment and favors state aid for their contribution in the household and educational work. Perevedentsev feels that such an investment is economically more profitable and pedagogically as well as population-policy-wise more effective than the expansion of children's institutions.
23. Charčev 1964, p. 231.
24. In West Germany in 1961 the proportion of three generation families among all households amounted to 9.14%; see Wurzbacher 1968, p. 117.
25. Charčev 1964, p. 180.
26. See p. 53.
27. Charčev 1964, pp. 232-233.
28. According to the 1897 census, 73.7% of the total population and 86.3% of the female population between the ages of 9 and 49 were illiterate. In 1913 the proportion of illiterates in the total population was still estimated at about 66%; by 1959 only 1.3% of the total population and 1.9% of the female population between the ages of 9 and 49 were so designated. See De Witt 1961, p. 72.
29. *Narodnoe chozjajstvo SSSR v 1961 godu*, p. 24.
30. *Strana Sovetov* 1967, p. 237.
31. *Vestnik statistiki* 1968, quoted in *Ost-Probleme* 1968, pp. 362-363.
32. Quoted in Hindus 1963, p. 287.
33. Vestnik statistiki 1968. Quoted in *Ost-Probleme* 1968, p. 362.
34. Ibid.
35. Kuznecova 1968.
36. Quoted in Zemcov 1965, p. 63.
37. Zemcov 1965, p. 63.
38. Studies in Hungary and Poland have resulted in similar conclusions. See Grušin 1967, p. 73, and Golod 1967.
39. See pp. 44-45.
40. The mother's overriding importance in education is also reflected in the minds of young people; see p. 85.
41. Charčev 1964, pp. 256-257.
42. Slesarev and Jankova 1967.
43. Golod reports about corresponding data from Poland (1967).
44. Since 1936, a strongly tabooed repressive sexual morality has prevailed in the Soviet Union; about the problem of sex education in the Soviet Union, see Harmsen 1967. The tabooing of sexuality and the persistence in sanctioning all sexual relations can be interpreted as instruments for

controlling and disciplining people. Indeed, the actual sexual behavior of Soviet youth does not seem to correspond to the social norms; premarital sex is equally as widespread as in Western societies (Kon 1966). Among other things, the fact that, in the past few years, the pedagogical taboo of sex education has been broken and been given increasing attention may be connected with the above fact as well as with the constant increase of divorce rates (see below). See Baskina 1968, Charčev 1966 a,b and 1968, Kon 1966, Kostjaškin 1964 and 1968.

45. *Narodnoe chozjajstvo SSSR v 1961 godu,* p. 204.
46. *Narodnoe chozjajstvo SSSR v 1965 godu,* p. 120.
47. *Narodnoe chozjajstvo SSSR v 1968 godu,* pp. 42-43.
48. This study by V. T. Lisovskij and S. Pelevinyj was published in *Nedelja* (The Week), 1966, Nr. 27. Several results are quoted in Laptenok 1967, pp. 121, 157, 167 and in *Sputnik* 1968, Nr. 4, pp. 114-115.
49. Charčev 1965.
50. See note 48.
51. Beljavskij 1967.
52. See p. 109.
53. *Na blago* 1961.
54. Charčev 1964, pp. 162ff.
55. Beljavskij 1967.
56. See p. 89.

CHAPTER 3

1. See pp. 18-20.
2. *Narodnoe obrazovanie v SSSR* 1967, p. 39.
3. "Dlja samych malen'kich" 1967.
4. *Ženščiny i deti* 1961, pp. 157-158.
5. Maslov 1965, p. 22.
6. *Ženščiny i deti* 1961, pp. 157-158.
7. *Narodnoe obrazovanie v SSSR* 1967, pp. 39-40.
8. Solov'ëv 1962, p. 132.
9. The reference is found in Charčev 1964, p. 291.
10. The reference is found in Šeremet'eva 1968.
11. See pp. 48-49 and 76-80.
12. See pp. 59-64.
13. See p. 61.
14. See p. 65.
15. L. Liegle, *Familie und Kollektiv im Kibbutz. Eine Studie ueber die erzieherischen Funktionen der Familie in einem kollektiven Erziehungssystem* (Weinheim: Beltz, 1971).
16. See p. 63.
17. See p. 48.

18. In the early Soviet period there were a number of representatives and propagandists among the Soviet and especially among the Ukrainian pedagogues and educational planners who were convinced about a full-time "societal education" in children's homes; see pp. 18-19 and Anweiler 1964, pp. 150ff, 173ff. However, even during the early Soviet period negative experiences with the children's homes arose which were similar to those Kotovščika and Charčev described.
19. See pp. 48-50.
20. See p. 40.
21. See the letter from a reader in *Komsomol'skaja pravda,* of December 11, 1968, advocating the opposite position.
22. *Narodnoe obrazovanie v SSSR* 1967, pp. 39ff.
23. *Spravočnik* 1967, p. 63.
24. "Edinaja sistema vospitanija" 1959.
25. *Spravočnik* 1963, p. 63.
26. Reprinted in Markova 1964, pp. 77ff.
27. See pp. 70-71.
28. Markova 1964, p. 31ff.
29. See pp. 71-72.
30. Markova 1964, p. 62, 77.
31. Markova 1964, p. 78.
32. "Učitel' i roditeli" 1963, p. 12.
33. See p. 47.
34. See Chapter 5.
35. "Programma-minimum" 1968.
36. See (among others) Mace 1963, pp. 246ff.
37. Markova 1964, pp. 11ff.
38. Krupskaja 1962 and Makarenko, *Works,* IV, pp. 13ff. pp. 367ff; also Markova 1964, pp. 11ff.
39. See (among others) Markova 1956b, pp. 30ff.
40. See (among others) Markova 1956a.
41. See (among others) *O vospitanii doškol'nikov* 1963, pp. 40ff.
42. Markova 1964, p. 23; and Radina 1955.
43. See pp. 23-25.
44. *O vospitanii doškol'nikov* 1963, pp. 22-23.
45. *O vospitanii doškol'nikov* 1963, pp. 76ff.
46. Sevčenko 1966, pp. 58-59.
47. Sevčenko 1966, pp. 65, 58.
48. Kondratova 1966, pp. 48-49.

CHAPTER 4

1. A study by Bernhard Schiff, entitled *Die Reform der Grundschule in der USSR,* undertaken in connection with the same research project which also

supported this study, discusses questions of psychosocial development and school education as well as the training of elementary school children. This study appears as part of the series of educational publications put out by the Osteuropa-Institut, Free University of Berlin (Volume 6).

2. For a discussion of the leisure time problem and the research being done in this connection in the Soviet Union, see Mitter 1966.
3. Davydov and Pelipenko 1967.
4. Zdorovskij and Orlov 1966, p. 72.
5. See Kondratova's research data (1968) mentioned above, p. 80.
6. See pp. 113-114.
7. See pp. 87-91 and 114-115.
8. See pp. 47-48, and Mansurov and Lunkov 1967, p. 93.
9. Zajcev 1965, p. 90.
10. Dunaeva 1968, p. 277.
11. Dunaeva 1968, p. 286.
12. Anweiler 1964, pp. 173ff, 372-373.
13. Anweiler and Meyer 1961, p. 288.
14. *Učitel'skaja gazeta* of March 15, 1960.
15. Kostjaškin 1967, pp. 54-55.
16. The magazine Vospitanie skol'nikov (Education of Pupils) which replaced *Skola-internat,* handles a wide range of questions about school education without focusing on the boarding school as the prototype.
17. Lindner 1966, p. 349, also below, p. 101.
18. Prokof'ev 1968, p. 16. Dormitories for out-of-town students were built for such central schools; this type of boarding school is called "škol'nye internaty" (dormitory school) or "internaty pri škole" (dormitories at school)—in distinction to "skola-internat" (boarding school).
19. "Škola-internat" 1965, Nr. 5, p. 7.
20. *Učitel'skaja gazeta* of June 4, 1968.
21. Prokof'ev 1968, p. 16.
22. Twenty-third Congress of the Communist Party, p. 419.
23. Anweiler 1964, pp. 107ff.
24. Žurin 1955, pp. 22ff.
25. Reprinted in Žurin 1955, pp. 133ff.
26. Reprinted in *Roditeli i deti* 1961, pp. 416ff.
27. Reprinted in Žurin 1955, pp. 147-148.
28. Gasilov 1968.
29. Žurin 1955, p. 122.
30. Reprinted in Žurin 1955, pp. 155-156.
31. *Sem'ja i škola* 1963, Nr. 1, p. 40.
32. *Sem'ja i škola* 1963, Nr. 12, p. 12.
33. See (among others) H.-G. Rolff, *Sozialisation und Auslese durch die Schule* (Heidelberg 1967).
34. See (among others) Zaporožec 1968.

35. The Report of the Commission for Public Instruction, Science and Culture in *Učitel'skaja gazeta* of May 14, 1968.
36. Semënov 1965, p. 44.
37. Kulikov 1966, p. 45.
38. Semënov 1965, p. 44.
39. Twenty-third Congress of the Communist Party, p. 112.
40. Semënov 1965, p. 45.
41. See p. 39.
42. *SSSR v cifrach v 1968 godu*, p. 11.
43. Ibid.
44. *Ost-Probleme* 1968, p. 485.
45. *SSSR v cifrach v 1968 godu*, p. 120.
46. Semënov 1965, p. 45.
47. *Informationsdienst* 1966, Volume 12/13, pp. 23ff.
48. "Novyj rubež" 1968.
49. In an interview published in the July 10, 1969, issue of *Komsomol'skaja pravda*, I. G. Petrovsky, President of Moscow University (MGU), said that "many children in the cities often call upon the services of tutors" to get better chances for admission into universities, particularly to the well-known MGU.
50. See pp. 47-48.
51. *Količestvennye metody* 1966, p. 203.
52. See the section on juvenile delinquency, particularly pp. 111-113.
53. Min'kovskij 1966, pp. 488ff.
54. Rutkevič 1966. Quoted in Yanowitch and Dodge 1968, p. 254.
55. "Sojuzniki" 1968.
56. For the origin and growth of these types of schools, see Anweiler 1968, pp. 106-107, 121.
57. For the reference to these data, the author wishes to thank Professor O. Anweiler, who found them in the following source: *Sibirskoe otdelenie Akademii Nauk SSSR; Naučnyj sovet po problemam obrazovanija; Nauka i prosveščenie; Naučnopedagogičeskij sbornik*. Vyp. I. Novosibirsk, 1965.
58. See the report "S kollegii Ministerstva prosveščenija RSFSR" (From the Collegium of the Ministry of Education of the RSFSR) in *Učitel'skaja gazeta* of January 27, 1968.
59. See (among others) Aitov 1966.
60. Rutkevič 1966. Quoted in Yanowitch and Dodge 1968, p. 255.
61. Anweiler 1966, p. 164, and *Strana Sovetov* 1967, p. 277.
62. According to Aitov (1966, p. 23), about 874,000 out of the 2.7 million 1966 secondary school graduates could be accepted in the universities; of the more than 4 million secondary school graduates in 1970, according to the directives of the 23rd Party Congress, only slightly more than in 1966, namely 940,000 (that is, less than one-quarter of the graduates) are to be accepted in the universities.

63. Aitov 1965, p. 5.
64. Šubkin 1965, p. 66.
65. Petrov and Filippov 1967, p. 77.
66. Šubkin 1965, p. 66.
67. Petrov and Filippov 1967, pp. 81-82. If one considers the fact that the group of working-class children within the surveyed school population is about twice as large as the group of salaried employees' children (including the children of the intelligentsia)—60% compared to 33% of the school population—and that, on the other hand, the group of working class children within the surveyed student body is hardly larger than the group of salaried employees' children and the children of the intelligentsia—48.0% compared to 47.1% of the student body—then the effect of the selection process on the social structure by the transition from the secondary school to the university becomes especially clear.
68. Quoted in Yanowitch and Dodge 1968, pp. 260ff. The fact that children of collective farmers form only 4.8% of the students in the Technical Institutes of Sverdlovsk and only 1.0% of the students in the State University ought not to be overlooked in this connection.
69. "Sistema obrazovanija" 1968, pp. 208-209.
70. Mention must be made of such measures as the preferred admission of young people with industrial experience and the development of the correspondence and evening study courses which were especially intensified under Khrushchev, as well as the "Organization of Preparatory Courses in the Universities," which were announced in a directive of the Central Committee of the CPSU and of the USSR Council of Ministers in the September 6, 1969 issue of *Pravda*. Such introductory courses are to facilitate university admission for secondary school graduates "from the ranks of progressive workers, collective farmers, and discharged military personnel." The university departments concerned will offer remedial courses preparatory to university study upon the initiative of the factories, organizations, collective farms, etc., to which the graduates belong.
71. Anweiler 1968, pp. 200-201 and W. Mitter: "Einheitlichkeit und Differenzierung als Problem der sowjetischen Schulreform" in O. Anweiler (editor), *Bildungsreformen in Osteuropa* (Stuttgart 1969), pp. 108-140.
72. See (among others) Zaporozec 1968.
73. See (among others) Kostjaškin 1967.
74. Hellmer 1966, p. 9.
75. See p. 11.
76. Hazard 1953, pp. 252-253.
77. Prochorov 1967.
78. Hellmer 1966, p. 23.
79. See pp. 53-54, where it is also pointed out that especially the steadily increasing divorce rates during the past few years in the Soviet Union are responsible for the increase in incomplete families.

80. Beljavskij 1967.
81. Charčev 1964, p. 277.
82. Charčev 1964, p. 276.
83. "Socializm i sem'ja" 1967, p. 139.
84. Zjubin 1966, p. 25.
85. Suvorov 1966.
86. See pp. 89-91.

CHAPTER 5

1. A survey of 250 families in Voronež (RSFSR) showed that "more than 77% of the children have no steady chores in the family" (Kaliničenko 1966, p. 196).
2. Volkova 1959, p. 86.
3. Zdorovskij and Orlov 1966, pp. 71-72.
4. Petuchov 1959, p. 18.
5. Zdravomyslov 1964.
6. See pp. 128-129.
7. In contrast, F. R. Filippov and his assistants report a large conformity between the vocational preparation in school-based work instruction and actual vocational choice—however, they do not touch upon the question of career desires. See "Sistema obrazovanija" 1968, p. 205.
8. Archangel'skij and Petrov 1967, p. 72.
9. Zdravomyslov and Jadov 1966, pp. 201, 206.
10. Ibid., pp. 201, 205-206.
11. Ibid., pp. 197, 206.
12. Murašév and Orel 1966.
13. Grušin 1967, p. 76.
14. Gurjanov 1966, pp. 154ff.
15. Gurjanov 1966, p. 184.
16. See p. 122.
17. See pp. 122-123.
18. Asratjan 1968, p. 41.
19. Mansurov 1967, pp. 78-79.
20. Mordkowitsch 1968, pp. 27-28.
21. Mal'kovskaja 1968.
22. Zotov 1967.
23. Mansurov 1967, pp. 83, 91.
24. Lisovskij 1967, p. 47.
25. Ibid., p. 51.
26. See p. 27.
27. Kaliničenko's research results, which indicate that Soviet parents are primarily oriented toward accomplishment, adjustment, and individual morality, essentially confirm the research data which were gathered in the

Research Center for Soviet Studies at Harvard University analyzing the value standards in three generations of Russian or Soviet emigrants. Cf. Inkeles and Bauer 1961, pp. 219ff.

28. See *betrifft: erziehung* 1968, Nr. 7, p. 14.
29. In contrast, Coser's (1950-1951) interpretation seems unreliable to me. Coser feels that the Soviet state consciously encourages an authoritarian family type; of course, one must remember that Coser is referring to the Stalin era. For the position of Soviet pedagogy after the Stalin era as opposed to authoritarian educational forms in the family, see pp. 79-80 and p. 147.

CHAPTER 6

1. Two interpretations are conceivable here. One can, as Inkeles and Bauer (1961, pp. 219ff) do, proceed from a strong continuity of familial value standards through the generations and establish an extensive agreement between Russian and Soviet family education with respect to the passing on of individualistic values. On the other hand one can also argue that the social change of society and of family structure, brought about by industrialization and collectivization, through the increase of the educational level, and the living standard, has, for its part, contributed to a strengthening of the individualistic-familial value orientation.
2. See note 15 to Chapter 3.

Bibliography

The titles of Russian newspapers and journals have been abbreviated as follows in the bibliography:

Došk. vosp.	Doškol'noe vospitanie
Koms. pravda	Komsomol'skaja pravda
Lit. gaz.	Literaturnaja gazeta
Nač. šk.	Načal'naja škola
Nar. obraz.	Narodnoe obrazovanie
Sov. ped.	Sovetskaja pedagogika
Učit. gaz.	Učitel'skaja gazeta
Vopr. fil.	Voprosy filosofii
Vopr. psich.	Voprosy psichologii

An English translation of all Russian as well as of all German titles appears in parentheses immediately following the original title. English language translations of the Russian or German entries may exist, but they have not been included in this bibliography. Those titles appearing in English are the original English language editions.

Ahlberg, R. *Die Entwicklung der empirischen Sozialforschung in der Sowjetunion* (The Development of Empirical Social Research in the Soviet Union). Reports of the Osteuropa-Institut at the Free University of Berlin, Philosophy and Sociology Series. Berlin: 60 (1964).
——— . "Die Sozialstruktur der UdSSR" (The Social Structure of the USSR). *Osteuropa,* 5/6 (1968), 353-368.
Aitov, N. A. "Nekotorye osobennosti izmenenija klassovoj struktury v SSSR" (Several Characteristics in the Change of Class Structure in the USSR). *Vopr. fil.,* 3 (1965), 3-9.
——— . "Vlijanie obščeobrazovatel'nogo urovnja rabočich na jich proizvodstvennuju dejatel'nost' " (The Impact of the Workers' Level of General Education on Their Productive Work). *Vopr. fil.,* 11 (1966), 23-31.
Andreev, Ju. "Sem'ja, moral', zakon. Čto novogo v proekte osnov zakonodatel'stva o brake i sem'e" (Family, Morality, and Law. The New Policies in the Legislation Project on Marriage and Family). *Izvestija,* 4/18/1968.
Antipin, E. "Partijnost' pedagogičeskogo dela" (The Party Spirit in Pedagogical Work). *Učit. gaz.,* 2/1/1969.

Anweiler, O. *Geschichte der Schule und Paedagogik in Russland. Vom Ende des Zarenreiches bis zum Beginn der Stalin-Aera* (History of the School and Pedagogy in Russia. From the End of the Tsarist Regime to the Beginning of the Stalin Era). Osteuropa-Institut at the Free University of Berlin, Educational Publications. Berlin: Quelle & Meyer, 1964.

_____. "Bildungspolitik und Sozialstruktur in der Sowjetunion" (Educational Policy and Social Structure in the Soviet Union). In *Sowjetgesellschaft im Wandel. Russlands Weg zur Industriegesellschaft*, edited by F. Meissner (Soviet Society in Transition. Russia's Path toward Industrialization). Stuttgart: Kohlhammer, 1966, 153-184.

_____. *Die Sowjetpaedagogik in der Welt von heute* (Soviet Pedagogy in Today's World). Heidelberg: Quelle & Meyer, 1968.

Anweiler, O., and Meyer, K. *Die sowjetische Bildungspolitik seit 1917. Dokumente und Texte* (Soviet Educational Policy since 1917. Documents and Texts). Heidelberg: Quelle & Meyer, 1961.

Apresjan, Z. "Partija i komsomol" (Party and Komsomol). *Pravda*, 10/18/1968.

Aptekman, D. M. "Priřiny živuřesti religioznogo obrjada kresřenija v sovremennych uslovijach. Po itogam konkretnogo sociologiřeskogo issledovanija" (The Reasons for the Survival of the Religious Custom of Baptism under the Current Conditions. The Results of an Empirical Sociological Study). *Vopr. fil.*, 3 (1965), 83-89.

Archangel'skij, L. M. "Individual'noe soznanie i moral'nye cennosti" (Individual Consciousness and Moral Values). *Vopr. fil.*, 7 (1968), 67-76.

Archangel'skij, L. M., and Petrov, Ju. P. "Žiznennye plany i idealy škol'noj moloděži. Po rezul'tatam ětiko-sociologiřeskich issledovanij" (The Life Plans and Ideals of School Children. The Results of Ethical-Sociological Studies). *Sov. ped.*, 6 (1967), 68-76.

Arkin, E. A. *Roditeljam o vospitanii. Vospitanie rebënka v sem'e ot goda do zrelosti* (For Parents on Education. The Raising of the Child in the Family from His First Year to Maturity). Moscow–Leningrad: 1949.

Asratjan, D. I. "O privleřenii obšřestvennosti k vospitaniju pionerov" (On Involving the Community in the Education of Pioneers). *Sov. ped.*, 10 (1968), 40-45.

Bahro, Horst. *Das Kindschaftsrecht in der Union der sozialistischen Sowjetrepubliken* (The Rights of Minors in the Union of Soviet Socialist Republics). Frankfurt–Berlin: Publications of the Scientific Society for the Rights of the Individual and Related Areas, Ltd., Metzner, 1966.

Balaguškin, E. G. "Stroitel'stvo kommunizma i razvitie brařnosemejnych otnošenij" (The Structure of Communism and the Development of Marriage and Family Relations). *Vopr. fil.*, 3 (1962), 31-38.

_____. "Liřnost' i sem'ja" (Personality and Family). In *Liřnost' pri socializme* (The Personality in Socialism). Moscow: 1968, 188-200.

Baskina, A. "Ne zver' i ne angel'. Vsluch ob odnom šřepetil'nom voprose." (Neither Animal nor Angel. Statements about a Taboo). *Lit. gaz.*, 11/27/1968.

Bebel, A. *Die Frau und der Sozialismus* (The Woman and Socialism). 25th ed. Stuttgart: Dietz, 1895.

Beljavskij, A. "Ostorožno–zakon" (Caution–the Law). *Lit. gaz.*, 4/26/1967.

Beresnevič, E. V. "Igra i vospitanie rebënka" (Play and the Education of the Child). In *O vospitanii doškol'nikov v sem'e* (On Raising Preschool Children in the Family). Moscow: 1963, 94-115.

Besedy s roditeljami o vospitanii detej v sem'e (Conversations with Parents on the Raising of Children in the Family). Series II. Moscow: 1957.

Bikžanova, M. A. *Sem'ja v kolchozach Uzbekistana* (The Family in the Kholchos Farms in Uzbekistan). Tashkent: 1959.

Bischoff, M. *Die Struktur und die Wandlung der sowjetischen Familie (um 1950): die Familie in der sowjetischen Gesellschaft* (The Structure and the Change of the Soviet Family [about 1950] : The Family in Soviet Society). Unpublished dissertation: University of Hamburg, 1956.

Blitsten, D. "Experiments with Family Life in Russia and in Israel." In Blitsten, D., *The World of the Family.* New York: Random House, 1963.

Boldyrëv, N. I. *Vospitanie kommunističeskoj morali u detej v sem'e* (The Education of Children for Communist Ethics in the Family). Moscow: 1960.

Brežnev, L. I. "Reč' na Vsesojuznom s'ezde učitelej" (Speech at the All-Union Teachers' Congress). *Nar. obraz.,* 7 (1968), 4-11.

Bronfenbrenner, U. Two Worlds of Childhood: U.S. and U.S.S.R. New York: Russell Sage, 1970.

Bucharin, N., and Preobraschensky, E. (Bucharin, N., and Preobraženskij, E.) *Das ABC des Kommunismus. Populaere Erlaeuterungen des Programms der Kommunistischen Partei Russlands (Bolschewiki)* (The ABC's of Communism. Popular Explanations of the Program of the Communist Party of Russia [Bolsheviks]). 3rd Ed. Hamburg: Verlag der kommunistischen Internationale, 1923.

Burštejn, V. Ja. "Predstavlenija mladšich škol'nikov o trude svoich roditelej" (The Conceptions of Elementary School Children of Their Parents' Work). *Nač. šk.,* 4 (1961), 64-67.

Čekalin, N. I. *Ljubov' i sem'ja* (Love and Family). Moscow: 1964.

Celikova, O. P. "Nravstvennyj ideal" (The Moral Ideal). In *Nravstvennost' i nravstvennoe vospitanie. Materialy naučnoj konferencii* (Morality and Moral Education. Proceedings of a Scientific Conference). Series V. Novosibirsk: 1962.

——— . "Rol' položitel'nogo primera v nravstvennom vospitanii" (The Significance of a Positive Example in Moral Education). *Sov. ped.,* 10 (1966), 9-18.

Charčev, A. G. "Brak i sem'ja v socialističeskom obščestve" (Marriage and Family in the Socialist Society). *Koms. pravda,* 4/23/1952.

——— . *Marksizm-Leninizm o brake i sem'e* (Marxism/Leninism on Marriage and the Family). Moscow: 1959.

——— . *Sem'ja v sovetskom obščestve* (The Family in Soviet Society). Leningrad: 1960.

——— . "O roli sem'i v kommunističeskom vospitanii" (On the Family's Role in Communist Education). *Sov. ped.,* 5 (1963), 62-72.

——— . *Brak i sem'ja v SSSR. Opyt sociologičeskogo issledovanija* (Marriage and Family in the USSR. A Study in Sociological Research). Moscow: 1964.

168   Bibliography

———. "O putjach dal'nejšego ukreplenija sem'i v SSSR" (On Methods toward Further Strengthening of the Family in the USSR). In *Social'nye issledovanij* (Social Science Studies). Moscow: 1965, 162-169.

———. "Sem'ja–jačejka obsčéstva" (The Family–the Cell of Society). *Pravda,* 7/25/1966 a.

———. "Eščé raz o sem'e" (Once Again on the Family). *Pravda,* 11/23/1966 b.

———. "Byt i sem'ja pri socializme" (Home Life and Family under Socialism). *Vopr. fil.,* 3 (1967), 12-19.

———. "Pravo, moral', byt" (Right, Morality, and Home Life). *Isvestija,* 6/20/68.

——— and Golod, S. I. *Professional'na ja rabota ženščin i sem'ja* (Occupational Work of Women and the Family). Leningrad: 1971.

——— and Jankova, Z. A. (eds.) Metodologrčeskie problemy issledovanija byta (Methodological Problems of Research on Everyday Life). *Social'nye issledovanija, 7* (1971).

Coser, L. A. "Some Aspects of Soviet Family Policy." *American Journal of Sociology,* 56 (1950/51), 424-434.

Davydov, G. P., and Pelipenko, L. K. "Nekotorye pedagogičeskie problemy ispol'zovanija vremeni i organizacii dejatel'nosti v sem'e učaščichsja 5-10 klassov" (Some Pedagogical Problems of the Use of Time and of the Organization of Family Activities among 5th through 10th Graders). 1967 manuscript, partially reprinted in *Nar. obraz.,* 7 (1968), 86-91.

De Witt, N. *Education and Professional Employment in the USSR.* Washington: National Science Foundation, 1961.

Die Grundlagen der kommunistischen Erziehung (Uebers. a. d. Russ.) (The Foundations of Communist Education. Translated from the Russian). Berlin: Volk und Wissen, 1964.

"Dlja samych malen'kich" (For the Youngest). *Učit. gaz.,* 4/29/1967.

Dodge, N. T. *Women in The Soviet Economy: Their Role in Economic, Scientific, and Technical Development.* Baltimore: Johns Hopkins Press, 1966.

Dragynova, T. V. *Vospitanie podrostka v sem'e* (The Education of Adolescents in the Family). Moscow: 1955.

Dunaeva, L. P. "Vzajmootnošenija podrostkov s roditeljami i vozniknovenie konfliktov v sem'e" (The Mutual Ties between Adolescents and Parents and the Origin of Conflicts in the Family). In *O nravstvennom vospitanii škol'nika* (On the Moral Education of the Pupil). Leningrad: 1968, 274-289.

"Edinaja sistema vospitanija" (A Uniform System of Education). *Sem'ja i škola,* 8 (1959), 4.

Eisenstadt, S. N. *Von Generation zu Generation* (From Generation to Generation). Munich: Juventa, 1966.

Engels, F. *Der Ursprung der Familie, des Privateigentums und des Staates. Im Anschluss an Lewis H. Morgans Forschungen* (The Origin of the Family, of Private Property, and of the State. A Follow-Up to the Research of Lewis H. Morgan). Berlin: Verlag Neuer Weg, 1946.

Eštokin, A. "Pokolenie vstupajuščee v žizn' " (The Generation Entering Life). *Sovetskaja Rossija*, 9/16/1965.

Fisher, R. T. *Pattern for Soviet Youth. A Study of the Congresses of the Komsomol, 1918-1954.* New York: Columbia University Press, 1959.

Flerina, E. A. *Vospitanie rebënka v sem'e ot trëch do sem'i* (The Raising of Children from three to seven in the Family). Moscow: 1950.

Gasilov, G. "Sojuz školy i ulicy" (An Alliance between the School and the Street). *Pravda*, 8/31/1968.

Geiger, H. K. "Changing Political Attitudes in Totalitarian Society: A Case Study of the Role of the Family." In Bell, N. W., and Vogel, E. F., *A Modern Introduction to the Family.* New York–London: Free Press, 1960, 173-188.

———. *The Family in Soviet Russia.* Cambridge, Mass.: Harvard University Press, 1968.

Gercenson, A. "Sociologija prestupnosti" (Sociology of Crime). Manuscript form, 1967.

Golod, S. "Ženščiny na rabote i doma" (Women at Work and at Home). *Lit. gaz.* 4/26/1967.

Goode, W. J. *World Revolution and Family Patterns.* Glencoe, Ill.: Free Press, 1963.

Grušin, B. A. "Slušaetsja delo o razvode. O tak nazyvaemych 'legkomyslennych brakach' " (A Divorce Case Is Tried. On the So-called Frivolous Marriages). *Molodaja gvardija,* 6 (1964), 164-191, and 7 (1964), 255-282.

———. *Svobodnoe vremja. Aktual'nye problemy* (Free Time. Current Problems). Moscow: 1968.

Grušin, B. A., and Čikin, V. V. *Ispoved' pokolenija* (The Confession of a Generation). Moscow: 1962.

Gurjanov, S. T. "Duchovnye interesy sovetskogo rabočego" (The Intellectual Interests of the Soviet Worker). In *Sociologija v SSSR* (Sociology in the USSR), Volume II. Moscow: 1966, 151-186.

Gurova, R. G. "Sem'ja, škola, ulica" (Family, School, and Street). *Sem'ja i škola,* 9 (1968), 8-9.

Gurova, R. G., and Cyrempilon, A. V. "Izmenenija v uslovijach žizni i oblike detej evenkov (1929-1966). Opyt sravnitel'nogo social'no-pedagogičeskogo issledovanija" (Changing Living Conditions and Personality Changes among Evenki Children. 1929-1966. A Study in Comparative Social Science–Pedagogical Research). *Sov. ped.,* 11 (1968), 58-69.

Halle, F. W. *Die Frau in Sowjetrussland* (Uebers. a. d. Amerikan.) (The Woman in Soviet Russia. Translated from the American). Berlin–Wien–Leipzig: Zsolnay, 1932.

Harmsen, H. (ed.) *Sexualerziehung in der UdSSR und in Mitteldeutschland. Zur Entwicklung und Organisation des Gesundheitswesens in Sowjetrussland, in osteuropaeischen Volksdemokratien und in Mitteldeutschland.* Bd. 35 (Sex Education in the USSR and in East Germany. Toward the Development and

Organization of the Health Service in Soviet Russia, in East European Peoples' Democracies, and in East Germany, Volume 35). Hamburg: Akademie fuer Staatsmedizin, 1967.

Hazard, J. N. *Law and Social Change in the USSR.* Toronto: Stevens Press, 1953.

Hellmer, J. *Jugendkriminalitaet in unserer Zeit* (Juvenile Delinquency in Our Time). Frankfurt: Fischer Buecherei, 1966.

Hindus, M. "The Family in Russia." In Anshen, R. N., *The Family: Its Function and Destiny.* New York: Harper & Brothers, 1949, 111-124.

———. *Haus ohne Dach. Russland nach viereinhalb Jahrzehnten Revolution.* (House without a Roof. Russia after Four and One-Half Decades of Revolution). Wiesbaden: Brockhaus, 1963.

———. *Die Enkel der Revolution. Menschliche Probleme in der Sowjetunion* (The Grandchildren of the Revolution. Human Problems in the Soviet Union). Wiesbaden: Brockhaus, 1967.

Informationsdienst zum Bildungswesen in Osteuropa. Osteuropa-Institut an der Freien Universitaet Berlin. Hrsg. vom Referat fuer Bildungswesen in Osteuropa. Heft 12/13 (Information Service for Education in Eastern Europe. Osteuropa-Institut at the Free University of Berlin. Published from a report for the Educational System in Eastern Europe). Volume 12/13. Berlin: 1966.

Inkeles, A., and Bauer, R. A. "Patterns of Family Life." In Inkeles, A., and Bauer, R. A., *The Soviet Citizen: Daily Life in a Totalitarian Society.* Cambridge, Mass.: Harvard University Press, 1961, 189ff.

Iovčuk, M. T. "Marksistsko-Leninskaja sociologija v SSSR i issledovanija problem duchovnoj žizni socialističeskogo obščestva" (The Marxist-Leninist Sociology in the USSR and Studies about Problems of the Cultural Life of the Socialistic Society). *Filosofskie nauki,* 4 (1967). Abridged German translation in *Ost-Probleme* 1968, 26-33.

Istorija pedagogiki. Učebnoe posoboe dlja doškol'nych pedagogičeskich učilišč (History of Pedagogy. A Textbook for Preschool Pedagogical Institutions). 3rd ed. Pod red. M. F. Šabaevoj. Moscow: 1961.

Jakovlev, N. M. "Izučenie idealov staršeklassnikov" (The Study of the Ideals of Upper-Grade Students). *Sov. ped.,* 12 (1965), 41-45.

———. "Rebënok i ego obščestvo. Social'no-psichologičeskij éskiz" (The Child and His Society. A Sociopsychological Study). *Vopr. psich.,* 4 (1966), 142-151.

Jaroslavskij, E. "Moral' i byt proletariata v perechodnom periode" (Morality and Everyday Life of the Proletariat in the Time of Transition). In Razin, I., *Komsomol'skij byt* (Life in the Komsomol). Moscow-Leningrad: 1927, 34-54.

Kaliničenko, V. P. "Socialističeskaja sem'ja kak institut vospitanija detej" (The Socialist Family as an Institution of Child Education). In *Voprosy kommunističeskogo vospitanija. Vypusk vtoroj. Isvestija Voronežskogo*

Gosudarstvennogo Pedagogičeskogo Instituta, Tom 73-j (Questions of Communist Education. Second Series. Reports of the State Pedagogical Institute at Voronež, Volume 73). Voronež: 1966, 192-204.

Khrushchev, N. S. "Vospityvat' aktivnych i soznatel'nych stroitelej kommunisticeskogo obščestva. Reč tovarišča N. S. Chruščëva na XIII s'ezde VLKSM" (On the Raising of Active and Aware Builders of the Communist Society. A speech by Comrade N. S. Khrushchev at the XIII Congress of the VLKSM). *Nar. obraz.,* 5 (1958), 4-12.

———. Za pročnyj mir vo imja sčast'ja i svetlogo buduščego naroda" (For a Lasting Peace in the Name of Happiness and of the Bright Future of the People). In *Vserossijskij s'ezd učitelej. Moskva 6-9 ijulja 1960 goda Stenografičeskij otčet* (Stenographic Minutes of the All-Russian Teachers' Congress, Moscow, July 6-9, 1960). Moscow: 1961, 5-29.

Koenig, R. "Entwicklungstendenzen der Familie im neueren Russland" (Developmental Trends of the Family in Modern Russia). In *Materialien zur Soziologie der Familie* (Information on the Sociology of the Family). Berne: Francke, 1946.

Kolbanovskij, V. N. *Ljubov', brak i sem'ja v socialističeskom obščestve* (Love, Marriage, and Family in the Socialist Society). Moscow: 1948.

Količestvennye metody v sociologii (Quantitative Methods in Sociology). Moscow: 1966.

Kon, I. S. "Polovaja moral' v svete sociologii" (Sexual Morality in a Sociological Perspective). *Sov. ped.,* 12 (1966), 64-78.

———. *Sociologija licnosti* (Sociology of the Personality). Moscow: 1967.

———. "Junost' iščet sebja" (Youth's Search for Identity). *Sem'ja i škola,* 8 (1968), 9-11.

Kondratova, V. "Formirovanie u detej doškol'nogo vozrasta uvaženija k roditeljam" (The Development of Respect for Their Parents among Preschool Children). *Sov. ped.,* 11 (1966), 47-55.

———. "Vzroslye i deti" (Adults and Children). *Nar obraz.,* 9 (1968), 83-85.

Konnikova, T. E. "Formirovanje obščestvennoj napravelennosti ličnosti škol'nika kak pedagogičeskaja problema" (The Forming of Societal Orientation in the Pupil's Personality as a Pedagogical Problem). In *O nravstvennom vospitanii škol'nika* (On the Moral Education of the Pupil). Leningrad: 1968, 3-28.

Korolëv, Ju. A. "Vzajmodejstvie morali i prava v bračnosemejnych otnošenijach" (The Interaction of Law and Morality in Marriage and Family Relations). *Vopr. fil,* 11 (1963), 75-85.

Kostjaschkin, É. G. (Kostjaškin, É. G.) "Die Entwicklung der ganztaegigen Erziehung im Schulwesen der Sowjetunion" (The Development of Full-day Education in the School System of the Soviet Union). *Bildung und Erziehung,* 4 (1969), 264-277.

———. "Pedagogičeskie aspekty polovogo vospitanija" (Pedagogical Aspects of Sex Education). *Sov. ped.,* 7 (1964), 43-51.

———. "Sem'ja i prodlënnyj škol'nyj den'" (The Family and the Lengthened

School Day). *Sov. ped.,* 4 (1967), 47-56.

——— . "Ličnoe sčastie–ne prostoe delo" (Personal Happiness–No Simple Affair). *Sem'ja i škola,* 10 (1968), 4-5.

Kotovščika, A. " 'Neobyčnye' deti" ("Exceptional" Children). *Lit. gaz.,* 10/29/ 1960.

——— . "O nich dumajut mnogie. Ešče raz o 'neobyčnych detjach' " (Many Think about Them. Once Again on "Exceptional" Children). *Lit. gaz.,* 7/25/1961.

Kovalëv, A. G. "Ob izučenii nravstvenno-psichologisčeskogo oblika škol'nika" (On the Study of the Moral-Psychological Character of the Pupil). In *Voprosy nravstvennogo vospitanija škol'nikov. Sbornik statej* (Questions of the Moral Education of School Children. Anthology of Essays). Leningrad: 1960, 121-132.

——— . *Psichologija ličnosti* (Psychology of the Personality). Second, improved, and expanded edition. Moscow: 1965.

Krasnogorskaja, L. I. *Rol' sem'i v vospitannii doškol'nika* (The Role of the Family in the Raising of the Preschool Child). Moscow: 1952.

Krupskaja, N. K. "Krepkaja sovetskaja sem'ja" (The Solid Soviet Family). In Krupskaja, N. K., *Pedagogičeskie sočinenija v. 10 tomach* (Pedagogical Works in 10 Volumes). Volume 6. Moscow: 1959, 318-325.

——— . *O vospitanii v sem'e. Izbrannye stat'i i reči* (On Education in the Family. Selected Essays and Speeches). Moscow: 1962.

Kruteckij, V. A., and Lukin, N. S. *Psichologija podrostka* (Psychology of the Adolescent). Moscow: 1959.

Kulikov, V. "Sovetskoe krest'janstvo" (Soviet Peasantry). *Kommunist,* 4 (1966), 91-96.

Kušner, P. I. "O nekotorych processach proizchodjaščich v sovremennoj kolchoznoj sem'e" (On Some Processes, Which Are Taking Place in the Contemporary Kolchos Family). *Sovetskaja etnografija,* 3 (1956).

Kuznecova, L. "Noša ne po pleču" (The Burden Is Too Heavy to Bear). *Lit. gaz.,* 2/15/1967.

——— . "Novyj lik madonny" (The New Face of the Madonna). *Lit gaz.,* 2/28/1968.

Lagutin, N. *Bjudžet sovetskoj sem'i* (The Budget of the Soviet Family). Moscow: 1967.

Laptenok, S. *Moral' i sem'ja* (Morality and Family). Minsk: 1967.

Lavrov, A. S., and Lavrova, O. A. *Vospitanie čuvstv* (The Education of Emotions). Moscow: 1967.

Lemberg, E. "Paedagogische Forschung in der Sowjetunion" (Pedagogical Research in the Soviet Union). In Lemberg, E. (ed.), *Das Bildungswesen als Gegenstand der Forschung.* (The Educational System as an Object of Research). Publications of the Institute for International Pedgogical Research. Volume 3. Heidelberg: Quelle & Meyer, 1963, 253-312.

Lenin, V. I. *Sočinenija. Izdanie 4-e* (Works, 4th Ed.). Moscow: 1941-1958.

Lenin ueber Volksbildung. Artikel und Reden (Lenin on Popular Education. Articles and Speeches). Berlin: 1966.

Levšin, L. A. *Pedagogika i sovremennost'* (Pedagogy and Today). Moscow: 1964.
——— . *Dajte pedagogičeskij sovet* (Give Some Pedagogical Advice). Moscow: 1965.
——— . "Semejnoe vospitanie" (Family Education). In *Pedagogičeskaja enciklopedija* (Pedagogical Encyclopedia). Volume 3. Moscow: 1966, Columns 818-828.
Lewytskyj, B. "Studenten und Schueler in der Sowjetunion" (Students and School Children in the Soviet Union). In *Aus Politik und Zeitgeschichte. Beilage zur Wochenzeitung Das Parlament* (On Politics and Contemporary History. Supplement to the weekly: *Das Parlament*), B 7 (1969), 2/15/1969, 31-46.
Lichačev, B. "Nužna bor'ba, a ne propoved' " (A Campaign Is Needed, Not a Creed). *Učit. gaz.*, 5/18/1967.
Lichačeva, N., and Mironov, M. "Na pročve revnosti i meščanstva" (Results of Jealousy and Petty-Bourgeois Attitudes). *Sem'ja i škola*, 2 (1964), 27-28.
Ličnost' pri socializme (The Personality in Socialism). Moscow: 1968.
Lindner, W. "Tendenzen und Probleme der Tageserziehung in einigen sozialistischen Laendern" (Trends and Problems of Full-day Education in Several Socialist Countries). *Vergleichende Paedagogik*, 4 (1966), 337-338.
Lisowski, W. T. (Lisovskij, V. T.) "Lebensplaene der sowjetischen Jugend" (Life Plans of Soviet Youth). *Jugendforschung* (Youth Research), 3/4 (1967), 45-53.
Lorimer, F. *The Population of the Soviet Union: History and Prospects.* Geneva: League of Nations, 1946.
Mace, D. and Vera. *The Soviet Family.* London: Doubleday, 1963.
Makarenko, A. S. *O vospitanii v sem'e. Izbrannye pedagogičeskie proizvedenija* (On Education in the Family. Selected Pedagogical Works). Moscow: 1955.
——— . "Ein Buch fuer Eltern" (A Book for Parents). In Makarenko, A. S., *Werke.* (Works). Volume 4. Berlin: Volk und Wissen, 1958, 13-36.
——— . "Vortraege ueber Kindererziehung" (Lectures on the Raising of Children). Ibid., 364-450.
——— . "Reden und Aufsaetze ueber Kindererziehung" (Speeches and Essays on the Raising of Children). Ibid., 451-538.
Mal'kovskaja, T. "Poka diagnoz" (Meanwhile a Diagnosis), *Koms. pravda*, 2/10/1968.
Mansurow, N. S. (Mansurov, N. S.) "Die Presse und die Jugenderziehung" (The Press and the Education of Youth). *Jugendforschung*, 1/2 (1967), 69-86.
——— . "Jugendforschung in der UdSSR" (Research on Youth in the USSR). *Jugendforschung*, 7 (1968), 65-74.
Mansurow, N. S., and Lunkow, J. G. (Lunkov, J. G.) "Die Formung des politischen Bewusstseins der lernenden Jugend" (The Formation of the Political Consciousness of Young Students). *Jugendforschung*, 1/2 (1967), 87-93.
Mar'enko, I. S. "Rol' sem'i v vospitanii sovetskogo patriotizma i proletarskogo internacionalizma u podrostkov" (The Role of the Family in the Education

of Young People toward Soviet Patriotism and Proletarian Internationalism). In *Besedy s roditeljami o vospitanii detej v sem'e* (Conversations with Parents on the Raising of Children in the Family). Series II. Moscow: 1957, 35-45.

Markov, V. S. "Socialisti̇́ceskij byt i formirovanie c̆eloveka buduśćego" (The Socialist Household and the Forming of the Man of the Future). In *Nravstvennost' i nravstvennoe vospitanie. Materialy nauc̆noj konferencii* (Morality and Moral Education. Working Papers for a Scientific Conference). Series V. Novosibirsk: 1962, 132-145.

Markova, T. A. *Podgotovka detej k s̆kole v sem'e* (The Child's Preparation for School in the Family). Moscow: 1956 a.

_____ . *Trudovoe vospitanie dos̆kol'nika v sem'e* (The Preschool Child's Education for Work in the Family). Moscow: 1956 b.

_____ . "Kak vospityvat' u detej poslus̆anie, aktivnost' " (How to Train Children in Obedience and Activity). In *O vospitanii doskol'nikov v sem'e* (On the Education of Preschool Children in the Family). Moscow: 1963, 40-48.

_____ . *Detskij sad i sem'ja. Posobie dlja studentov-zaoc̆nikov dos̆kol'nych otdelenij pedagogic̆eskich institutov* (Kindergarten and Family. A Handbook for Correspondence Course Students at the Preschool Departments of Pedagogical Institutes). Moscow: 1964.

Marx/Engels ueber Erziehung und Bildung. Zusammengestellt von Prof. P. N. Grusdew (Marx/Engels on Education and Upbringing. Compiled by Prof. P. N. Grusdew). Berlin: Volk und Wissen, 1966.

Maslov, P. P. *Dochod sovetskoj sem'i* (The Income of the Soviet Family). Moscow: 1965.

Materialy XXII s'ezda KPSS (Working Papers for the XXII Congress of the CPSU). Moscow: 1961.

Medynskij, E., and Petruchin, J. "A. S. Makarenko a vospitanii detej v sem'e" (A. S. Makarenko on the Education of Children in the Family). In Makarenko, A. S., *O Vospitanii v sem'e. Izbrannye pedagogic̆eskie proizvedenija* (On Education in the Family. Selected Pedagogical Works). Moscow: 1955, 3-19.

Meek, D. L. *Soviet Youth. Some Achievements and Problems. Excerpts from the Soviet Press, edited and translated by Dorothea L. Meek.* London: Routledge & Kegan Paul, 1957.

Meissner, B. (ed.) *Sowjetgesellschaft im Wandel. Russlands Weg zur Industriegesellschaft* (Soviet Society in Transition. Russia's Path toward Industrialization). Stuttgart: Kohlhammer, 1966.

Mel'nikova, T. "Ideal'noj sem'ej javljaetsja ta, gde . . ." (The Ideal Family is, where . . .). *Koms. pravda*, 6/15/1966.

Min'kovskij, G. M. "Detskaja prestupnost' " (Juvenile Delinquency). In *Pedagogic̆eskaja ènciklopedija* (Pedagogical Encyclopedia).Volume 3. Moscow: 1966, Columns 488 ff.

Mitter, W. "Das Freizeitproblem im Spiegel sowjetischer Publizistik" (The Problem of Free Time as Reflected in the Soviet Press). *Bildung und Erziehung*, 3 (1966), 194-210.

Mordkowitsch, W. G. (Mordković, V. G.) "Zur Entwicklung der gesellschaftlich-politischen Aktivitaet der Jugend" (On the Development of the Socio-political Activity of Youth). *Jugendforschung,* 7 (1968), 25-38.

Murašëv, S., and Orel, V. "Student i obščestvennye nauki" (The Student and Social Sciences). *Koms pravda,* 4/20/1966.

Na blago i sčastie naroda. Sbornik dokumentov (For the Good and Happiness of the People. A Collection of Documents). Moscow: 1961.

Narodnoe chozjajstvo SSSR v. 19.. godu. Statisticeskij ežegodnik (The National Economy of the USSR in 19.. A Statistical Yearbook). Moscow: 19. . .

Narodnoe obrazovanie v SSSR 1917-1967 (Public Education in the USSR 1917-1967). Pod red. M. A. Prokof'eva, P. B. Zimina, etc. Moscow: 1967.

Naumova, N. F. "Social'naja obuslovennost' emocional'nogo otnošenija k trudu" (The Social Conditioning of the Emotional Attitude toward Work). In *Sociologija v SSSR* (Sociology in the USSR). Volume 2. Moscow: 1966, 138-150.

Nikitina, V. "Ostrov materej v more problem" (The Island of Mothers in a Sea of Problems). *Koms. pravda,* 12/11/1968.

"Novyj rubež" (A New Horizon). *Učit. gaz.,* 9/3/1968.

O vospitanii doškol'nikov v sem'e (On Raising Preschool Children in the Family). Moscow: 1963.

O vospitanii škol'nika v sem'e. Pedagogičeskie sovety roditeljam (On Raising the School Child in the Family. Pedagogical Advice for Parents). Pod red. A. A. Žochova. Moscow: 1954.

"O Vsesojuznom seminare po doškol'nomu vospitaniju" (Notes of the All-Union Seminar on Preschool Education). *Došk. vosp.,* 12 (1968), 84-86.

"Obščestvennost', sem'ja i pionerskaja organizacija" (The Public, the Family, and the Pioneer Organization). *Sov. ped.,* 5 (1963). 3-10.

Obščie osnovy pedagogiki (General Foundations of Pedagogy). Pod red. F. F. Korolëva, V. E. Gmurmana. Moscow: 1967.

Ol'šanskij, V. B. "Ličnost' i social'nye cennosti" (Personality and Social Values). In *Sociologija v SSSR* (Sociology in the USSR). Volume 1. Moscow: 1966, 470-530.

Osipov, G. V., and Ščepanskij, Ja. (eds.) *Social'nye problemy truda i proizvodstva. Sovetsko-pol'skoe sravnitel'noe issledoranie* (Social Problems of Work and Production: A Soviet-Polish Comparative Study). Moscow: 1969.

"Otvetstvennost' školy i učitelja" (The Responsibility of the School and the Teacher). *Nar. obraz.,* 12 (1967), 2-10.

XX. Parteitag der Kommunistischen Partei der Sowjetunion (Twentieth Party Congress of the Communist Party of the Soviet Union). Dusseldorf: 1956.

XXI. Parteitag der Kommunistischen Partei der Sowjetunion (Twenty-First Party Congress of the Communist Party of the Soviet Union). Berlin: 1959.

XXIII. Parteitag der Kommunistischen Partei der Sowjetunion (Twenty-Third Party Congress of the Communist Party of the Soviet Union). Verlag Presseagentur Nowosti, 1966.

Pavlova, N. " 'Robinzon' sredi ljudej" (A "Robinson" among Men). *Koms. pravda,* 12/4/1968.

Pedagogičeskij slovar' v dvuch tomach (Pedagogical Dictionary in Two Volumes). Moscow: 1960.

"Pedagogika. Kurs lekcij" (Pedagogy. A Lecture Course). Pod red. G. I. Ščukinoj. Moscow: 1966.

Perfil'evskaja, D. "Tak nazyvaemye 'trudnye' " (So-called Problem Children). *Nar. obraz.,* 4 (1966), 65-66.

Perova, G. Ja. "Škola, sem'ja i obščestvennost' " (School, Family, and Public). *Sov. ped.,* 1964, 3-11.

Petrov, Ju. P., and Filippov, F. R. "Žiznennye plany vypusknikov srednych škol i jich realizacija" (The Life Plans of Secondary School Graduates and Their Realization). In *Sociologiceskie problemy narodnogo obrazovanija* (Sociological Problems of Public Education). Sverdlovsk: 1967, 73-82.

Petrova, K. L. "Edinstvo učebnoj i vneučebnoj raboty—važnejšee uslovie vsestoronnogo razvitija učaščichsja" (The Unity of Curricular and Extracurricular Work—A Very Important Condition for the Well-Rounded Development of Students). *Škola-internat,* 5 (1965), 2-9.

Petuchov, N. N. "Rol' sem'i v vospitanii u detej kommunisticeskogo otnošenija k trudu" (The Role of the Family in Educating Children for a Communist Attitude toward Work). In *Vospitanie detej v sem'e. Sbornik lekcij* (The Raising of Children in the Family. A Collection of Lectures). Leningrad: 1959, 3-21.

Platonova, A., and Kovalevskij, K. "Pervoe zveno" (The First Step). *Učit. gaz.,* 2/10/1968.

Podgalo, A. "Brigady kommunisticeskogo truda—voploščenie idej Lenina" (The Brigades of Communist Work—The Realization of Lenin's Ideas). In *Voprosy ekonomiki,* 4 (1960). German translation in *Ost-Probleme,* 1960, 378-380.

Problemy byta, braka i semi (Problems of Household, Marriage, and Family). Vil'njus: 1970.

Prochorov, V. S. "O gruppovoj prestupnosti nesoveršennoletnych" (On the Group Delinquency of Minors). In *Vestnik Leningradskogo Universiteta,* 11 (1967). Quoted in Lewytskyj, B., op. cit., 39.

"Proekt Osnovy Zakonodatel'stva Sojuza SSR i Sojuznych Republik o brak i sem'e" (The Basic Law Project of the USSR and the Union Republics on Marriage and Family). *Isvestija,* 4/10/1968.

Programma vospitanija v detskom sadu (Program for Education in Kindergarten). Moscow: 1962. Revised edition, 1970.

"Programma-minimum pedagogičeskich znanij dlja samoobrazovanija roditelej" (Minimal Program of Pedagogical Knowledge for the Self-Education of Parents). *Sem'ja i škola,* 10 (1968), 17-19.

Prokov'ev, M. A. "O sostojanii i merach dal'nejšego ulučšenija raboty srednej obščeobrazovatel'noj školy" (On the Current Situation and Measures on Further Improving the Work of the General Secondary School). *Nar. obraz.,* 7 (1968), 12-26.

Radina, K. D. *Ateisticeskoe vospitanie detej v sem'e* (The Atheistic Education of Children in the Family). Leningrad: 1955.

Ramm, Thilo. "Die kuenftige Gesellschaftsordnung nach der Theorie von Marx und Engels" (The Future Social Order According to the Theory of Marx and Engels). In *Marxismusstudien*. Zweite Folge. Edited by I. Fetscher. (Studies on Marxism. Second Series). Tübingen: Mohr, 1957, 77-119.

Roditeli i deti. Vospitanie detej v sem'ye (Parents and Children. The Raising of Children in the Family). Moscow: 1961.

Rostovceva, O. P. "Novye formy sodružestva školy, sem'i i obščestvennosti" (New Forms of Cooperation between School, Family, and Public). *Sov. ped.*, 4 (1963), 67-72.

Ruettenauer, I. *A. S. Makarenko. Ein Erzieher und Schriftsteller in der Sowjetgesellschaft* (A. S. Makarenko. An Educator and Writer in Soviet Society). Freiburg: Herder, 1965.

Rumjancev, A. M. "Vstupajuščemu v mir nauki" (To the Young Scientist). *Koms. pravda*, 6/8/1967.

Rutkevič, M. N. *Žiznennye plany molodëži. Sociologičeskie issledovanija*, vypusk II (The Life Plans of Young People. Sociological Research). Series II. Sverdlovsk: 1966.

Sagimbaeva, R. "Ne tol'ko rabotnica . . ." (Not Only a Working Woman . . .). *Lit. gaz.*, 8/14/1968.

Schlesinger, R. *The Family in the USSR. Changing Attitudes in Soviet Russia.* Documents and Readings, Edited with an Introduction by Rudolf Schlesinger. London: Routledge & Kegan Paul, 1949.

Selivanov, V. I. "Pervičnye sel'skie kollektivy i jich vlijanie na formirovanie ličnosti" (Primary Rural Collectives and Their Influence on Personality Formation). In *Sociologija v SSSR* (Sociology in the USSR). Volume 1. Moscow: 1966, 457-469.

Semënov, V. "Social'naja struktura sovetskogo obščestva" (The Social Structure of Soviet Society). *Kommunist*, 11 (1965), 39-48.

"Sem'ja i ee rol' v stroitel'stve kommunizma. Marksizm-Leninizm o social'noj suščnosti sem'i. V pomošč' partijnoj učebe" (The Family and Its Role in the Building of Communism. Marxism/Leninism on the Social Character of the Family. A Guide for Party Schools). *Sov. ped.*, 4 (1966), 103-117.

Šeremet'eva, E. "Kogda skladyvaetsja charakter. Eščë raz o materjach i malyšach" (When the Foundations of Character Are Laid. Once More on Mothers and Small Children). *Koms. pravda*, 11/15/1968.

Sevčenko, M. D. "Ateisticeskoe vospitanie i preodolenie nasledovanija det'mi religioznych semejnych tradicij" (Atheistic Education and the Prevention of Children Taking Over Religious Family Traditions). In *Novye issledovanija v pedagogičeskich naukach* (New Research in the Pedagogical Sciences). Volume 8. Moscow: 1966, 55-60, and Volume 9. Moscow: 1966, 65-69.

Šimbirëv, P. N., and Ogorodnikov, I. T. *Pedagogika. Učebnik dlja pedagogičeskich institutov* (Pedagogy. Textbook for Pedagogical Institutes). Moscow: 1954.

Simirenko, A. *Soviet Sociology. Historical Antecedents and Current Appraisal.* Chicago: Quandrangle Books, 1966.

"Simpozium po issledovaniju problem sem'i i byta" (Symposium on the Study of Problems in the Family and Home Life). *Sov. ped.,* 6 (1967), 154-156.

"Sistema obrazovanija i social'noe sbliženie ljudej umstvennogo i fizičeskogo truda" (The Educational System and the Social Rapprochement of Intellectual Workers and Laborers). In *Klassy, social'nye sloi i gruppy v SSSR* (Classes, Social Strata, and Groups in the USSR). Moscow: 1968, 202-215.

"Škola-internat–obrazcovoe vospitatel'noe učreždenie" (The Boarding School— A Model Educational Institution). *Nar. obraz.,* 6 (1958), 16-17.

Slastenin, V. "Protiv intellektual'noj apatii" (Against Intellectual Apathy). *Učit. gaz.,* 1/7/1969.

Slesarev, G. A. "Voprosy organizacii truda i byta ženščin i razširennoe vosproizvodstvo" (Questions of Work Organization, Women's Home Life, and Increased Birthrates). In *Social'nye issledovanija* (Social Science Studies). Moscow: 1965, 156-161.

Slesarev, G. A., and Jankova, Z. A. "Ženščina na promyšlennom predprijatii i v sem'e" (Women's Problems in the Factory and in the Family). 1967 manuscript. This study has meanwhile been published in a reader under the title: *Social'nye problemy truda i proizvodstva* (Social Problems of Work and Production). Moscow: 1969.

Slovar' dlja roditelej. Semejnoe vospitanie (Dictionary for Parents. Family Education). Moscow: 1967.

"Socializm i sem'ja. Naučnaja žizn' " (Socialism and Family. Scientific Life). *Vopr. fil.,* 7 (1967), 137-140. The materials of this symposium have meanwhile been published under the title: *Problemy byta, braka i sem'i* (Problems of Household, Marriage, and Family). Vil'njus: 1970.

Sociologičeskie problemy narodnogo obrazovanija (Sociological Problems of Popular Education). Sverdlovsk: 1967.

"Sojuzniki–i vsegda" (Always Allies). *Lit. gaz.,* 8/14/1968.

Solomencëv, M. S. "O proekte osnov zakonodatel'stva Sojuza SSR i Sojuznych Republik o brake i sem'e. Doklad predsedatelja Komissii zakonodatel'nych predloženij Soveta Sojuza deputata M. S. Solomencëva" (On the Basic Law Project of the USSR and the Union Republics on Marriage and Family. An Address by the Chairman of the Commission for Legislation Suggestions in the Federal Council, Deputy M. S. Solomencëv). *Pravda,* 6/27/1968.

Solov'ëv, N. Ja. *Sem'ja v sovetskom obščestve* (The Family in Soviet Society). Moscow: 1962.

Sorokina, A. I. *Lehrbuch der Vorschulerziehung* (Uebers. a. d. Russ.) (Textbook on Preschool Education. Translation from the Russian). Berlin: 1962.

Spravočnik po doškol'nomu vospitaniju (Handbook for Preschool Education). Moscow: 1967.

SSSR v cifrach v 1967 godu. Kratij statističeskij sbornik (The USSR in Numbers in the year 1967. A Brief Statistical Compendium). Moscow: 1968.

Stankov, A. G. *Polovaja žizn' i sem'ja* (Sex Life and Family). Kiev: 1958.

Strana Sovetov za 50 let. Sbornik statističeskich materialov (Fifty Years of the Soviet Nation. A Compendium of Statistical Information). Moscow: 1967.

"Stroitel'stvo kommunizma i sem'ja. Navstreču XXII s'ezda KPSS" (The Structure of Communism and the Family. Toward the XXII Party Congress of the CPSU). *Sem'ja i škola*, 6, 6-9.

Strumilin, S. G. "Rabočij byt i kommunizm" (Everyday Life of the Worker in Communism). *Novyj mir*, 7 (1960). German translation in *Ost-Probleme*, 1960, 651-655.

Šubkin, V. N. "Vybor professii v uslovijach kommunističeskogo stroitel'stva" (Choice of Occupation under the Conditions of the Communist Structure). *Vopr. fil.*, 8 (1964), 18-28.

———. "Molodëz vstupaet v žizn'" (Youth Enters Life). *Vopr. fil.*, 5 (1965), 65-70.

———. "Vybor professii. Po materialam sociologičeskogo issledovanija molodëži Novosibirskoj oblasti" (Career Choice. From the Data of a Sociological Study among the Young People of the Novosibirsk Area). *Sov. ped.*, 2 (1968), 56-57.

Suchomlinski, W. A. (Suchomlinskij, V. A.) *Ueber die Erziehung des kommunistischen Menschen* (Uebers. a. d. Russ.) (On the Education of Communist Man. Translation from the Russian). Berlin: Volk und Wissen, 1963.

———. "Etjudy o kommunističeskom vospitanii" (Studies on Communist Education). *Nar. obraz.*, 4, 6, 8, 9, 10, and 12 (1967).

Suvorov, M. "Ešče raz—kto vinovat?" (Once Again—Who Is Guilty?). *Nar. obraz.*, 8 (1966), 82-85.

Svadkovskij, I. F. *Nravstvennoe vospitanie detej* (The Moral Education of Children). Moscow: 1962.

———. "Vysokaja otvetstvennost'" (A Great Responsibility). *Sem'ja i škola*, 1 (1961), 2-4.

Swerdlow, G. M. (Sverdlov, G. M.) *Sovetskoe zakonodatel'stvo o brake i sem'e* (The Soviet Legislation on Marriage and Family). Moscow: 1961.

———. *Mutterschaft, Ehe und Familie im Sowjetgesetz* (Motherhood, Marriage, and Family in Soviet Law). Berlin: Verlag der Sowjetischen Uilitärverwaltung in Deutschland, 1946.

Terent'eva, L. N. "Opyt izučenija sem'i i semejnogo byta latyšskogo kolchoznogo krest'janstva" (Studies on the Family and Everyday Family Life among the Latvian Kolchos Peasants). In *Sovetskaja etnografija*, 3 (1958).

Timasheff, N. S. "The Attempt to Abolish the Family in Russia." In Bell, N. W., and Vogel, E. F., *A Modern Introduction to the Family*. New York-London: Free Press, 1960, 55-63.

Titarenko, V. Ja. "Sem'ja kak faktor nravstvennogo vospitanija. Avtoreferat dissertacii" (The Family as a Factor of Moral Education. Dissertation). Leningrad: 1967.

"Učitel' i roditeli—vernye sojuzniki" (Teachers and Parents—True Allies). *Sem'ja i škola,* 12 (1963), 12, 32.

Urlanis, B. "Skol'ko nado imet' detej?" (How Many Children Should You Have?). *Lit. gaz.*, 5/1/1968.

Volfson, S. Ja. *Sociologija braka i sem'i* (Sociology of Marriage and Family). Moscow: 1929.

———. "Socializm i sem'ja" (Socialism and Family). In *Pod znamenem Marksizma,* 1936, 31-69. English translation in Schlesinger, R., op. cit., 280-315.

Volkova, E. I. *Otec i mat' kak vospitateli* (Father and Mother as Educators). Moscow: 1956.

———. "Vospitanie otvetstvennogo otnošenija k domašnemu trudu u molodeži" (The Education of Youth for a Responsible Attitude toward Housework). *Sov. ped.,* 10 (1959), 86-92.

Vorožejkin, E. M. *Brak i sem'ja* (Marriage and Family). Moscow: 1965.

Vospominanija o V. I. Lenine (Remembrances of V. I. Lenin). Volume 2, Moscow: 1957.

Wagenlehner, G. "Die Entwicklung des Kommunismus in der Sowjetunion" (The Development of Communism in the Soviet Union). In *Aus Politik und Zeitgeschichte.* Beilage zur Wochenzeitung *Das Parlament.* (On Politics and Contemporary History. A Supplement to the weekly *Das Parlament*). B 36/65, 7/8/1965, 14-24.

"Women in the USSR." In *Soviet Sociology* (IV), 3 (1965/66), 52-59.

Wurzbacher, G. (ed.) *Die Familie als Sozialisationsfaktor* (The Family as a Socialization Factor). Stuttgart: Enke Verlag, 1968.

Yanowitch, M. "Soviet Patterns of Time Use and Concepts of Leisure." In *Soviet Studies,* 15 (1963), 17-37.

Yanowitch, M., and Dodge, N. "Social Class and Education: Soviet Findings and Reactions." In *Comparative Education Review,* 3 (1968), 248-267.

Zajcev, V. L. "Predstavlenija učaščichsja ob istočnikach nravstvennogo vlijanija. Materialy massovogo anketirovanija" (Students' Ideas on the Sources of Moral Influencing. Survey Results). *Sov. ped.,* 12 (1965), 89-93.

Zaporožec, A. V. "Rol' social'nych uslovij žizni i vospitanija v psichičeskom razvitii rebënka" (The Role of the Societal Conditions of Life and Education for the Psychic Development of the Child). *Došk. vosp.,* 2 (1965), 29-37.

———. "Detstvo. Sem'ja i jasli" (Childhood. Family and Nurseries). *Pravda,* 1/8/1969.

Zdorovskij, G. E., and Orlov, G. P. "Pravil'noe ispol'zovanie svobodnogo vremeni škol'nikov—odno iz sredstv vospitanija" (The Appropriate Utilization of the Pupils' Free Time as a Means of Education). *Sov. ped.,* 6 (1966), 71-75.

Zdravomyslov, A. "Problemy tekučesti rabočej sily" (Problems of Fluctuation in the Working Forces). *Trud,* 12/2/1964.

Zdravomyslov, A., and Jadov, V. A. "Otnošenie k trudu i cennostnye orientacii ličnosti" (The Attitude toward Work and Individual Value Orientation). In: *Sociologija v SSSR* (Sociology in the USSR). Volume 2. Moscow: 1966, 187-207.

Zemcov, V. V. "Rezervy rosta i racional'noe ispol'zovanie svobodnogo vremeni rabočich" (Growth Potential and Rational Use of Free Time by Workers). *Vopr. fil.*, 4 (1965), 61-69.

Zenščiny i deti v SSSR. Statističeskij sbornik (Women and Children in the USSR. A Statistical Compendium). Moscow: 1961 and 1969.

Zjubin, L. M. *Kto za èto v otvete?* (Who Is Responsible for That?). Leningrad: 1966.

Zotov, Jr. " 'Fiziki' v komitete. Zametki komsomol'skogo rabotnika" ("Physicists" on the Committee. Notes of a Komsomol Functionary). *Koms. pravda*, 6/21/1967.

Zuev, D. "Ne prichoti radi. Zametki o vospitanii detej v sem'ye" (Not from Whim. Notes on the Raising of Children in the Family). *Pravda*, 1/22/1967.

Žurin, B. I. *Roditel'skaja obščestvennost' v pomošč škole* (The Parents' Public as a Support of the School). Second, improved edition. Moscow: 1955.

Zvorykin, A. "Možno li sproektirovat' sčast'e?" (Can Happiness Be Planned?). *Koms. pravda*, 1/12/1968.

Index